March 9, 1990 ב"ה

Our Dear Uncle Sholem,

May you celebrate many, many more healthy, happy birthdays together with your dear family - Bis hundert & Zwanzig Yuhr.

All our love,

Sylvia & Michael

מסורה

The ArtScroll Series®

Rabbi Nosson Scherman / Rabbi Meir Zlotowitz
General Editors

Around the Maggid's Table

Around the

by Rabbi Paysach J. Krohn

Published by
Mesorah Publications, ltd

Maggid's Table

More classic stories and parables
from the great teachers of Israel

FIRST EDITION
First Impression . . . December, 1989

Published and Distributed by
MESORAH PUBLICATIONS, Ltd.
Brooklyn, New York 11232

Distributed in Israel by
MESORAH MAFITZIM / J. GROSSMAN
Rechov Harav Uziel 117
Jerusalem, Israel

Distributed in Australia & New Zealand by
GOLD'S BOOK & GIFT CO.
36 William Street
Balaclava 3183, Vic., Australia

Distributed in Europe by
J. LEHMANN HEBREW BOOKSELLERS
20 Cambridge Terrace
Gateshead, Tyne and Wear
England NE8 1RP

Distributed in South Africa by
KOLLEL BOOKSHOP
22 Muller Street
Yeoville 2198
Johannesburg, South Africa

ISBN
0-89906-562-7 (hard cover)
0-89906-563-5 (paperback)

Typography by Compuscribe at ArtScroll Studios, Ltd.

Printed in the United States of America by Noble Book Press
Bound by Sefercraft, Quality Bookbinders, Ltd. Brooklyn, N.Y.

הרב שלום מרדכי הכהן שבדרון

שערי חסד, ירושלים

בס"ד

עש"ק י"ה קודש - לחודש אדר א' תשמ"ט. פה גלות נויארק.

לכבוד ידידי אהובי, הר"ר פסח, ומזכה הרבים בהפיצו ספר
הנקרא באנגלית "THE MAGID SPEAKS" אשר ידיו כוננוהו מראש ועד סוף
בלשון צח וצח, ובכוונת הלב. ואכן קראוהו ולמדו בו יותר מעשרים
אלף איש. אנשים נשים וטף. בכל קצוי תבל. ועדיין לא נס ליחו -
וחדשים לבקרים נוספים עוד איום ליום לשתות מימיו "אין מים אלא
תורה"! אשרי לו ואשרי חלקו! הה"ר הרב וכו' מוה"ר פסח יוסף
קראהן שליט"א. שזכה וזיכה בזכות אביו הגדול בתורת חיים
ואהבת חסד" באופן נפלא מאד. אשר לא רבים ימצאו כמוהו.
כידוע לכל מכיריו, הה"ה הרה"ג ופו' מוה"ר אברהם זלמן ז"ל.
ותבלח"ט אלמנתו - היא הרבנית הדגולה מנשים באהל תפארת מרת
הינדא תחי' לאוי"ש. שאומנם סייעה ברוחה ומגנן לבן סופרים לאת
בנה החשוב הנ"ל בהרבה מאמרים בספר כיד ה' הטובה עלי.

ועתה אם שמוע - בישן, תשמעו - בחדש! אשר אוותה נפשו של ידידי
הנ"ל להוציא עוד ספר בסיפורי מעשים מגדולי הדורות לזכות את הרבים
עוד ועוד. בבחינת תלמיד המחכים את רבו - כי לקט ואסף איזה
אלפים כרכים וכרכים של הנהגות ומעשים, תורתם ומשליהם. בתורה ויראת
שמים ומדות טובות. הכל מדברי ומדברותי בצאתו וביאו ממסד ועד
הטפחות. ובידים מעמדי להסריך על ידו, ומעט ראיתי ואמרתי
ואמת. כי לא עלה בידי - מחמת טרדותי העצומים בה' ברוב הבית - להתעסק
אתו כבספר הראשון. אבל המעט שראיתי וזמעתי מאמינו - ייטב לב הכל!
כי כמעשהו בראשון כך בשני יהלך בדרך הנכונה. ורבים ילכו לאורו.
ויתנני לברכו בברכת כהן הדיוט שיצליח בכל דרכיו ובכל מעשיו.
ובפרט בספר אשר מתכונן להוציא.

נאום: ידידו וידיד כל המצפה לכבודו.

שלום מרדכי הכהן שבדרון.

מרדכי גיפטר
ישיבת טלז

RABBI MORDECAI GIFTER
28570 NUTWOOD LANE
WICKLIFFE, OHIO 44092

בע״ה

כ״ז תמוז תשמ״ט

מאד שמחתי לשמוע שידידי הר״ר פסח קראהן שליט״א מכין לדפוס ספר שבו ימצא המעיין אוצר מחשבה מפי גדולים שבדורות עברו, דורות שבהם הרביצו תורה ויראה טהורה. ומובטחני שכל המעיינים יושפעו מהדברים לבקש להתגדל כפי מה שרצו בעלי המאמרים. יתברך ר׳ פסח בעבודתו וידע כל ימיו אך טוב.

מנאי, אוהב תורה ולומדיה,

מרדכי גיפטר

RABBI
ISRAEL GROSSMAN
BATEI WARSAW
JERUSALEM, ISRAEL

ישראל גרוסמן
רב ור"מ ודומ"ץ
בפיה"ק ירושלים תובב"א
מחבר ספרי שערי כתובות שערי גיטין
שערי קדושין שערי ב"ק שו"ת הליכות ישראל
שו"ת משכנות ישראל שו"ת נצח ישראל
בתי ורשה ירושלים

Tel. 287056 .טל

בס"ד י"א אדר א' תשמ"ז

הגיעני היום בשבחו של ידידי היקר והנכבד רודף צדקה וחסד אוה"ת
רחים רבנן ודחיל רבנן הרב ר' פסח קראהן שליט"א
בן הרבני יקר הצדיק רב פעלים בבית המדרש וכו' מוהר"ר אברהם זעליג ז"ל,
אשר עומד להוציא ספר שני לתולדות הצדיקים. וכמעשהו בראשון
כך מעשהו בשני. ופוק חזי מאי עמא דבר. שכבר יצא בשלושה מהדורות
ותהלת הספר מלא בפי כל. כולם מהללים ומשבחים תוכן הספר.
וגם ספרו החדש מכיל ספורים נפלאים לעורר הלבבות
לתקון המדות ולהתחזקות באמונה ובהשגחה פרטית.
וחכם מה הוא אומר. החכם את שהוא בעצמו. זהו מה שאומר
הרב רבי פסח שלא מדרוש בדרשות לרבים ובספרים נחמדים,
ורק בדבר ומעורר חברי ללומדים בקביעות עתים לתורה.
וכן לבא לעזרת מי שזקוק לעזרה. ואשרי חלקו שזכה בכך
וברכתי נאמנה לו שיזכה את הרבים מתוך הרחבת הדעת
ושלות הנפש ויתוסף תעצומות עוז. ועסי"ת יעלה כל
מעלות לרבים לטובה,

בברכת ידידו דו"ש מלונ"ח
ישראל גרוסמן

הרב ישראל גרוסמן
מחבר ספרי שערי ב"ק
ושערי כתובות ושד
וחבר רב ור"מ בפיה"ק ירושלים ת"ו
שכונת בתי ורשה
RABBI I. GROSSMAN Jerusalem - Israel

דוד קאהן

ביהמ"ד גבול יעבץ
ברוקלין, נוא יארק

בס"ד

לפה מפיק מרגליות, אומן במלאכת שמים
אהובי יקירי הרב ר' פסח יוסף קראהן שליט"א

באתי עוד הפעם ללמוד לבני יהודה קשת והנה כתבת דברי הימים – ספר הישר לדורות מידות נכונות ולחזק ידים רפות לתורה ולהתעודד על ידי מסירת סיפורים. הייתי עד ראיה בעצמי, שדקדקת לחפש אחר המקור של כל סיפור להוכיח אם אמת הוא, ונתקשרת עם המקור הראשון של המעשה ובמקום שהיה אפשר עם בעל העובדא. תמהתי על מה שבזבזת כל כך הרבה זמן וממון למטרתך הנ"ל היות והמעשיות טובות הנה והתועלת שתבא מקריאתן לכאורה שוה היא בין אם אירעו בדיוק כמו שהנך מוסר אותן בין אם לא היה ככה, ומה העבודה הזאת לכם (פירוש, מה הטורח הזה שאתה מטריח את עצמך ואחרים)

אמנם נוכחתי לדעת שהצדק אתך בעבודתך הקודש, דאדרבה דכולהו היא מצות סיפור יציאת מצרים שנצטוינו בה, שעל ידה משפיע האב על כל יוצאי חלציו למיניהם – שהרי כנגד ארבעה בנים דברה תורה: לחכם הרי מדריכו בדרך ה' בפרטי המצות והנהגות טובות; לרשע הוא מעוררו לתשובה; לתם מודיעו מה שאירע ומה שנעשה שיכיר בהנהגת השי"ת כפי כחו ותפיסתו; ולשאינו יודע לשאול פותח לו ומניח עמו היסוד של כל הדעות והדבקות שעורו על כלל ישראל ושבכלל "בעבור זה" לקיים מצותיו של הבורא ית"ש. והרי אנו מקדימים הסיפור לבנים אלו בברוך שנתן תורה לעמו ישראל", ואמרו בעבודה זרה (ד,ב) דתורה דכתיב בה אמת אין הקב"ה עושה לפנים משורת הדין, נ"א שכדי שהסיפור ימלא מטרתו להשפיע על הארבעה בנים, לכל אחד לפי יכלתו, צריכים למסור הסיפור בתורת "תורה" ולא בתורת סיפור בעלמא, שיצא האמת לאמיתו.

והנני מברך אותך שכשם שזכית בחיבוריך הקודמים כן תמשיך בהצלחתך, ורכב על דבר אמת.

אוהבך ומוקירך ודורש שלומך
דאהבה ויקר
דוד קאהן
יום תבר מגל תשמ"ט

◆§ Table of Contents

Part F: Views and Perspectives

Author's Preface

הריני מזמן את פי
להודות ולהלל ולשבח את בוראי.

It is with feelings of gratitude that I present this work to the reading public: gratitude to *Hashem*, for allowing me to complete this work of stories and parables gleaned from some of today's most inspirational members of *Klal Yisrael;* and gratitude to the many people who encouraged me with this project by giving me countless hours of their precious time for the sake of this endeavor.

R' David Singer, the noted *rav* of the Sefardishe Shul in Boro Park, recently recounted to me an interesting anecdote concerning the Minsker *Maggid*, R' Binyamin Shakovitzky (1863-1938).

The *Maggid* was once invited to give a *drashah* (lecture) in a village far from his home town of Minsk. As he stepped up to the podium from where he would deliver his *drashah*, he looked out at the multitudes that had gathered to hear him. *Talmidei chachamim* (Torah scholars) sat in the audience, along with countless *baalei battim* (lay people) of the community. Women and children as well had assembled in this hall to listen to the *Maggid*.

The *Maggid* was overcome with awe at the size of the gathering. He had been prepared to begin his *drashah* one way, but now instead he spoke in a more personal manner. "As many of you know," he began, "this is my first time in your village. In order to make my way here, I hired a *baal agalah* (wagon driver) to bring me. We traveled for quite a while on lonely and deserted roads until we came to a crossroads. We had to turn either right or left. We were helpless because there was no one around of whom to ask information. But then the driver noticed a small tin sign on a tree in front of us. We walked up to the sign to read it and there, in hand-written letters, was the name of your village, along with an arrow pointing to the road on the right.

"We took that road and, as you see, we arrived safely. However, as we came into this village a thought occurred to me. I realized that back at the crossroads we had required direction — we were lost — and yet we relied on a mere tin sign, and only because we felt the information was correct.

"I, too," said the *Maggid*, "am standing before you, merely as a tin sign prepared to give direction to those who will listen. I am not here to give you my own personal thoughts, but the thoughts and messages of the great people from whom I have learned and gleaned. The information, I believe, is correct. I am here merely to present it."

I feel the same way.

The episodes, incidents, insights and perspectives of the people mentioned in this book speak for themselves. I thank *Hashem* for giving me the opportunity to bring them to you, the reader.

Two years ago, I had the wonderful opportunity to be in *Eretz Yisrael* for *Sukkos*. The *Yom Tov* had been ushered in by a magnificent kaleidoscope of vendors of all ages selling their wares in the crowded streets of Geulah and Meah Shearim. The colorful scope of their items ranged from huge green Moroccan *esrogim*, to eight-foot-long stalks of furry willows (to be used as *schach*, to cover *sukkos*). There was the widest array of *lulavim* and *hadassim* as well as the most beautiful *sukkah* decorations imaginable. The joyous anticipation in the streets of Jerusalem for the upcoming *Yom Tov* had been almost tangible.

Yom Tov itself was a unique experience. *Sukkos* stood on almost every one of the *mirpesot* (porches) which draped the endless rows of apartment houses. Walking along almost any street in Jerusalem, one might hear the *HaMotzi* blessing being recited over bread in one *sukkah*, a *niggun* (song) being sung in a second one, *Bircas HaMazon* (Grace after Meals) coming from a third. The endless sounds of children's chatter and silverware's clatter completed the musical mosaic for the casual passerby.

But now, after the first two days of the holiday itself, it was the first night of *Chol HaMoed* (the intermediate days of the holiday) for us Diaspora Jews. Various institutions were celebrating with music and dance their *Simchas Beis HaShoevah* and the festivities were in full swing. Music and songs poured into the night from loudspeakers all over the city.

As it is the custom of many in Jerusalem to visit prominent *rabbanim* in their homes during *Yom Tov*, a group of us drove to the Shaarei Chessed section of Jerusalem with great anticipation. We were going to the *sukkah* of the world-renowned *Maggid* of Jerusalem, R' Sholom Schwadron.

A *maggid* is a multi-faceted *darshan* (lecturer) who can deliver colorful *drashos* on a variety of topics while simultaneously weaving a fascinating tapestry of stories and parables around his words — be they harsh rebuke or gentle encouragement. A *maggid* of the past usually traveled from city to city, even from country to country, delivering *drashos* that always attracted great crowds. His unique delivery blended with his magnificent *maggid's* melody made his *drashos* unforgettable.

One of the last of this breed is the man known throughout the Jewish world as the *Maggid* of Jerusalem, R' Sholom Mordechai (HaKohen) Schwadron. For more than forty years he has moved and inspired audiences in Israel, Europe, Canada and America. He is one of a kind, and perhaps the last of a kind. (For a detailed history of *maggidim*, see ArtScroll's *The Maggid Speaks*.)

My relationship with R' Sholom began in 1964 when he first came to America. At that time my late father, R' Avrohom Zelig Krohn, *z"l*, had the foresight to open our home to R' Sholom and to R' Yisroel Grossman of Jerusalem, two people he had never met before, who came to the United States on behalf of *Chinuch Atzmai*. (An incredible chain of events leading up to that invitation is described in detail in the introduction to *The Maggid Speaks*.) R' Sholom remained in my parents' home for close to six months. A long-standing friendship between our families thus began, and on R' Sholom's subsequent visits to America, and during our trips to *Eretz Yisrael*, being around R' Sholom and following him to his *drashos* became an integral part of our lives.

R' Sholom is known for his electrifying *drashos* of fire and silk. His warmth, good cheer and personification in his private life of all that he demands from his public audiences have made him, over the last forty years, a magnet that attracts a sea of Jewish humanity wherever he goes. It is a thrill to be in his presence.

When we entered R' Sholom's *sukkah* we saw we were not the first ones there. R' Sholom, who was seated at the head of the table, dressed royally in his golden *tish bekesha*, bedecked with his *shtreimel*, and surrounded by his children and grandchildren, was holding court. His mood was expansive, for in addition to his immediate family members there were present two Sephardic gentlemen, a *rosh yeshivah* from Ashdod, a nephew from England, and numerous Americans — all sitting around his table and listening attentively to his every word and nuance. Music blared in the background from the *Beis Knesses HaGra*, the *shul* behind R' Sholom's home, as yet another yeshivah in Jerusalem celebrated the *Simchas Beis HaShoevah*. Music played, adults danced and children sang, providing the perfect harmonious backdrop.

And in this brightly decorated *sukkah* R' Sholom was telling a story about a *gadol* (great Torah sage). The people listening nodded their approval and the *Maggid's* brother-in-law, R' Rafael Dovid Auerbach, excitedly exclaimed, "*Noyra noyra'oys* (awesome of awesomes!)" in jestful imitation of R' Sholom's familiar reaction to a noteworthy story. R' Sholom went on with another story that taught *yiras Hashem* (respect of G-d), and his son, R' Yitzchok, countered with a parable. This reminded the nephew from England of a marvelous story that had occurred in London years ago. "*Oi!*" exclaimed R' Sholom. "I meant to ask you about that one!" Everyone listened, enraptured, to the gripping tale.

The women, R' Sholom's daughters and granddaughters, stood outside the small *sukkah*, listening with relish to the stories they must have heard a thousand times before. And so it went. One of R' Sholom's sons-in-law chimed in with a *maiseh* (story). "Is that the way it happened?" asked R' Sholom. "I seem to remember it was slightly different." Playfully he admonished his listeners, "One must always tell a story exactly the way he heard it!"

The *rosh yeshivah* from Ashdod told an outstanding story about a *gadol* that he had heard when he was studying in the Telshe Yeshiva in Cleveland. R' Sholom listened intently, laughed heartily and then exclaimed, "*Pilay ployim* (wonder of wonders)!" One day, he would be sure to tell this story himself.

For the next few hours people darted in and out of R' Sholom's *sukkah* in Shaarei Chessed, listening to a story, telling a story, coming by to say "*Gut Yom Tov*" and staying to bask in the ambience of the colorful *Maggid*. On and on the talk continued into the night: a story, a parable, a debate about the veracity of a tale, a discussion about whether the lesson taught was noteworthy.

I was spellbound. The comments, the quips, the episodes and the incidents that flew verbally back and forth across the table were thrilling and mesmerizing. Each was either a lesson in *ahavas Hashem* (love of G-d), *zehirus b'mitzvos* (being careful in *mitzvah* observance), or *bein adam l'chaveiro* (care and concern for a fellow Jew). There was no place in the world where I would rather have been than right where I was. It was one of the experiences in life that one wishes one could hold on to forever, a series of moments to eternalize and internalize.

I shall always remember that night for the pure joy and exhilaration I felt at being "Around the *Maggid's* Table." It is the essence of that delight and excitement that I have tried to capture in this book which I now present to the reading public.

Acknowledgments

No words can adequately express the warm feelings of love, admiration and *hakoras hatov* that my family and I all have for the Maggid of Jerusalem himself, Rav Sholom Schwadron. Our lives have been remarkably enhanced by our association with him over the last twenty-five years.

Once again as with the writing of *The Maggid Speaks,* he allowed me almost endless access to his time both here and in Israel. For this volume he gave me stories of his own, listened and commented on many that I had assembled from others and most of all encouraged me constantly in this endeavor. In acknowledgment and recognition I dedicate this volume to him.

This book, *Around the Maggid's Table,* is a combination of stories and parables that I heard either from R' Sholom or from others who graciously told of fascinating incidents which they had experienced or heard from reliable sources. Almost every single person to whom I spoke appreciated the value of making an inspirational but little-known story available to the public.

For me to have been involved with the following people was an experience and an honor that I will always treasure. Anyone familiar with Jewish leaders in Torah *chinuch* (education) today, will surely recognize many of the names listed alphabetically below. Each of them gave me access to his time; each of them tried to help as best he could. I thank *Hashem* that I had the merit and the opportunity to spend time with such outstanding individuals:

R' Yisroel Belsky (Brooklyn), R' Lipa Brenner (Brooklyn), the *Rosh*

Yeshivah of Chevron R' Simcha Zisel Broide (Jerusalem), R' Moshe Chodosh (Jerusalem), R' Dovid Cohen (Brooklyn), R' Yaakov Galinsky (Bnei Brak), R' Lipa Geldwerth (Brooklyn), R' Abba Zalke Gewirtz (Cleveland), the *Rosh Yeshivah* of Telshe R' Mordechai Gifter (Cleveland), R' Eliezer Ginsburg (Brooklyn), the *Rosh Yeshivah* of Emek Halachah R' Tuvya Goldstein (Brooklyn), R' Moshe Grossman (Brooklyn), R' Yisroel Grossman (Jerusalem), R' Yitzchok Dovid Grossman (Migdal HaEmek), R' Pinchus Hirschprung (Montreal), R' Avrohom Kabalkin (Jerusalem), R' Yechiel Meyer Katz (Montreal), R' Aryeh Katzin (Brooklyn), R' Moshe Kasirer (Forest Hills), R' Kolman Krohn (Lakewood), R' Herschel Mashinsky (Monsey), R' Reuven Meletzky (Jerusalem), R' Zelig Prag (Brooklyn), R' Avrohom Moshe Rabinowitz (Brooklyn), R' Simcha Nosson Segal (Ashdod), R' Yaakov Silverfarb (Bnei Brak), R' Chaim Shapiro (Baltimore), R' Avrohom Shkop (Brooklyn), and R' Peretz Steinberg (Kew Gardens Hills). Additionally, the following distinguished individuals gave me of their valuable time for the sake of this book: Mr. Willie Bauman (Englewood), Mr. Yehuda El'Chonen (Detroit), Mr. Bezalel Fixler (Kew Gardens), Mr. Moshe Gold (Brooklyn), Mr. Isaac Handler (Brooklyn), Mr. Zev Schlesinger (Kew Gardens), Mr. Moshe Sukenik (Kew Gardens) and Mr. Harry Wolpert (Baltimore).

Although the aforementioned people told me almost tenfold the amount of material that appears in this book, the process of sifting and selecting which stories and parables to write and print was my responsibility. I pray that I have chosen well and that I have been able to transmit the inspiration I found in these selections.

❦ ❦ ❦

I am grateful to Mr. David Schild of Teaneck and Mrs. Chani Friedman of Chicago who, despite their busy schedules, devoted countless hours to reading, analyzing and commenting on every story and parable in this book. Their perspectives enhanced my own perspective of what was being written, and many of their suggestions have been incorporated into the manuscript for the benefit of the reading public.

My mother, תחי׳, Mrs. Hindy Krohn, from whom I obtained an

appreciation for the written word, was for the past two years involved with the research and writing of her own book (*The Way It Was*, recently published by ArtScroll/Mesorah). Yet she constantly made my writings a priority as she corrected, edited and commented on the selections for this work. Her guidance and counsel were invaluable. May she reap much deserved *nachas* from her children and grandchildren.

I am deeply indebted to my brother, R' Kolman Krohn of Lakewood, New Jersey, for his counsel and extensive comments on practically every selection in this work.

I express a specific note of appreciation to Mrs. Nina Ackerman Indig of Bayswater, New York, who served as editor for this book. Her corrections, changes and pursuit of consistency added immeasurably to the production of this work. The reading public will gain from her diligence, as she is becoming recognized as one of ArtScroll's finest editors.

My *rebbe*, R' David Cohen, of Brooklyn, added input into almost every facet of this work. His daily concern for the success of this venture was a source of strength and encouragement, just as his constant advice and guidance have been for more than fifteen years. I can never thank him enough.

Special thanks are due to the Ner L'Meah organization in Israel, which provides cassette recordings and videotapes of Torah education, for supplying me with numerous cassettes of lectures by R' Yaakov Galinsky and other noted speakers in Israel. Here in New York, R' Moshe Grossman made available to me many exceptional recordings of discussions he had with R' Sholom Schwadron; Nachum Lehman of the Yeshivah of Staten Island guided me with technical computer assistance, and the Lehrers of Kew Gardens were always busy checking sources and references whenever I needed this done.

The name ArtScroll today has become a household word which is synonymous with the dissemination of Torah in the English language on its highest level. It has been my good fortune to become associated at ArtScroll with such outstanding individuals as R' Nosson Scherman, R' Meir Zlotowitz, R' Sheah Brander, and R' Avie Gold who, in their pursuit of excellence, have set standards in the presentation of Torah and *yahadus* for generations to come. As a cohesive unit, they have in the last thirteen years brought the heritage of Torah to tens of thousands who might otherwise have been bereft of it. Their daily diligence personifies the dictum that Moshe *Rabbeinu* expressed in The Song at the Sea, "זֶה קֵלִי וְאַנְוֵהוּ — This is my G-d and I shall glorify Him" (*Shemos* 15:2). May *Hashem* accept the work of their hands.

I am grateful to the entire team at ArtScroll/Mesorah, each in his or her own field of expertise: Shimon Golding, Michael Horen, Yosef Timinsky, Michael Zivitz, Yitzchok Saftlas, Mrs. Faygie Weinbaum, Mrs. Esther Feierstein, Mrs. Menucha Silver, Mrs. Zissi Landau, Mrs. Suri Maline, Sheila Tennenbaum, Lea Freier, Bassie Goldstein and Faigie Zlotowitz.

Thanks to Menachem Adelman of Brooklyn and Moshe Poupko of Jerusalem for the beautiful photography on the cover.

After having spent close to five consecutive years working on two previous *sefarim* (books), it was not my intention to begin another one right away. However, more than anyone else, it was my wife Miriam who encouraged me to become involved in this particular project so soon, for in her role as both a parent and teacher she understood the potential *chinuch* value inherent in stories about *tzaddikim* and *tzidkaniyos*. The benefits that we and our children have reaped from our involvement with this project are due to her foresight.

I thank Hashem for the opportunities He has given me. May He extend his mercy and kindness towards me, my wife Miriam, תחי', and our children, שיחיו, so that we can together grow to emulate in the finest manner those written about in these pages.

ואני תפלתי לך ה׳ עת רצון אלקים ברוב חסדך ענני באמת ישעך.

Paysach J. Krohn — פסח יוסף קראהן
Kew Gardens, New York — ח״י חשון תש״נ
Nov. 16, 1989

Introduction

A Maggid and His Message

Introduction

◆ *A Maggid and His Message*

A visiting *maggid* attracts different people for different reasons. Some are attracted by the powerful message which the *maggid* will undoubtedly deliver at his *drashah* (lecture). Others want to hear the dramatic story or parable that he will recount with inimitable eloquence. For a third group, the attraction lies in the unique melody, the haunting rhapsody that emphasizes and embellishes the words that he speaks and the pictures that he verbally paints. And finally, for some nothing equals the power of the personality and presence of the *maggid* himself. For this group it is not so much what the *maggid* says, but the way in which he says it that makes him so captivating.

Perhaps the most widely known *maggid* in the Jewish world today is the famed *maggid* of Jerusalem, R' Sholom Mordechai (HaKohen) Schwadron. A vestige of the old-time *maggid* who would travel to countless cities and deliver thunderous *drashos,* R' Sholom (the author and editor of more than twenty-five *sefarim*) has delivered his *drashos* throughout Israel, Europe and America. Inevitably he leaves a lasting impression; inevitably people clamor for more.

An incident that occurred in Glasgow, Scotland, years ago, vividly portrays the attraction and the influence of a *maggid* such as R' Sholom.

In the 1940's, R' Sholom traveled from *Eretz Yisrael* to England.

He visited and lectured in various cities, including Gateshead, Manchester and London. From there he traveled to Scotland, where he spent a *Shabbos* in the city of Glasgow.

He was told that he could find a *minyan* of *shomrei Shabbos* (Sabbath observers) in the *shul* located in the Gorbals section of town, where R' Binyamin Beinish Atlas was the *rav.* At that time, Glasgow had close to twenty-five thousand Jewish inhabitants, but a mere hundred were *shomrei Shabbos.*

During his stay, the news came from Israel (then called Palestine) that the Arabs had been carrying out pogroms against Jews throughout the country, and were readying themselves for war.

The Chief Rabbi of England, Rabbi Dr. Sir Israel Brodie (1895-1979), proclaimed a *Yom Tefillah* (day of prayer) on behalf of the people of Palestine. Throughout England and Scotland Jews were to gather in their local synagogues, and in Glasgow announcements were made that R' Sholom Schwadron, the *maggid* of Jerusalem, would deliver a keynote address.

R' Sholom was puzzled about his being asked to speak. He knew not a word of English, and for the most part, the Jews in Glasgow did not know Yiddish or Hebrew. But still, to have refused would have been disrespectful and so he consented.

On Sunday afternoon more than eight hundred people crowded into R' Atlas' *shul* in Gorbals. Men, women and children came to pray and be inspired. R' Leib Rubenstein, of a *shul* in Giffnock, a suburb of Glasgow, led the assembled in the recitation of *Tehillim* (*Psalms*). Many speakers delivered prepared addresses, and then it was time for the *maggid* of Jerusalem to take the podium. R' Sholom, by virtue of his being a resident of Jerusalem, represented the Jews victimized by Arab horrors.

R' Sholom put on his *tallis* (prayer shawl), mounted the steps towards the *Aron Kodesh* (Holy Ark), kissed the curtain covering the Ark, and turned to face his audience, which was waiting in anticipation. As he looked around he saw an endless sea of eager faces on people with whom he could not communicate verbally.

But nevertheless he began — in Yiddish. He cited a verse in *Tehillim* (102:1) and roared it dramatically in a melody that stunned every listener into rapt attention. In a pleading, haunting voice he called out, "תְּפִלָּה לְעָנִי כִי יַעֲטֹף — A prayer of the afflicted man as he is cloaked (in a prayer shawl)."

"We have gathered here," R' Sholom said, "because we all share the pain and affliction of our brothers and sisters in *Eretz Yisrael.*" He then went on to tell the following parable:

> A chronic alcoholic and drunkard was one day making his way home from work. He had earned a few shillings which he was bringing home so that his wife and family would have money for food. But on the way he passed a tavern. The temptation was too great and so he entered, ordered a few drinks, spent the money he had and dropped into a drunken stupor.
>
> He awoke an hour later, realized what he had done and began to worry. How would he tell his wife and children? He knew they were relying on him, and so instead of going directly home he went to the house of his father, who lived nearby.
>
> "Father," he said, "I did a foolish thing but I need money for my family. Please help me."
>
> The father, a compassionate man, gave his son the money he needed. The son thanked him, but on the way home he passed the same tavern again. Once again he could not resist the temptation. He went inside and ordered drinks with the money that he had received from his father.
>
> After the last penny was gone, he began thinking about the foolishness of his actions, and what the repercussions would be for his wife and children. Once again he made his way to his father's house, and asked him for some money for the sake of his family that was counting on him.
>
> The father chastised his son and warned him not to walk down that same street again, but to go directly home via another route.
>
> The son followed his father's advice, but on that different route, too, there was a tavern, and for the third time the son could not contain his craving for whiskey. He entered the bar, ordered drinks, and spent every last penny he had on alcohol.

Now when he came to his senses he realized that he was in deep trouble. The only one who could bail him out was his father — but how could he face him? And so he wrapped himself in a shawl so that his father wouldn't be able to see his face, and made his way to his father's home.

He knocked on the door, and when his father opened it the son said, "Father, I cannot face you because I am humiliated by my actions, but I plead for your help for the sake of my family."

R' Sholom paused for a moment and then cried out, "We have gathered here today in Glasgow to plead to our Father in Heaven for the sake of our brothers and sisters in *Eretz Yisrael.* But how can we show our face to *Hashem?* Ours is a face filled with embarrassment, for we have acted irresponsibly! *Shabbos* observance has been neglected, *kashrus* has been forsaken, *taharas hamishpachah* (family purity) has been disregarded. How can we show our face to *Hashem?* Thus we are all here," R' Sholom said as he tugged at his *tallis*, "just like the man that King David described — עָנִי כִּי יַעֲטֹף — an afflicted man wrapped in a prayer shawl, embarrassed to face *Hashem.*" And then in his inimitable *maggid's* melody, R' Sholom cried out and pleaded, "Come, my dear brothers and sisters! Together let us spill out our hearts to *Hashem!*"

As R' Sholom now looked out over his audience, he could see that people were crying. Somehow he had touched them. He continued his talk in Yiddish, exhorting them to repentance, encouraging them to make commitments anew and to continue with their heartfelt prayers for the people struggling in *Eretz Yisrael.*

The gathering eventually dispersed, but a number of people tarried in the *shul,* and formed a circle around R' Sholom. "Rabbi," a man called out in English, "when and where are you speaking next?"

R' Sholom motioned to the man that he did not understand what he was asking, as he did not speak English. Someone explained that the man wished to know where R' Sholom's next *drashah* would be given. R' Sholom smiled and said, through an interpreter, "Tell me — I don't speak English and you don't speak Yiddish, so why would you care to hear me again?"

The man thought for a moment and then replied, "*Rebbe*, my mind may not have understood your words, but my heart understood your message."

Now, decades later, when R' Sholom reflects on that incident in Glasgow, he says, " 'יִשְׂרָאֵל אֲשֶׁר בְּךָ אֶתְפָּאָר — Israel, in you I take pride' (*Yeshayahu* 49:3). Every Jewish heart yearns to be inspired, for in the recesses of the soul of even the most estranged and alienated Jew there exists a tiny spark that is fueled by a craving to be virtuous and a desire to be distant from evil." (See *Rambam, Hilchos Geirushin* 2:20.)

A *maggid's* magnificent message, coated with stories and parables, can cause the flickering sparks of *Yahadus* in his listeners to ignite.

R' Sholom, though, says that as well intentioned as any in his audience may be, listening alone is not enough. They must react! To bring across his point he employs a famous parable from the noted Dubno *maggid*, R' Yaakov Krantz (1740-1804).

> The Dubno *maggid* once described how a man from a small village came to a big city for a visit. During his stay he heard a tremendous clamoring, as sirens and whistles seemed to wail endlessly. When he inquired as to why there was such noise, he was informed that there was a fire somewhere in town and that the whistles and sirens were actually signals as to where the fire was, so that firefighters could put it out.
>
> The visitor thought that this warning system was a very clever idea, and so he went and purchased some sirens and whistles for his own community. A few weeks later there was a fire in his village. Immediately he ran for his sirens and whistles and tooted until he was blue in the face. But the fire raged on and destroyed everything in its path. He was

astounded and furious. He ran back to the big city and complained to the storekeeper that he had been cheated. "The sirens and whistles didn't work for me or for my villagers," he complained. "Everything was burnt to a crisp."

"You are quite foolish," said the shopkeeper. "The whistles and sirens can only tell you where the fire is, but it is the people themselves who have to react to put out the blaze."

"And that," says R' Sholom, "is the same with every *maggid* and every speaker. The *maggid* can only 'blow the whistle' and let the people know where the fire [of evil inclination] is burning, but the people themselves must put out the blaze. Simply listening to *drashos* and stories can be a pleasant pastime, but it won't put out the fire!"

Part A:

Caring

◆§ *Voices*

When R' Sholom Schwadron tells this story, he prefaces it by saying that it is one of the most magnificent he has ever heard. The sensitivities displayed here by the great R' Yosef Chaim Sonnenfeld (1848-1932), the *rav* of the Old City of Jerusalem, are simply extraordinary. As R' Sholom says, "No one but a R' Yosef Chaim would even think of having such empathy, which of course is all the more reason that every one of us can learn so much from this story."

In the early 1900's a certain R' Nachum was the regular *baal tefillah* (leader of services) for the *Mussaf* prayers on the *Yamim Nora'im* (High Holy Days) in the *shul* where R' Yosef Chaim Sonnenfeld was the *rav*. The *shul*, located in the Old City of Jerusalem, was filled to capacity every *Rosh Hashanah* and *Yom Kippur*, and to have been selected as this highly regarded congregation's *baal tefillah* for these holy days of prayer was indeed a great honor.

One year, a few weeks before *Rosh Hashanah*, R' Nachum suddenly passed away. After mourning their dear friend, the elders of the congregation approached R' Yosef Chaim and asked, "What shall we do about getting a *baal tefillah*? Shall we begin to search for a candidate?"

The *rav* told the people not to be concerned — he would see to it that there would be a worthy *baal tefillah* in due time. Days passed, and no mention was made of the topic. Soon it was merely five days before *Rosh Hashanah* and the elders, along with some others in the congregation, were somewhat apprehensive that such an important position as *baal tefillah* had not yet been filled. A bit impatient, they approached R' Yosef Chaim a second time.

Once again the *rav* assured them that a *baal tefillah* would be found and that they needn't worry nor give the matter any additional thought. And so they let the matter go, but still they were curious.

The eve of *Rosh Hashanah* arrived. Tomorrow the *baal tefillah* would be standing at the *bimah* leading the *Mussaf* prayers. And still no one had any idea who the *baal tefillah* would be. The people simply could not contain themselves any longer. "*Rebbe*," they protested, "tomorrow the *baal tefillah* must show up, and you haven't said a word to us as to who he will be, nor did you even let us search for one."

"I've told you a few times," the *rav* said, "that there is nothing for any of you to worry about. The matter will be taken care of." Bewildered and confused, each person made his way home, puzzled by the *rav's* strange behavior.

The next day there was a sense of anticipation in the air. The *Shacharis* (morning) prayers were concluded, the Torah was read, and the *shofar* was about to be blown. There was a nervous tension in the old *shul* so strong that everyone could feel it.

All eyes were on the saintly man, R' Yosef Chaim Sonnenfeld. Suddenly he got up from his seat and walked straight to where the son of the deceased R' Nachum was sitting. He bent over the young man and said softly to him, "You are to be the *baal tefillah*. Go up to *daven Mussaf* just as your late father did."

The young man was speechless! He was the last one in *shul* to even remotely consider the possibility of being asked to *daven*. He began to protest, "But I am not at all prepared; I didn't look over the *davening* before *Yom Tov!*"

R' Yosef Chaim answered him in a calm voice, "You have heard your late father *daven* here for many years. You are familiar with his manner of *davening*. Go to the *bimah* and do your best. You will be fine."

The young man obeyed the *rav* and approached the *bimah*. The elders were aghast but they said nothing at the moment, choosing rather to wait until after *davening*.

After *Mussaf*, a group of esteemed *baalei battim* (lay people) went over to the *rav*, and said respectfully, "We accept your decision that R' Nachum's son should have been the *baal tefillah*, but we just wonder how you could suggest that he lead the congregation when the *halachah* clearly states that an *avel* (mourner) may not pray at the *amud* (lectern, where the *chazzan* leads the congregation in prayer) during the High Holy Days." (See *Orach Chaim* 581:1; *Mishnah Berurah* §7.)

R' Yosef Chaim scanned the surprised group and then answered softly, "Do you know who was sitting and *davening* in the *ezras nashim* (ladies' section) of our *shul*? R' Nachum's widow. You can well imagine the grief and sorrow that she is feeling, especially on this very day, when her late husband would have been the one to lead us in *Mussaf*. Imagine the pain she would have felt if someone else would have begun to *daven* the *tefillah* she used to hear her husband *daven* every year. Her crying and pain would have been heard and felt by us all!

"I wanted to minimize the widow's grief as best I could, and so I decided to place someone at the *amud*, as close in her eyes as possible to her husband — and who better than her own son? The Torah warns us numerous times about causing pain to a widow, and thus I felt compelled to act as I did. Appointing R' Nachum's son surely outweighed the law of not permitting an *avel* to be a *chazzan* on the High Holy Days. For after all, it does also say in *halachah* that if there is no one else available, the mourner may indeed be the *chazzan*. In this case, for the sake of the widow, I felt it was as if there really was no one else." (See *Mishnah Berurah* 581:7.)

◆§ *To Seize the Moment*

The Talmud (*Sotah* 13a) commends Moshe *Rabbeinu* for having the presence of mind to think about the concerns of others at a time when most were occupied with their own personal welfare.

It is explained that as the Jews were preparing to leave Egypt they had the opportunity to take for themselves a great deal of the Egyptians' valuable possessions (see *Shemos* 12:36). Moshe *Rabbeinu,* however, was concerned with other matters. He remembered the promise made to Yosef many years earlier, before Yosef died, that when the Jews finally left Egypt his remains would be taken to be buried in *Eretz Yisrael.* Thus, as all the people were gathering the spoils of Egypt, Moshe sought Yosef's remains, found them, and took them along in fulfillment of the ancient promise.

The Talmud attributes the verse in *Mishlei* (10:8) "חֲכַם לֵב יִקַּח מִצְוֹת — A wise man takes *mitzvos*" to Moshe's deed. The following incredible incident which R' Yisroel Grossman, a *dayan* (rabbinical judge) in Israel, witnessed many years ago, would certainly fall into this exalted category.

The year was 1945, and the Arabs were throwing grenades in many Jewish areas. Sirens wailed and people ran frantically to shelters. R' Yisroel himself was in one of the shelters in Jerusalem when he heard the terrible news that one of his students had been hit by a grenade and now lay dying in the Bikkur Cholim Hospital in downtown Jerusalem.

Because he was the boy's *rebbe* (teacher) he felt that he had to go to the child. He ran through the streets to the hospital, trying to avoid open spaces where he would be an easy target for an Arab's gunshot or grenade.

As he was about to enter the hospital he saw in the distance the famed *tzaddik* R' Arye Leib Levin (1885-1969) running with another man towards the hospital. He waited until the two men came to the door, and watched as they entered the building.

As the three of them walked into the hospital's main corridor, they were confronted by the horrible sight of many bodies covered with sheets — the fatal casualties of the Arab attacks. R' Yisroel was about to search for a nurse to ask about his *talmid's* whereabouts, when he saw an unbelievable thing. R' Arye Leib Levin had walked over to a body, lifted the white sheet that covered it, and was ordering the man who accompanied him to photograph the faces of the deceased.

Going from one body to the next, R' Arye Leib and the photographer lifted each sheet, snapped a picture, and lowered the sheet back over the body. R' Yisroel was appalled. He knew R' Arye Leib's reputation as a man of tremendous *ahavas Yisrael* (love of one's fellow Jew) — but how could he be so insensitive at a time like this? R' Yisroel thought that perhaps R' Arye Leib desired to have these pictures taken so that they could be sent abroad to show the world evidence of the Arab atrocities. But still, R' Yisroel felt this was wrong.

"R' Arye Leib," R' Yisroel called out. "Where is *kavod hames* (respect for the dead)?"

"R' Yisroel," the saintly R' Arye said calmly, "you may believe me that what I am doing is for a distinct purpose. I am not a *rav,* but when I heard all the grenades exploding and realized that people were being killed, I investigated and found out that a new graveyard had been opened to bury these people en masse immediately. If the dead men are not properly identified, then their wives will remain *agunos* (woman who are uncertain regarding their husband's fate) and may never be able to remarry! I thought that perhaps these pictures would aid the *rabbanim* responsible for determining their status."

R' Yisroel was speechless as R' Arye Leib continued. "I ran out of my shelter to find a photographer. I couldn't find one that would come with me at first. Even when I finally found this one, the sirens had been going for so long that he was afraid to step outside. I tried to explain to him the importance of what we must accomplish — but still he was hesitant. Then I told him, 'I promise you that you and I will share equally in the reward for this *mitzvah* in *Olam Haba.*' It was only then that he agreed to come along."

Now, years later, R' Yisroel ponders with amazement: Who else at a time like that would have even thought of the plights of people he had never even met? Only R' Arye Leib.

Just like Moshe *Rabbeinu* many years before.

A Little Boy's Esrog

Very often we tend to pay attention to others only if we feel they are as important as, or more important than, we are. We listen to their problems, try to fulfill their requests, and bestow on them our finest social graces. To show concern and care for a "less important" individual sometimes takes a conscious effort. However, for an adult to regard the feelings of a child other than his own, indeed takes a very special person.

This beautiful episode, which took place in Jerusalem, portrays the beauty of a special man's character.

In Jerusalem many years ago there lived an exceptional man, a well-known *talmid chacham* (Torah scholar) and *askan* (one involved with community affairs), known as R' Zalman R' Nusson's. The man's name was actually R' Zalman, and it was his father who was R' Nusson, but a century or more ago it was common to call a man in this manner, especially if two people in town had the same first name. Thus he came to be known as R' Zalman R' Nusson's.

R' Zalman was regarded as one of the most respected *esrog* experts in Jerusalem. Hundreds of people would make their way to his home during the days before *Sukkos* to get his opinion on the beauty and *kashrus* of the *esrog* and *lulav* they were considering. If R' Zalman said it was beautiful, then you knew it was beautiful. If he showed any doubt whatsoever, the person would return the *lulav* or *esrog* in question and pick another one.

It happened one year that an extraordinary number of people came to R' Zalman. Even on *erev Yom Tov* the flow of people did not stop. Finally the last person left, and R' Zalman prepared some clothes and made his way to the *mikveh* to immerse himself before the holiday. On his way to the *mikveh* he was approached by a young boy, Aharon, the son of the well-known *talmid chacham,* R' Avrohom Moshe Katzenellenbogen.

"R' Zalman," the young lad called out, "could you please look at my *esrog?* My father got it for me, and I would like your opinion on it."

"My child," R' Zalman said as he rushed on, "I know your father. You can be sure that if he bought you the *esrog* it's perfectly kosher. There is no need to worry about it." And with that R' Zalman continued on his way.

Young Aharon was devastated. He had wanted to be just like the grownups and have the expert examine his own precious *esrog*, but the expert was obviously too busy. True it was late, just hours before *Yom Tov*, but it was hard for the boy to understand that. He went home dejected, but did not say anything about the incident to anyone.

The next morning, the first day of *Yom Tov*, R' Avrohom Moshe, the young boy's father, was sitting in his *sukkah* learning from a *sefer* before he left for *shul*. Suddenly he heard a knock at the door. He was surprised that anyone would be coming to his home this early. It was, after all, before *davening*. When he got to the door he was even more startled to see his good friend R' Zalman standing there.

"*Gut Yom Tov!*" R' Avrohom Moshe exclaimed. "To what do I owe this pleasure so early in the morning?"

"Is your son Aharon up yet?" R' Zalman asked, as he entered the *sukkah*.

"Is that whom you came to see?" R' Avrohom Moshe asked in surprise.

"Yes," replied R' Zalman with a smile, not saying anything more.

R' Avrohom Moshe ran hurriedly to his son's room and called out, "Aharon, Aharon, get up! You have a special visitor." Aharon forced his eyes open and asked, "This early in the morning? Who is it?"

He could hardly believe it when his father told him that it was none other than R' Zalman. The boy quickly washed *negel vasser* (water poured on the hands in the morning for spiritual purity) and came out to the front room where his visitor was waiting. "*Gut Yom Tov*, Aharon," R' Zalman began. "I came here to see your *esrog*."

The boy blushed with embarrassment and pleasure. "But you told me yesterday that the *esrog* was fine," the boy blurted out.

"Yes," said R' Zalman. "I did actually tell you that, but then I realized that I should have checked it before I made any statement.

I was a bit rushed yesterday, but I thought I had better have a look at the *esrog* before you use it for the first time this morning."

The child's father observed all this in stunned silence. He had no idea that his son had even met R' Zalman the previous day, and now, listening to their conversation, he began to understand what had happened right before *Yom Tov*.

The young boy beamed with pride and ran to get his *esrog*. He watched carefully as the expert R' Zalman scanned every centimeter of the little *esrog*, turning it slowly and peering at it from all angles as the light from the window shone on it. The child waited for R' Zalman's appraisal. "Young man," the elderly R' Zalman said, "that which I told you yesterday wasn't enough. Your *esrog* is so magnificent that I would be willing to trade with you — your *esrog* for mine — if you would agree."

The young boy smiled. "No, thank you," he said. "I would like to use the one my father bought for me, but it would not have been the same without your approval."

As the elated boy went back to his room, R' Avrohom Moshe could not help but marvel at the sensitivity that R' Zalman had displayed towards his son. It was obvious to him that R' Zalman had come to his home, not because he felt the *esrog* should be looked at, but rather to uplift the crestfallen child.

As R' Zalman rose to leave, he turned to R' Avrohom Moshe and said, "*Ah kindt is oichet ah mensch.* (A child is also a person.)"

The child eventually grew up to be a *melamed* (teacher) in a *yeshivah ketanah* (elementary school) in Jerusalem, where he retold the story to his *talmidim* (students). One of these students was later to become the famed *Maggid* of Jerusalem, R' Sholom Schwadron, and it is through R' Sholom that we know the story today.

◆§ A Link in the Chain

There is a phrase in the *Shabbos Minchah Shemoneh Esrei* (Sabbath afternoon service) "וּמִי כְּעַמְּךָ יִשְׂרָאֵל — Who is like Your nation of Israel." At times we hear about certain individuals in *Klal Yisrael* who perform such exemplary acts that one can only view their behavior with awe, and acknowledge that indeed no nation is blessed with people like those of the Jewish nation.

The following story is a case in point. Despite the fact that the people in the story undoubtedly deserve public acclaim, the nature of the episode is somewhat sensitive and thus the actual names of the people involved have been changed.

In the 1960's a man in his mid-forties passed away, leaving his wife and children. The oldest son, Yosef, in his early twenties at the time, left the yeshivah in which he was studying and took over his father's business so that he could support his mother and brothers and sisters. The people in his neighborhood were extremely fond of this particular family, and many of them made special efforts to assist the family in various ways. One evening during the *shivah* (week of mourning), for example, some members of the family went down to the basement of their home, only to find it filled with enough food to last for months. To this day they have never been able to figure out who put it there and when!

Yosef, who was now suddenly at the helm of his father's business, struggled daily as he sought to maintain the clients and associates that his father had acquired during his lifetime. As he was young and relatively new on the job, competitors tried to take advantage of Yosef's inexperience. Each day brought new worries and fears. But Yosef labored on, for his entire family depended on him.

A number of weeks after the *shivah*, a local businessman, Mr. Chaim Hans, approached Yosef in *shul* one morning and said, "I realize that things are not easy for you and the family at the moment. I would like to help by giving you this money to ease your burden somewhat. Please accept it." The envelope he held out contained two thousand dollars.

Yosef was reluctant to take the money because he didn't want to accept charity. Understanding this, Mr. Hans explained, "This is not *tzedakah;* it is a loan which doesn't have a due date. You may repay it whenever you wish. Please don't feel pressured."

Both Yosef and his mother were very grateful for the money, and were determined to try to pay it back as soon as possible.

A year and a half went by, and, although Mr. Hans helped the young man in other ways as well, no mention was ever made of the loan. Finally Yosef and his mother felt that they could afford to pay back the entire sum. Yosef called Mr. Hans at his office, told him that he wished to see him, and was invited to come by.

At their meeting Yosef thanked his benefactor again for the kindness that he had extended to the family, and told him that he was happy to now be able to pay back the loan in its entirety.

Mr. Hans smiled at Yosef and said, "Thank you for your intentions, but I don't want the money back."

Yosef was startled. "What do you mean, you don't want the money?" he asked. "When you first gave it to me, I told you that I didn't want to accept it because I didn't want to accept charity. You assured me that it was a loan. And as a loan it's my obligation to pay it back — and so here I am!"

Mr. Hans smiled gently at the young man and said, "Sit down. I have a story to tell you." And then, in his dignified and kindly manner, he told Yosef the following:

"A number of years ago I was having a very difficult time in business. I owed various people money, and I was on the verge of bankruptcy. At that time a man in our neighborhood, Mr. Louis Stein, approached me and said, 'I realize that you are in a difficult financial position. Here, let me give you some money. Hopefully it will be of some benefit to you. Please accept it.'

"At that time," Mr. Hans continued, "I told Mr. Stein that I simply could not accept money from him. But he reassured me by insisting that it was not *tzedakah* that he was giving me, but a loan with no time limit for repayment. I could pay it back whenever I wished. On that basis I took the money, because I really did need it at the time. Then a few years later when business, *baruch Hashem* (thank G-d), became better, I went to return the sum to him.

"When I presented him with an envelope containing the money, Mr. Stein refused to take it. I began to argue with him and said, 'You must take the money! You said that it was a loan, not charity! I have come to repay it.'

"Mr. Stein smiled at me and said, 'Chaim, it was indeed a loan, and you do have to pay it back . . . but not to me. I want you to pay back the loan in the following manner: One day in the future, when you come across a person or a family who needs the money, pass it along . . . as a loan. And when they come to pay it back, explain the terms of the loan to them, as I just explained them to you."

Mr. Hans smiled broadly at Yosef, who was awe struck by what he was hearing, and continued. "The money I gave you was indeed a loan, and now it's your turn and obligation to pay it back in the very same manner I paid back my loan. I chose to pay it to you; someday you and your mother will pass the money on to someone else."

And that's exactly what they did.

◆§ *A Request of a Lifetime*

Life is filled with decisions. Every day each one of us must make many of them. Some are major and some are minor, but every decision we make should be one that we are prepared to live with.

Decisions require varying degrees of thought, wisdom and foresight. Sometimes, though, a man must make a choice that could alter his life's course forever. He may not even have the luxury of time for consultation with friends or family. Thus the particular decision he makes comes from the depths of his heart and reveals his inner self and his definition of life's priorities.

In this incredible incident recently told by R' Yisroel Grossman, a *dayan* (judge) in Jerusalem, about his father R' Zalman, we learn, by way of a difficult decision he made, the values of an extraordinary Jew.

R' Zalman Grossman was an extremely pious Jew in Jerusalem who manifested a unique approach in his loving observance of *Shabbos*. From sunset on Friday afternoon until after reciting *Havdalah* on Saturday night, he did not sleep.

He explained his custom to his children by telling them, "The Talmud (*Shabbos* 119a) refers to *Shabbos* as a beautiful queen. Thus every Jew on this day is to be considered a king who has an opportunity to spend time with the queen." He would then tell his children a parable. "There was once a king who slept very little. People in his kingdom would ask him why he conducted himself this way and he would answer, 'When I sleep, I am like everyone else. I don't feel like a king. It is only when I am awake and aware of who I really am that I realize I am the king.' Therefore," R' Zalman continued, "why should I waste, by sleeping on *Shabbos*, even one moment of this wonderful opportunity that I have to spend the day with the *Shabbos* Queen?"

Thus R' Zalman would spend the entire *Shabbos* either learning *mishnayos*, saying *Tehillim*, singing *zemiros*, or praying with great fervor. As poor as he was, on *Shabbos* R' Zalman personified royalty.

In the year 1912, when Israel (then called Palestine) was under Turkish rule, poverty was rampant throughout the country. People were literally starving, and there was little opportunity for employment. R' Zalman had no choice but to leave Israel for a few years and come to America to find a means of livelihood by which to support his family back home. He borrowed money for a ticket, boarded a ship and began the long voyage over the Mediterranean Sea and across the Atlantic Ocean.

The first Friday night on board, R' Zalman decided that he would conduct himself as he did at home. He would observe *Shabbos* with the same intensity as he did every week. After he *davened*, sang *Shalom Aleichem*, recited in song the prayer *Ribbono shel Olam* and sang *Aishes Chayil*, he made *Kiddush* and ate his *Shabbos* meal. Throughout the meal — which he ate alone — he sang *zemiros* and peered into one of the many *sefarim* he had taken along.

Afterwards he sat by himself in a corner and began learning *mishnayos.*

What he hadn't been aware of was that, beginning halfway through his meal and continuing later as he was learning *mishnayos* and the *sidrah* of the week, a man was standing off to the side and observing him. For hours the man watched in amazement as R' Zalman absorbed the beauty and radiance of *Shabbos.* Eventually the man went off to sleep but R' Zalman was up all night.

In the morning, the man again observed the intensity and sweetness of R' Zalman's *tefillos.* He watched how R' Zalman made *Kiddush,* sang *zemiros* once again and ate his meal, completely involved with the sanctity of *Shabbos*. Throughout the afternoon and then at *Minchah* and *Shalosh Seudos* (the third *Shabbos* meal) the man continuously observed R' Zalman. Finally, after *Havdalah* the gentleman made his way to where R' Zalman was standing.

He began to speak with respect and awe. "I observed you for hours this past *Shabbos.* I have never in my life seen anyone become as involved with the beauty of *Shabbos* as you were. I cannot begin to tell you how touched I was by your demeanor. You may not know who I am, but my name is Baron Rothschild."

R' Zalman was quite surprised by this man's words and even more surprised that he had been watched over *Shabbos.* The two men got into a short conversation about their respective backgrounds, and the more the baron spoke to R' Zalman the more fascinated he became with him. Then the baron made a startling statement. "R' Zalman, I would like to honor any one request that you may have. I will give you fifteen minutes to think about it, and then let me know what I can do for you."

R' Zalman couldn't believe this sudden turn of good fortune. All he had to do now was ask Baron Rothschild for a substantial amount of money and he could then take the first boat back to Israel and spare himself the humiliation of collecting funds for himself and the members of his family.

R' Zalman went back to his berth to consider the matter. But the more he thought about it, the more a plight of a different kind came to mind.

Just two days before he left Israel, R' Zalman's brother, R' Shlomo Levi, had come to talk to him. R' Shlomo Levi was one of the founders of Mishmar HaYardein, a *moshav* (settlement) in the northern part of *Eretz Yisrael,* near Syria. R' Shlomo Levi explained to his brother that Mishmar HaYardein, along with its two neighboring *moshavim* — Rosh Pinah and Yesod HaMalah — were infested with malaria. Children and old people were dying every day as a result of this horrible disease, and young parents were confined to bed and could not work to support their families. The situation was worsening with each passing day. There simply was not enough medicine for everyone. "When you go to America," R' Shlomo Levi begged, "please don't forget about the children and their elders. Families are being decimated because there is not enough money for medication. Every dollar that you send us will help save lives."

Now, sitting in his berth all alone, R' Zalman was in a terrible quandary. His natural inclination was to try and save his own family from the clutches of extreme poverty and starvation — but what about the hundreds and hundreds of people in his brother's community up North? After a few agonizing minutes he made up his mind and went outside to meet with the baron.

"Have you decided what you would like?" asked the baron.

"Yes, Your Honor," replied R' Zalman. "I have a brother who is in involved with three communities in northern Israel. The area is plagued by rampant malaria that is causing the deaths of countless children and their parents. If you could somehow arrange for doctors to go to those communities and treat the sick, that would be the greatest favor you could do for me."

The baron shook hands with R' Zalman and told him he would try to do his best. The rest of the trip was uneventful, and R' Zalman eventually came to New York, where he set up an office in the Lower East Side to collect funds for the Yeshivah Ohel Moshe in Jerusalem.

About four months after he arrived, R' Zalman received a letter from his brother, R' Shlomo Levi. After preliminary greetings, the letter read, "My dear brother Zalman, I don't know how I can begin to describe what has gone on here during these last few weeks. Out of nowhere, like manna from Heaven, doctors and nurses came into our towns with truckloads of health supplies and medications. They opened three different pharmacies, dispensed pills to the sick, gave injections to those who needed them and prescribed medications. Almost immediately people stopped dying. You could see the health of the community improving day by day. A twenty-four-hour period actually went by during which there was not one reported death. We are all so grateful to *Hashem* for this sudden turn of events. For the first time in weeks people are actually smiling and hopeful."

R' Zalman could not believe what he was reading. The baron had actually complied with his request! R' Zalman continued reading the letter. "My dear brother, you needn't worry about us. *Hashem* has taken care of us. Worry about your own problems and may you and yours be helped as we were helped."

R' Zalman read the letter a second time, absorbing every word. When he finished, he buried his face in his hands and wept. He had performed the ultimate act of *chessed* (kindness) — for no one in Mishmar HaYardein or in the neighboring *moshavim* even knew that he was responsible for the countless lives which were being saved.

Years later R' Zalman would tell his children, "I cried for another reason as well. I cried because I was so grateful to *Hashem* for giving me the strength to overcome my natural inclination to save my own family first. It took a certain courage to think of others at that very difficult period in my life. That I should have been able to muster that strength and see the fruits of my action was overwhelming. How fortunate I was to be able to benefit in some way the people of *Klal Yisrael!*"

And the people in the *moshavim* never knew why they were helped!

❦ ❦ ❦

After a number of years R' Zalman returned to *Eretz Yisrael*, where he raised his distinguished family. However, before leaving the shores of America, this holy man lived through yet another incredibly inspirational incident (see the story "Royal Rescue," page 126).

⸙ Rise and Shine

The Talmud (*Berachos* 9b) teaches that *vasikin* (extremely devout people) would get up very early each morning to *daven Shacharis,* timing their prayers so that they would begin to recite the *Shemoneh Esrei* at sunrise. And, although few people are able to maintain such a schedule, this is the optimal time for *davening.*

When R' Isser Zalman Meltzer (1870-1953), the *Rosh Yeshivah* of Yeshivas Eitz Chaim in Jerusalem (and father-in-law of R' Aharon Kotler [1891-1962]), was getting on in years, he had a *bachur* living in his home to attend to his needs.

One evening, R' Isser Zalman called the *bachur* to his room and said, "I have been thinking that perhaps now, at this stage of my life, I should begin to *daven k'vasikin.* Tomorrow morning I will get up early, wake you, and then together we'll go to a *shul* not too far from here where they have a daily *vasikin minyan.*"

The *bachur* readily agreed and offered to wake up early himself and then wake R' Isser Zalman. The *Rav,* however, insisted that he be the one to get up first. "After all," he said, "it is only because of me that we are going to be changing our regular schedule."

The student, though, was so excited with the anticipation of doing something special with a *gadol hador* that he could hardly fall asleep.

Several times throughout the night the young *bachur* awoke, each time looking at his watch to see if it was time to prepare to go. When he realized it was still too early, he would doze off again for a while. Finally the hour came when he knew that R' Isser Zalman should be coming to wake him. He waited in bed, not daring to get up and wake R' Isser Zalman. An hour passed and still R' Isser Zalman had not stirred. The *bachur* figured that perhaps the *Rav* had overslept. By this time, he knew, they had missed the time for *vasikin*, so he went back to sleep with the thought that the next day he would make sure to wake R' Isser Zalman for the *vasikin minyan*.

A while later, at the time that he customarily awoke each day,

R' Isser Zalman came out of his room. Upon seeing the youth he said, "My child, don't for a moment think that I overslept. Late last night as I was lying in bed, it occurred to me that I have been *davening* for years in the *shul* that we go to every morning. There are many older men there, true *tzaddikim*, who wait every morning for me to greet them and wish them a good day. It occurred to me that if I now left that *minyan* and began *davening* somewhere else, they would have *agmas nefesh* (anguish). So I made a calculation and decided that it is not worth *davening k'vasikin* if it would mean causing aggravation even to a few precious Jews. For that reason I have decided to continue *davening* at our regular *minyan*." And with that, R' Isser Zalman relinquished for himself the idea of *davening k'vasikin*.

"That," says R' Sholom Schwadron emphatically, "is *ahavas Yisrael*. And these men never realized what R' Isser Zalman had given up on their behalf!"

◆§ *A Time to Wait*

Great people seem to have time for everyone. It's the little people who always seem too busy to give of their time for others. The following story is heart warming, not merely for the loving concern depicted by a *gadol hador* (great Torah scholar of a generation) for a young boy, but also because it is an extraordinary lesson about time, patience and priorities.

This incredible incident was retold by R' Kalman Epstein, a *Rosh Yeshivah* in Yeshivah Shaar HaTorah, of Queens. The incident happened many years ago to his uncle, R' Leib, when he was fourteen years old.

Leib studied in a *yeshivah ketanah* in Russia, and was on his way home for vacation. His train was scheduled to come into the town station at 1:00, Thursday afternoon, when he would board it for the day-long trip to his home in Stutchin, in Poland. Leib knew that even if the train were to be on time, he would get home just a few hours before *Shabbos.*

But the train was far from punctual. It didn't pull into the station until Thursday evening, and it was after dark when Leib finally boarded. By Friday morning Leib realized that there was no way for him to manage to get to Stutchin in time for *Shabbos*. He would have to spend *Shabbos* elsewhere.

He asked the conductor where the train would be making stops. He reasoned that if he recognized one of the towns as a *Yiddishe* place, he would get off and hope that he would be invited home by someone. To his delight, the conductor told him that one of the stops would be in a town not far from Radin.

Leib was thrilled, for his great-uncle — the Chofetz Chaim himself — lived in Radin. Leib's grandfather was the Chofetz Chaim's brother. Surely he would be able to spend *Shabbos* with the great *tzaddik* of Radin! When the train stopped, Leib took his packages and got off, asked directions to Radin, and made his way as fast as he could to the house of his great-uncle.

When he got to the house he was greeted cheerfully by the Chofetz Chaim's wife, who said that her husband had already left for *shul*. She explained that he usually went to *shul* quite early, because it was his custom to learn with the people assembled there before *davening* began. She suggested that Leib rest up a bit before he went off to *shul* himself.

Having had no sleep the previous night because of the bumpy train ride and his uncomfortable seat, the exhausted boy fell asleep almost immediately.

When he awoke, he realized that the Chofetz Chaim was already sitting at the *Shabbos* table, reading from a *sefer*. The Chofetz Chaim greeted Leib warmly, told him to wash *negel vasser* (ritual washing after one has slept), *daven Kabbalas Shabbos* and *Maariv*, and then they would sit down to eat the *Shabbos seudah.*

After Leib finished *davening*, the Chofetz Chaim went and called his wife to join them. He recited *Kiddush*, and the three of them — the elderly *Rav*, his wife, and the young fourteen-year-old boy — ate the *Shabbos seudah* together.

After the *seudah*, the Chofetz Chaim excused himself and went to his room to sleep. Leib lay down once again on the same couch where he had previously taken his nap. He tried to sleep again, but couldn't. Having just slept a little while earlier, he found it hard to doze off again. He got up and went to the kitchen. On the counter he noticed a small clock. He picked it up, read the time, and opened and closed his eyes in disbelief. The watch seemed to be working — but it read 4:00! How could it possibly be 4:00 in the morning? It couldn't be just a few hours before daybreak! He looked outside and saw that it was totally dark, so he could not figure out what time it really was. Confused, he went back to the couch and eventually fell asleep.

When he awoke the next morning he went to the kitchen, where he saw the *rebbetzin*, the Chofetz Chaim's wife. "*Gut Shabbos,*" he began, bowing his head slightly in respect. Then he asked the question which had been troubling him. "Last night, after we ate the *seudah,* I couldn't fall asleep and so I came here into the kitchen. I saw a clock that said it was 4:00 in the morning. Was that clock working properly? What time did we actually finish the *seudah*?"

"Yes," she answered. "It was indeed very late when we finished."

"But the *seudah* didn't take that long," protested the puzzled Leib. "What time did we start eating? Did I sleep that long when I first got here?"

"I'll tell you what happened," said the *rebbetzin.* "When the *Rav* came home from *shul* you were in a very deep sleep. I wanted to wake you up so that you could hear *Kiddush,* but my husband wouldn't let me. He said that you were exhausted from your long trip, and suggested that I let you rest. He said he would wait to make *Kiddush* until you got up. However, as time was getting on he didn't want me to wait for him, so he instructed our son Aharon and me to make *Kiddush* and eat the *seudah.* My husband sat and learned, waiting until you awoke. We had arranged that when you did wake up he would come and get me, and we would all sit together in your honor for the *Shabbos seudah.*"

The *rebbetzin* added, "You did indeed sleep for quite a few hours, but the *Rav* insisted that he would not start his Friday night *seudah* without his special guest."

Aside from everything else that is magnificent in this story is the fact that neither the Chofetz Chaim nor his wife would have said anything to the boy about their astounding behavior if he had not happened to ask about it.

◆§ *A Blessing with No Strings Attached*

When one is a parent or a teacher, he or she has ample opportunity to criticize or chastise a child who has done something wrong. The instinctive way to do this is to lash out and berate the offender. It takes wisdom and patience, though, to be encouraging and yet critical at the same time. The Talmud (*Sotah* 47a) says, "לְעוֹלָם תְּהֵא שְׂמֹאל דּוֹחָה וִימִין מְקָרֶבֶת – Reject with the left [hand] and draw near with the right [hand]." The following episode is a beautiful example of this teaching.

A young fellow appeared before R' Chaim Ozer Grodzinsky (1863-1939), the *gadol hador* (acknowledged Torah leader) of his time, to get a *brachah* (blessing) so that he would not have to go to the Soviet Army. The hazards of war were frightening, and the term of service could be almost endless — usually twenty to twenty-five years — especially if the Soviet authorities knew that the inductee was Jewish.

In the course of his discussion with the young man, R' Chaim Ozer asked him, "Do you wear *tzitzis* (a four-cornered fringed garment worn by Jewish males)?"

The boy was embarrassed to admit the truth but he wouldn't lie to the man to whom he had come for a blessing, and so he looked down and said honestly, "No."

The conversation continued and R' Chaim Ozer asked, "Do you at least put on *tefillin* (phylacteries) every day?"

The boy hesitated for a moment, and then said in a low voice, "*Rebbe,* I can't lie to you. I don't."

"What about *Shabbos?*" asked R' Chaim Ozer. "Do you observe *Shabbos?*"

Once again the boy couldn't look the *rav* in the face and so, staring at the ground, he said, "*Rebbe,* I must tell you that I am not religious and I am not a Sabbath observer."

Silence permeated the room as the frightened boy waited for R' Chaim Ozer's next words. He was sure that he would be asked to leave immediately, or be rebuked strongly. He braced himself for the harsh words that he knew must come. But instead, R' Chaim Ozer said softly to him, "I give you a *brachah* that the Soviet authorities should be as disappointed in you as I am."

The boy thought his heart would melt as he understood at once both the rebuke and the blessing of R' Chaim Ozer. He nodded his thanks and left the room at once.

Two weeks later he came back to R' Chaim Ozer and said, "*Rebbe,* I wanted to tell you that your *brachah* helped. I was rejected by the Army." Then he lifted up his shirt and showed R' Chaim Ozer the *tzitzis* that he was now wearing.

The young man wore *tzitzis* and *tefillin*, and observed *Shabbos* for the rest of his life!

⊰§ *A Viennese Table*

In the 1930s, poverty was rampant in Eastern Europe. Numerous people left their homes and headed westward to Austria, seeking employment and the opportunity to enhance their financial status. Many Jews settled in the capital city of Vienna, the home of an established vibrant Jewish community.

Throughout the Jewish districts in Vienna it was known that the industrious R' Dovid Schlesinger (the son-in-law of the noted *Moreinu* R' Yaakov Rosenheim, 1870-1965) was exceptional in his acts of *chessed* (benevolence) and his house was open to all wayfarers. When strangers appeared in *shul* and seemed to have no place to go, he would invite them for a meal. Hardly a *Shabbos* passed without several guests at his table.

His son R' Zev, of Kew Gardens, New York, recently told this story.

One afternoon two young men came from Poland to seek employment in Vienna. They made their way to the headquarters of Zeirei Agudath Israel, a religious organization for young men. It was only hours before *Yom Tov*, and the two fellows were worried that they would have no place to eat that evening. "No problem," they were told, "just make your way to the Schiff *shul* [the main synagogue in Vienna, referred to by that name because it was on Schiff Street], and make sure that R' Dovid Schlesinger sees you both. You will undoubtedly be invited to his home."

Close to three hundred people *davened* in the Schiff *shul* every *Shabbos*, and even more were there on *Yom Tov*. Almost everyone had a designated seat, and so guests and travelers would all congregate in the last rows of the *shul*. Throughout the *davening* the two young men tried to make eye contact with Mr. Schlesinger, but they couldn't be sure he had noticed them.

When the *davening* was over and people began to file out of the huge *shul*, the two boys stationed themselves at the end of the main aisle in the middle of the *shul* so that, as Mr. Schlesinger walked towards the doorway, he would most certainly have to see them.

Sure enough, Mr. Schlesinger was making his way down that aisle, accompanied by another man. The two of them were deeply engrossed in conversation. As he came towards the two boys Mr. Schlesinger nodded to them, said *"Gut Yom Tov,"* and went on. They watched in dismay as he then walked with the other gentleman out of the *shul*.

They couldn't believe it! He was the only person they had been counting on — and now he had left without them! What were they to do? They stood around for a while and finally, not being sure what to do next, they too left the *shul*.

They stood outside in the dark, looking around hopelessly. After about five minutes they saw a man running towards them. As he came closer they recognized him. It was Mr. Schlesinger! "Boys, would you please do me the honor of joining us for the *seudah* tonight?" he asked breathlessly. The startled fellows were only too happy to extend this 'honor.' They could hardly accept fast enough!

They walked alongside their host as he made his way home, but they couldn't help wondering why he hadn't invited them when he first saw them in *shul*. Was he hoping that someone else would invite them? Did he think they had already been taken care of?

By the middle of the meal their curiosity had gotten the best of them. They just had to ask him. "While we appreciate your gracious invitation to us," one of the boys said, "we can't figure out something. Didn't you see us in *shul* as you were leaving? Why did you leave and then come back for us?"

R' Dovid gave them his warmest smile and explained. "Do you gentlemen recall that when I was walking down the aisle, I was walking with another man?"

"Yes," they nodded.

"Well, at one time that man was a very wealthy person but now, unfortunately, he has lost all his money. I knew that if I were to invite you while he was standing there he would feel compelled to invite one of you as well. He would have insisted that one of you go to his home and the other to mine. But I know that now he simply cannot afford to have guests. He hardly has enough money to feed his own family, and therefore I could not have possibly invited you while I was talking to him. However after I had walked with him down the block as I usually do, and he turned the corner, I was able to rush back here. I was hoping that you would both still be outside the *shul* — and thank G-d you were — so that you could grace our table."

The *chessed* of *hachnasas orchim* (inviting guests) is indeed praiseworthy. Enhanced as it was here with kindness and consideration, it is simply extraordinary.

◆§ *House Guests*

It is said that outside the house of the Maharsha (R' Shmuel Eliezer Eidels, 1555-1631), head of the *beis din* (religious court) in Ostroh, Poland, and author of a noted Talmudic commentary, there was a placard on which was written the verse from *Iyov* (31:32), "בַּחוּץ לֹא יָלִין גֵּר דְּלָתַי לָאֹרַח אֶפְתָּח — Let no stranger sleep outside, my doors are open for guests." Indeed, it was well known that the Maharsha's home was open to all wayfarers, regardless of their station in life.

The Maharsha stressed the careful wording of *Chazal* (the Talmudic scholars) in their teaching in *Avos* (1:15), "הֱוֵי מְקַבֵּל אֶת כָּל הָאָדָם בְּסֵבֶר פָּנִים יָפוֹת – Receive every person with [your] cheerful countenance." The dictum specifically states, "כָּל הָאָדָם – every person," indicating that it is proper and obligatory to greet all individuals in a friendly manner, regardless of their positions in life.

The following story, told by R' Sholom Schwadron, involves the Brisker *Rav*, R' Yosheh (Yosef) Ber Soloveitchik (1820-1892), author of *Beis HaLevi*, who, as the Maharsha did generations earlier, displayed an attitude of uniform concern to all members of *Klal Yisrael*.

It happened one bitter cold evening that R' Yosheh Ber had to travel to another town, through a blinding snowstorm, to take care of an important matter. The roads were getting impassable, and finally R' Yosheh Ber and his wagon driver realized they would have to stop somewhere and stay overnight.

It was already very late. The wind was howling and visibility was extremely poor, but the wagon driver thought he remembered coming across an inn somewhere in this area, so he continued on. After traveling a bit more they came upon the inn, and the driver told the Brisker *Rav* to wait in the wagon while he went to knock on the door. The driver knocked and knocked but there was no answer. He continued banging on the door and still there was no answer.

He came back to R' Yosheh Ber and said, "I think we will have to continue on. There doesn't seem to be anyone here."

"There has got to be someone there," said R' Yosheh Ber. "Just knock as hard as you can."

The driver — a huge strong fellow — knocked until the owner, who had been sleeping upstairs, thought the door would be shattered. The owner came to his window and yelled down, "What do you want so late at night? Can't you see this place is closed?"

The owner had indeed heard the knocking earlier, but he didn't feel like getting out of his warm comfortable bed to welcome a traveler who happened to need lodgings so late at night.

"We are freezing out here and it is dangerous for us to travel further. Please open up so we can come inside," the wagon driver yelled back.

"You couldn't find any other place?" the innkeeper shouted downward.

"We must get out of the cold or we'll freeze to death," the driver roared into the frozen night.

The innkeeper slowly got out of bed, grumbled something under his breath, and came downstairs to see just who was making all the noise. When he opened the door, the driver ran to get the Brisker *Rav*, who had been waiting in the shelter of the covered wagon.

The two men made their way into the inn where the innkeeper made it obvious that he was in no mood to tend to them. He told his guests to unpack their things in a side room which was near the washrooms. The room was cold, but to the two travelers it was a great improvement over being outdoors. The *Rav* and his driver tried to make themselves comfortable in the tiny room as they settled in for the night.

About half an hour later a tremendous din came from outside — the noise of people banging on the front door. "Open up in there!" someone called from the other side of the door. "The *Rebbe* and his *chassidim* are here!"

The owner, who had just fallen asleep, couldn't help but hear the commotion outside. He ran to the window and saw that indeed there were close to twenty people outside his door. That meant good business, and so he ran downstairs and opened the door with a smile. "Come right in out of the cold," he said warmly. "I have room for all of you."

The *chassidim* ushered their *rebbe* [some versions of the story say that it was R' Aharon Koidonover (1839-1897)] in ahead of them, and soon a band of twenty *chassidim* followed. The owner invited them all into his main dining room, assuring them they would be made comfortable, and convincing them how lucky they were to be able to spend the night at his inn. The owner brought out whiskey and cake and passed around the drinks until everyone felt warm. Soon songs and lively conversation broke out as the guests celebrated the fact that they had indeed found a place to spend the night, and were saved from continuing their perilous journey through the frozen darkness.

As their partying continued, the *Rebbe* had to leave the room for a moment to wash his hands. As he walked towards the washroom he noticed two people shivering in the side room. The Brisker *Rav*, who heard the *Rebbe* coming, pulled his hat over his eyes so that he would not be recognized. But the *Rebbe* entered the room, walked over to the man hidden under the hat, and lifted the brim.

"*Oy vay*! Brisker *Rav!*" he exclaimed, recognizing the Torah luminary immediately. "What are you doing here in this cold room? Who put you here?" The *Rebbe* didn't wait for an answer but insisted that the *Rav* and his driver get up immediately and come with him. The two followed the *Rebbe* into the huge room where the *chassidim* had gathered.

As the *Rebbe* walked in with the two behind him, everyone stood up. "Do you see who is in the inn with us?" the *Rebbe* asked out loud. "The *gadol hador*, R' Yosheh Ber."

And with that he led the *Rav* to the head of the table where he seated him, disregarding his protests.

Soon the owner of the inn came in with more food, and the *Rebbe* tore into him verbally. "How could you have put the Brisker *Rav*, the *gadol hador*, in that small cold room? Where is your *kavod haTorah* (honor befitting a Torah scholar)? He was freezing in there. You must ask the *Rav* for *mechilah* (forgiveness)!"

Everyone turned to see what the innkeeper would do, and slowly he began talking to the Brisker *Rav*. "I am sorry," he said. "I didn't realize who you were."

The Brisker *Rav* peered at the innkeeper through icy eyes and said aloud, "I cannot be *mochel* (forgiving)."

The *Rebbe* angrily turned towards the innkeeper. "Then you must ask for forgiveness again," the *Rebbe* said. "You obviously mistreated the *Rav* and his driver, so you must beg his pardon a second time." And once again the innkeeper asked for forgiveness and once again the Brisker *Rav* refused to grant it.

The *Rebbe* continued to address the innkeeper, saying, "Your sin is so great that your end will be a bitter one unless you somehow get the *Rav* to forgive you."

The innkeeper now pleaded with the *Rav* to forgive him, but the *Rav* remained silent. People began to wonder amongst themselves why the *Rav* was being so obstinate. Finally, as the innkeeper, along with everyone else, waited on edge to hear what R' Yosheh Ber would say, the *Rav* began to speak softly.

"My dear friend and host, of course I will forgive you. But first I would like to explain something to you and to all who are here. Many of you are aware that this *Shabbos* we will read [as the Torah portion of the week] *Parshas Vayishlach.*

"In the *parshah* we find that the children of Yaakov were angered when they learned that their sister Dinah, the daughter of our Patriarch Yaakov, had been defiled by the immoral man, Shechem. The verse states (*Bereishis* 34:7) 'וַיִּחַר לָהֶם מְאֹד, כִּי נְבָלָה עָשָׂה בְיִשְׂרָאֵל לִשְׁכַּב אֶת בַּת יַעֲקֹב, וְכֵן לֹא יֵעָשֶׂה — The men (Yaakov's children) were distressed and were fired deeply with indignation, for he (Shechem) had committed an outrage in Israel by defiling the daughter of Jacob — such a thing may not be done.'

"Why," asked R' Yosheh Ber, "did the Torah add the last part of the verse, 'וְכֵן לֹא יֵעָשֶׂה — Such a thing may not be done?' The Torah had already expressed the anger of Dinah's brothers (in the first part of the verse) at the outrage that had been committed.

"The answer," continued the Brisker *Rav*, "is that the Torah is telling us that 'such a thing may not be done' under any circumstances, regardless of whether it was to the family of Jacob or to any other family.

"And that," said the *Rav*, "is the problem here. You are begging my pardon because I am the Brisker *Rav*. That's not why you should be asking forgiveness. You should be asking forgiveness because it was wrong of you to behave like that to any Jew that may have come to your inn. No one should be left out in the cold waiting, and then be the subject of your derision.

"I harbor no ill feelings towards you," continued the *Rav*. "Quite the contrary. I forgive you and I would greatly appreciate if the very next time you come to Brisk, you will be a guest in my home!"

The innkeeper was without words for he was in an emotional quandary. On one hand he was gratified and relieved that the burden of guilt had been lifted from his shoulders by his having been forgiven, while on the other he felt humbled by the lesson he had just been taught. Slowly he walked up to where the *Rav* was sitting, bowed his head respectfully, and told the *Rav* that he would indeed welcome the opportunity to be a guest at the *Rav's* home. The *Rav* smiled warmly, and everyone drank *l'chaim* as the rest of the evening was spent in a warm and friendly atmosphere.

By the next morning the storm had subsided and everyone prepared to continue on his own particular way. The innkeeper bade everyone farewell, and as he watched the travelers fade into the distance, he realized that a change had come over him because of the special individuals who had by chance spent an evening at his inn.

❦ ❦ ❦

A number of weeks later the innkeeper had an occasion to be in the city of Brisk, and true to his word he made his way to the home of R' Yosheh Ber. The *Rav* went out of his way to serve the innkeeper personally, and saw to it that the man's accommodations met the highest possible standards.

As the guest personally experienced the quality of the *Rav's* *hachnasas orchim* (hospitality) and saw how the *Rav* went out of his way to make him comfortable, the transformation that had begun a few weeks ago became complete. The innkeeper returned to his roadside inn having learned, both by instruction and example, how to treat a fellow Jew. From then on his inn became a model of hospitality and good cheer as he became the most noted host in the entire region.

In the Heat of Rage

A man who suffers humiliation and degradation can, as a result, be broken in spirit. If the humiliation is public, the individual might even wish he were dead. Indeed, the Talmud (*Bava Metzia* 58b) teaches, "כָּל הַמַּלְבִּין פְּנֵי חֲבֵירוֹ בָּרַבִּים כְּאִלּוּ שׁוֹפֵךְ דָּמִים — If anyone publicly humiliates another person, it is as though he spills [his] blood."

Obviously there are levels of humiliation, and as the Talmud (*Bava Kama* 83b) further states, "הַכֹּל לְפִי הַמְּבַיֵּשׁ וְהַמִּתְבַּיֵּשׁ — It all depends upon [the status of] the one who humiliates and the one who is humiliated."

Regardless of how humble a person may be, he must be realistic in seeing himself as others see him. A person of prominent position — whether a parent, teacher, or community leader — who truly views himself as simple and insignificant still has the responsibility in his interactions with others to treat them with an understanding of how they perceive him personally.

The following story, retold by R' Chaim Shapiro of Baltimore, makes us realize the pain that a *rav,* R' Yisroel Yaakov Lubchansky (d. 1941), endured in order not to embarrass someone — even one who, many might feel, would have well deserved it.

In the town of New Baranovich, Poland, in the 1920s and '30s, there was no electricity, nor was there an oil or gas system for heating people's homes or *shuls.* The only heat produced for the *shul* came from the stove against its back wall. The unfortunate beggars who traveled from city to city relied on the *shul's* being kept warm overnight, for there they would sleep on the benches. It was the *shammas'* job to keep the wood burning in the potbellied stove, so that those who came to learn in *shul* in the evening, and those who arrived very early in the morning — before dawn — to learn or say *Tehillim* (*Psalms*), would be warm and comfortable.

Quite often, though, the *shammas* was negligent in performing this duty, and thus it had become an unspoken rule that the beggars who traveled from town to town would themselves, if necessary, feed the potbellied stove throughout the night from the stockpile of wood left alongside the stove by the *shammas.* However, if there were no beggars stopping over, or if those sleeping in the *shul* were lazy, by the time morning came the *shul* would be freezing. The *shammas* would then be rebuked by the people who came to *daven* and learn in the morning.

R' Yisroel Yaakov Lubchansky was the *rav* in the town of New Baranovich. In order to protect the *shammas,* who was very often negligent in his job, R' Yisroel Yaakov would leave his house very early in the morning while it was still dark outside, go to the *shul,* gather up the wood, pile it in the stove, light a fire and blow at the coals until he saw that the fire caught — all to make sure that it was warm for the early morning *mispalelim* (people who came to pray).

After a while the people began to take for granted that the *shul* would be warm every morning, and they complimented the *shammas* for his fine and dedicated work. The *shammas,* in turn, thought that it was the beggars who, in their own self-interest, were keeping the stove warm. Nevertheless he accepted the compliments, rationalizing that it was he who was nice enough to let the beggars sleep in the *shul* in the first place.

One winter morning, while it was still dark outside, R' Yisroel Yaakov came in as he did every day, to pile the wood into the oven. The *shammas* happened to arrive early that day, and noticed a man stoking the fire. "Good morning," the *shammas* called out as he made his way towards the stove. R' Yisroel Yaakov knew that if the *shammas* would realize that it was the *rav* who was actually doing the work which he, himself, was supposed to be doing, the man would be embarrassed, so he didn't reply.

R' Yisroel Yaakov hoped that the *shammas* would just go about his business of collecting *siddurim* and putting away *sefarim.* But, instead, the *shammas* became offended. "Good morning!" he yelled defiantly, sure that he was addressing a beggar. He waited for a reply. R' Yisroel Yaakov went about his work, putting his face closer to the stove to make sure that the *shammas* did not recognize him. If he answered, the *shammas* would realize at once who he was. R' Yisroel Yaakov just nodded his head and continued to blow at the coals so they would light the wood.

In a fit of rage, the *shammas* approached the 'beggar' from behind and kicked him, almost pushing the *rav* into the stove.

"What do you mean, you ingrate? You don't even answer when someone talks to you?"

By this time R' Yisroel Yaakov's face was in the stove, and he was choking and coughing from the smoke that was seeping into his lungs. The *shammas* gave him one more shove and walked away. By this time the *rav's* beard had caught on fire!

Realizing that the *shammas* had walked away, R' Yisroel Yaakov quickly turned away from the stove, and without a word ran out of the *shul,* hiding his face so that no one should recognize him. When R' Yisroel Yaakov came to *shul* later that morning with part of his beard missing, the people assumed that an accident had occurred in his own home.

❦ ❦ ❦

It was only years later, when R' Yisroel Yaakov had taken the position of *Mashgiach* in R' Elchonon Wasserman's yeshivah in Baranovich, that a family member revealed what had actually happened.

The Talmud (*Sotah* 10b) states: "נוֹחַ לוֹ לְאָדָם שֶׁיַּפִּיל עַצְמוֹ לְתוֹךְ כִּבְשַׁן הָאֵשׁ וְאַל יַלְבִּין פְּנֵי חֲבֵירוֹ בָּרַבִּים — It is better for one to throw himself into a burning furnace rather than humiliate another person publicly." R' Yisroel Yaakov Lubchansky, a man in our times, lived by that credo literally.

❧ *Departure Delayed*

R' Shneur Kotler (1918-1982), *Rosh Yeshivah* of Beth Medrash Govoha in Lakewood, New Jersey, was known not only for his outstanding Torah scholarship, but also for his extraordinary sensitivities to the feelings of others. This story, told by his *talmid,* R' Gavriel Finkel, is typical of the way R' Shneur showed his consideration towards others.

R' Shneur was in New York for a wedding. He had made the trip from Lakewood even though he was under intense pressure to get back as soon as possible for an important meeting later that night in his yeshivah office. A year earlier, the father of the *chassan* (groom) had done the yeshivah a favor, and R' Shneur felt that it was only right to reciprocate and participate in the gentleman's family *simchah.*

As R' Shneur and the young man who had driven him to New York made their way into the wedding hall, R' Shneur said, "Please be sure to be waiting right at this door immediately after the *chuppah* (wedding ceremony). I must get back to Lakewood as soon as possible." Naturally, the young man agreed to the *Rosh Yeshivah's* request.

After the *chuppah,* the young man made his way to the main entrance. Within moments R' Shneur was there. "I have to stay a little while longer," said R' Shneur to his driver, "but I should be ready in about ten minutes."

The young man thought that perhaps some important matter had come up which demanded R' Shneur's attention, and so he watched to see just where it was that R' Shneur was going. However, the *Rosh Yeshivah* didn't seem to be going anyplace specific. He chatted with a few people who came over to him, he made his way to the father of the *chassan* and wished him *Mazel Tov,* and then went to the father of the *kallah* (bride) and wished him *Mazel Tov* as well.

After a while R' Shneur once again met the driver at the door and said, "I'm sorry, but I must stay just a bit longer, and then we will be on our way."

It was almost twenty minutes later when R' Shneur returned to the appointed place, and finally the *Rosh Yeshivah* and his *talmid* began the trip back to Lakewood.

In the car, R' Shneur turned to the young man and said, "You are probably wondering why I felt that we should stay the extra time. Let me explain. You see, at the *chuppah* I was not given a *kibud* (an honor). There were many important people there, and I'm sure the families were very careful about whom to honor with the recitation of the seven wedding blessings. However, it occurred to me after the *chuppah* that if I were to leave right away, someone may think that I left because I was either embarrassed or insulted that I had not been given a *kibud*. Perhaps even the father of the groom might feel that I left early because I was upset. That would have put a damper on his *simchah*. I therefore felt it my obligation to stay a little bit longer so that it could not possibly seem that anyone had offended me in any way."

Cause for Alarm

Throughout his life, R' Yaakov Kaminetzky (1892-1986), the *Rosh Yeshivah* of Yeshivah Torah Vodaath in Brooklyn, was known for the original quality of his insight. In this episode we witness an unusual display of sensitivity to others.

In the year 1955, R' Yaakov Kaminetzky was called to travel out-of-town to settle a dispute between two religious institutions. At the time, one of his former *talmidim*, Rabbi Monni Weisberger, was working for Torah Umesorah (the umbrella organization of yeshivah day schools in America). R' Yaakov asked Rabbi Weisberger to accompany him as his interpreter. R' Yaakov understood English, but felt that in a matter where it was vital for every fact to be understood, it was imperative to have someone with him who could translate exactly what each party was saying.

Rabbi Weisberger was thrilled to have the opportunity to spend time with, and be of assistance to, his *rebbe*, and so he readily agreed to accompany him. As R' Yaakov had presumed that his *talmid* would agree to accompany him, he said, "I thought you would consent to come with me, so I have already purchased a ticket for you." The two were to meet Sunday morning at Penn Station, at 7:00 A.M.

On *Shabbos* night R' Yaakov called Rabbi Weisberger. "I just remembered that you recently got married. Aren't you still within the *shanah rishonah* (first year of marriage)?"

"Yes, that's correct," answered his *talmid*.

"If that's the case," said R' Yaakov, "there are those who hold that it is not proper, unless for reasons of earning a livelihood, for a husband to leave town within the first year of marriage.* Ask your wife whether she would like to come along. I will arrange for someone to take her to tour the city while we are occupied with the *din Torah* (religious adjudication)."

Rabbi Weisberger asked his wife whether she would like to join them, and after a moment's thought she said that yes, she would. The *talmid* relayed the message to his *rebbe*, who then smiled and said, "I thought she would say that, and so I purchased a ticket for her as well."

(Rabbi Weisberger feels that R' Yaakov did not wait to purchase the additional ticket on Sunday morning when they would all meet at Penn Station, for R' Yaakov understood that were he to wait, Rabbi Weisberger would then insist on paying for his wife's ticket himself. This way it would be too late, because the ticket would already have been purchased.)

Sunday morning, when Rabbi and Mrs. Weisberger met R' Yaakov at Penn Station, R' Yaakov — who was usually cheerful and upbeat — appeared haggard and exhausted. After greeting his *rebbe*, Rabbi Weisberger said to R' Yaakov, "The *Rosh Yeshivah* looks a bit tired."

"I didn't sleep last night," replied R' Yaakov. He then went on to explain. "Last night it was very hot, and I had to keep the window open in the room where I sleep. (This was before it was common for everyone to have air conditioners.) I knew that in order to meet you here at 7:00 A.M. in the morning, I would have to be up by 4:00 A.M." (R' Yaakov had a *seder* [routine] of learning before he *davened* every morning, and with the train scheduled to leave so early in the day, R' Yaakov's regular routine would have had to start that much earlier.)

"I set my alarm for 4:00 A.M.," R' Yaakov went on, "and then I remembered that the *goy* (gentile) who lives next door, a very fine man, is a very light sleeper. I know that the only day on which he can sleep late is Sunday morning, and I didn't want my alarm to go off that early for it might wake him. It says (*Vayikra* 5:23), 'וְהֵשִׁיב אֶת הַגְּזֵלָה — And one shall return that which he stole.' It is an

* See *Sefer HaChinuch, Mitzvah* 581; *Devarim* 24:5.

obligation to return an item if one stole it, but for *gezel sheinah* (stealing someone's sleep), it is impossible to make restitution. Therefore, I decided not to set the alarm at all. For that reason I was up all night, learning, and that's why I appear so tired."

☙ *Health, Education and Welfare*

We all know that is it proper and laudable to be concerned for the welfare of others. The following story retold by R' Lipa Geldwerth, however, happening when it did, goes almost beyond the scope of human imagination.

When the wife of the Tshebiner *Rav*, R' Dov Berish Weidenfeld (1879-1965), was very ill, she spent the last few weeks of her life in an Israeli hospital. With each passing day she became weaker and weaker. Finally one afternoon, in a special unit in the hospital, away from her room, she passed away. When the Tshebiner *Rav* was informed of his wife's passing he gasped and cried softly to himself.

After a few moments, though, he set aside his own grief, turned to those around him and urgently said, "Make sure they do not tell my wife's roommate that my wife passed away. She herself is a very sick lady and the two of them had became friendly over the last few days. If she hears the terrible news about her friend, it could *chas veshalom* (Heaven forbid) have a harmful effect on her and make her situation even more perilous than it is. See to it that she is merely told that her friend was transferred."

❦ ❦ ❦

Even in grief, there is greatness.

◆§ A Touch of Class

On a visit to Montreal, I heard this touching story from R' Pinchus Hirschprung, who is one of the world's outstanding *beki'im* (knowledgeable experts) in *Shas* (Talmud) and *poskim* (*halachic* literature).

R' Hirschprung was one of the prominent students in the world-famous Lubliner yeshivah, which for years had been headed by the renowned R' Meir Shapiro (1887-1934). In 1939 R' Hirschprung was asked to travel to America on behalf of the yeshivah. He thought that it would be helpful to get a letter of recommendation concerning the yeshivah from the *gadol hador* (outstanding Torah scholar of the generation), R' Chaim Ozer Grodzinsky (1863-1939), and so he traveled to a small town outside Vilna where R' Chaim Ozer was recuperating from a serious illness.

R' Hirschprung explained the nature of his visit to R' Chaim Ozer, who readily agreed to write the letter on behalf of Yeshivas Chachmei Lublin. R' Chaim Ozer, in his kindness, wrote a letter, then rewrote it a second and yet a third time just to be sure that his words were forceful enough in explaining to people why it was so imperative to help the Lubliner yeshivah in its hour of need.

After R' Chaim Ozer had completed the letter, he and the young *talmid* from Lublin began 'talking in learning.' A number of people gathered around to listen as dozens of Talmudic passages were cited and countless commentaries were quoted verbatim — from memory! The people assembled listened with astonishment as the great sage verbally fenced with the young *talmid*.

Then R' Chaim Ozer quoted a *gemara* (Talmudic passage) from the tractate *Yoma*. He cited it as being on *daf mem tes* (p. 49). The young *talmid* suggested that it was actually on *daf mem ches* (p. 48).

"No," insisted R' Chaim Ozer, "if I remember correctly, it's on *mem tes* (49)."

The young man, who was already known as an accomplished *talmid chacham* with a phenomenal memory, was positive that it was *mem ches* (48). He asked R' Chaim Ozer, "Perhaps we can check it out. Is there a *gemara* readily available?"

"It's not necessary," said R' Chaim Ozer as he touched the young *talmid's* arm gently, so as not to let him go get the *gemara*. He smiled softly as he continued. "I see your mind is young and sharp, and I am already an old man. You are probably right, not I. Why look it up? I might be embarrassed."

The young *talmid* felt bad for R' Chaim Ozer. He was aged and ailing and now his mind was forgetting. The conversation continued and eventually the young man got up to leave with the letter in hand. He thanked R' Chaim Ozer profusely for his time and effort, not realizing that he was never to see R' Chaim Ozer again — for two weeks later the great sage passed away.

Shortly after he left, the young man went to check the *gemara* to see who indeed was right, he or R' Chaim Ozer. When he found the passage he was startled. *He* was wrong and R' Chaim Ozer was right! The passage cited was indeed on *daf mem tes* (49).

R' Hirschprung says that it was then, after he looked up the *gemara*, that he understood why R' Chaim Ozer didn't want him to check it out in front of those assembled in the room. For it was he, the *talmid*, who would have been embarrassed, and R' Chaim Ozer, in his kindness, wanted to save him from that humiliation. So instead of checking the source, R' Chaim Ozer made a disparaging comment about his own (non-existent) human failing.

✤ *They Also Serve, Who Stand and Wait*

When R' Sholom Schwadron tells this story, he prefaces it by saying that he feels this is one of the most beautiful stories he has ever heard. It is actually a story within a story, that blends sensitivity and caring together with interesting insights. R' Sholom heard this story from the children of R' Yehoshua (Shea) Brim, the main character in this narrative.

R' Shea, who lived in Jerusalem, was a quiet man of great piety who performed his acts of kindness in unassuming ways. Only after he had passed away did stories surface as to how much he had actually helped so many. In each situation he had made a fellow Jew's problem his own personal problem.

It seems that a number of years ago a terrible tragedy occurred in Brodie's Houses, an apartment complex in Jerusalem. Just two weeks before the holiday of *Pesach*, a young man suddenly passed away, leaving a large family behind. He was a man who had always struggled financially, and now his family was left destitute, with very few relatives in Israel who could be of assistance.

Aside from the terrible travail that the family would have to deal with in the long term, there was the immediate pressing problem regarding the upcoming *Yom Tov. Pesach* is a time when the father of a household is the dominant figure as he conducts the meaningful *Pesach seder* for his family. Who now was going to be able to conduct the *seder* for the bereaved widow and her young children?

R' Shea looked for a candidate who would be willing to forgo his own *seder* at home, but couldn't find one. Finally, just a few days before the holiday, he located a young man learning in a yeshivah, with no relatives of his own in Israel, who said that he would be willing to conduct the *seder* for the family.

The night of *Pesach* arrived, and as R' Shea left his home to go to *shul* he told his wife that he might be a bit detained because he wanted to check, on the way home, that everything was working out at the home of the widow. Once in *shul* R' Shea began to look around for the young man who had agreed to conduct the *seder*, but he was nowhere to be found. R' Shea wondered whether perhaps the fellow had forgotten about his commitment, or maybe he was simply *davening* in another *shul*. That would be strange, though, because R' Shea and the fellow had agreed to walk together from R' Shea's *shul* to the home of the family in Brodie's Houses. When the *davening* ended, R' Shea once again searched the *shul* but he couldn't find the young man.

R' Shea left the *shul* with his children and told them to go on home to wait for him there. He hoped to be home shortly himself. He also hoped that he would meet the fellow outside Brodie's Houses so that he could take him to the home of the widow and her children. But when he got to the complex, the young man was nowhere to be seen; and when R' Shea walked into the apartment itself, no one was there but the young mother and her children.

The children were scampering all over the apartment and the mother seemed to be walking around aimlessly. After waiting a short while, R' Shea decided to conduct the *seder* himself. He called everyone to the table and then slowly and patiently he made *Kiddush,* gave everyone at the table a small piece of the *karpas,* had the children ask the Four Questions, and began to retell the story of the Exodus from Egypt — all this as his wife and family, along with his own widowed mother, were sitting home and waiting for him.

R' Shea sat with the family as they ate their meal (although he alone did not eat*). He enlivened the table with his conversation and *zemiros* (songs) until finally the mother and children ate the *afikoman.* By the time he was ready to leave, some of the small children were already asleep, for he had been there for close to three hours! The young widow thanked him profusely, and R' Shea made his way home.

When he came into his house, his wife, his mother, and his children were waiting for him with mixed feelings. On one hand, they understood that he had probably helped that family in their moment of sorrow. On the other hand, here in his own home he had kept a widow (his mother) waiting, in addition to his own children, who had been looking forward to this night for months. R' Shea began to conduct the *seder* by once again reciting the *Kiddush* — this time for his own family. However, because it was already very late, the children hurried through the *Mah Nishtanah* (the Four Questions, traditionally asked by the children at the beginning of the *seder*), they all drank each of the four cups of wine at the proper point in the *seder,* had their meal, and made sure to eat their *afikoman* — all before midnight, as is required by *halachah.***

After their *seder* was over, the children of R' Shea respectfully approached their father. "We understand that you wanted to help the widow and her family," they began, "but what about your own family? We were kept waiting for hours! And besides, what about

* See *Orach Chaim* 484:1.

** See *Orach Chaim* 477:1.

your own mother? She is an older woman, and she too is a widow! Why did you favor the widow there over the widow here?"

R' Shea understood that their questions were justified. Patiently he said to them, "My dear children, your questions are legitimate. I will answer them with a story that happened to me many years ago with the Chazon Ish."

This is the story he told them.

❀ ❀ ❀

Many years earlier, R' Shea and a group of friends were studying in yeshivos in Bnei Brak. One of the older fellows in their group was having a difficult time finding a *shidduch* (partner in marriage). One day a number of the young men in the group were told that the Chazon Ish wished to see them. Immediately they made their way to the home of the great sage.

After inquiring as to their own personal welfare, the Chazon Ish said to them, "As friends of this young man [with the *shidduch* problem], it is your obligation to work on his behalf as diligently as possible to find him a suitable partner in marriage." The Chazon Ish stressed the importance of this *mitzvah* and encouraged them to do whatever they could.

The young men obeyed his directive and dedicated themselves totally to the effort. They contacted everyone they knew, they made calls, they visited people, they spoke, they cajoled — and finally they were told about a girl who would be suitable for their friend. The young man was introduced to the young lady, and within a short time the two of them decided to marry.

The young men in the group were thrilled. They had accomplished what they had set out to do, and now they couldn't wait to tell the Chazon Ish. They ran to his home to announce that they had fulfilled their mission. The Chazon Ish was overjoyed. The boys informed the great sage that later that same evening there would be a *t'na'im* (official engagement) and they invited the Chazon Ish to come, for they assumed he would want to participate in this wonderful *simchah*.

The Chazon Ish told them that indeed he would like to come, but that he was occupied at the time with certain matters; however, he asked that once all the people were assembled and the families were ready to make the *t'na'im*, they should please call for him and he would come.

That evening the families and friends got together, the *chassan* and *kallah* made their entrance, and after some joyous singing two young men (one of them was R' Shea) were sent to bring the Chazon Ish to the festivities.

When R' Shea and his friend came to the home of the Chazon Ish the door to his room was open, so they knocked softly and walked in. They saw that he was involved in a detailed discussion with a man and a woman. The Chazon Ish realized that the young men had entered, but they understood that they could not interrupt him. They were sure that he would finish with the people shortly and then make his way with them to the *t'na'im* of the new *chassan* and *kallah*.

But the Chazon Ish was in no rush. The two people had a very long list of items written on a sheet of paper from which they were reading. The man would mention an item and the woman would say, "Should we buy this?" If the Chazon Ish said, "No," they would go to the next item. If he said, "Yes," one of them would ask, "How much should we pay for it? Is that the cheapest price we can get it for?" Over and over the same questions were asked for every single item on that sheet. Patiently and carefully the Chazon Ish thought about each item mentioned and then gave his opinion as to whether they should stock the item or not.

Finally, after more than an hour, the man and the woman rose to leave. They couldn't stop thanking the Chazon Ish for his valuable time. Only then did the Chazon Ish get up to go with the two young men.

"You must be wondering," began the Chazon Ish, before the two young men could even ask, "why I kept you waiting so long, and what was so important about my discussion with those two people. Let me explain. You see, that husband and wife are survivors of the concentration camps. They recently came to *Eretz Yisrael*, hoping to rebuild their lives. They decided to open a store and they came to me for help. I couldn't help them with money, so the least I could do is help them with advice. Every *shekel* they invest is important for their future and so I tried, to the best of my ability, to help them decide what to purchase for their store. It is my *mitzvah* to assist them, but it is not only my *mitzvah* — it is your *mitzvah* as well — because by your waiting you also had a share in that *mitzvah*, as did all the people who were kept waiting at the *t'na'im*. We all had the obligation to help those two get started in business again so they could begin a new life."

❦ ❦ ❦

"And that is the reason," said R' Shea to his children, late into the night, that *Pesach*, "why I went to the widow with the young children and helped them with their *seder* before coming home. Because all of us — myself, you, your mother and grandmother — as members of *Klal Yisrael* had the obligation to help her. By your waiting patiently for me to come back, you too shared in the *mitzvah* of helping that unfortunate family through this *seder* night."

Friday Night Visit

David *HaMelech* wrote in *Tehillim* (41:2), "אַשְׁרֵי מַשְׂכִּיל אֶל דָּל — Praiseworthy is he who cares wisely for the impoverished." All of us are interested in doing favors for others, for it is the basic nature of a Jew to be compassionate and caring. The Talmud (*Yevamos* 79a) says, "שְׁלֹשָׁה סִמָּנִים יֵשׁ בְּאוּמָּה זוֹ: הָרַחֲמָנִים וְהַבַּיְשָׁנִין וְגוֹמְלֵי חֲסָדִים — There are three distinguishable features of this nation: They are merciful, modest and benevolent."

Yet many times, in our zealousness to do a favor, we fail to take into consideration the feelings of its recipient. It is indeed possible, for example, that a sick person may not want visitors, then *not* to go see him would be doing him a favor. It is possible that a dear friend might need a loan, but for him to know that we are aware of his dire financial straits might be humiliating to him. If such is the case, then arranging for him to get the money he needs through a third party would be appropriate. Part of doing *chessed* is being sensitive to the total person in need. Thus, when and how one does a favor is of vital importance.

The verse quoted above teaches us that a man should plan his benevolence with intelligence and foresight.

An example of this occurred a while back in Jerusalem, involving a noted Sephardic Torah scholar and *kabbalah* teacher, Chacham Rabi Salamon Mutzafi (1900-1974). His actions bespoke insight and concern for the total person.

It happened that one of the prominent *rabbanim* of Jerusalem fell ill and was bedridden for months on end. He could no longer go to *shul* nor make any public appearances. After a while, Chacham Mutzafi began to visit the *Rav* every Friday night on his way home from *shul*. He would spend quite a bit of time with the *Rav*, discussing the pressing issues of the day and seeking his counsel on problems he had faced throughout the past week.

After a number of weeks during which he made these Friday night visits, some of his family members asked Chacham Mutzafi, "Why do you go and visit the *Rav* on Friday nights? Your family is kept waiting for you. The *Rav* you visit is bedridden at home and is there every day and every night of the week. Why not visit him in the middle of the week?"

Chacham Mutzafi replied, "I am sure that on Friday night the *Rav* remembers his days of glory. In years gone by, every Friday night this *Rav* would make his way home from *shul* accompanied by many of his congregants. He would tell them the *divrei Torah* (words of Torah) he had thought of during the week, and would discuss the various *she'eilos* (questions of Jewish law) about which he had been consulted. Now, as an invalid, he has none of that honor. Friday night must be the saddest time of the week for him. For what he had, he no longer has. It is for that reason that I go to cheer him up specifically at that time. Even though some of my family members may be somewhat inconvenienced, this is a price worth paying in order that this great *talmid chacham* should not experience any anguish on the night of the holy *Shabbos*."

◆§ *Bang-up Job*

This story like the previous one displays an ingenuity in dealing with those who are less fortunate.

Many years ago there was a young man, a fellow in the *kollel* (advanced yeshivah for married men) of a prominent American yeshivah, who was financially strapped. Although the *kollel* he attended offered a weekly stipend, his expenses for food, shelter, and school tuition for his children exceeded by far the small amount of money he received from his yeshivah. To make matters worse, he could rely on very little financial assistance from his parents or in-laws.

Other members of the *kollel* tried to help this young *talmid chacham* financially, but he refused all assistance. He and his dedicated wife were content to live on the meager funds they could put together by combining his *kollel* check and her paycheck from a teaching job.

There was one fellow in the *kollel* though, R' Yisroel, who was known for the ingenious ways he devised to do charitable deeds. He was a person who would inconspicuously place note pads and pencils in every telephone booth throughout the yeshivah so that they would be available to anyone who happened to be making a call. He also paid for wall clocks to be put up in various rooms where *shiurim* (lectures) were given, for the benefit of those who studied there throughout the day. In his own unobtrusive way he made sure to be of service to others. It bothered R' Yisroel no end that he couldn't figure out a way to help his financially troubled friend.

One day he hit upon a brilliant plan. He called the young *talmid chacham* and said, "I was down at the grocery and the owner told me that he just got in some cases of fish in cans that were damaged. The food inside is perfect, but he is afraid that the women will be hesitant to buy the fish when they see the condition of the cans. He is selling them on a first-come-first-served basis for two-thirds off the regular price. I know that you are in middle of learning, but I'm going back to the store now — so if you want I can buy a whole case for you at the cheaper price."

The *masmid* (diligent one) was very grateful for his friend's thoughtfulness. "Yes, yes!" he answered eagerly. "I certainly could use such a bargain."

R' Yisroel rushed to the grocery as quickly as he could and bought a few cases of canned fish. He immediately took it home, got a few hammers and, together with his children, banged up the cans and tore off some of the labels so that the cans would indeed appear damaged. He then called the *masmid*.

"I have the fish in my house," R' Yisroel said joyfully. "It's yours whenever you want it."

That evening the young *talmid chacham* came to R' Yisroel's home to pick up the smashed cans of fish. He gave R' Yisroel twenty dollars (for fish that was valued at over sixty), and thanked him profusely.

It never occurred to the *masmid*, who was totally involved in his learning, to find out if anyone else had taken advantage of the 'bargain.'

◆§ *About Face*

Just about everyone wants and needs attention. Quite often, those very people who seem independent and aloof are the ones who are inwardly crying out to be recognized. The hard exterior shown to others is merely a covering for a broken heart. One never knows when the voice from within will pierce through. A sensitive person, though, is more likely to hear this voice when it does cry out.

The following story — told by R' Kalman Drebin of Brooklyn about his close friend, R' Yosef Geffen* — took place many years ago when R' Yosef was a *talmid* in the Novardok yeshivah in Bialystok. Today R' Yosef is a man very much in demand by people with personal problems. The sensitivity displayed by him in this story allows us to understand why.

* The name has been fictionalized by personal request.

In the yeshivah of Novardok, where R' Avrohom Yoffin (1887-1970) was the *Rosh Yeshivah,* there were no dormitory facilities for the *talmidim.* Instead, each student was responsible to find and maintain his own living quarters. Most of the students rented rooms in nearby buildings. Most of the owners of these buildings were happy to have them as tenants. But there was an exception.

One building, where more than twenty rooms were occupied by *talmidim,* was owned by a bitter woman who had very little use for yeshivah *bachurim.* The woman, a widow who lived with her young son, constantly ridiculed and criticized each and every one of the *talmidim* who rented from her. At times she created havoc in the building. For example, on one Friday afternoon, she suddenly turned off the water supply. On another, she shut the electricity for no apparent reason. Soon her harassment became too much for the *talmidim* to tolerate. They realized that even though the building was close to the yeshivah, it simply was not worth the trouble of living there. One by one, they began to seek new quarters. Soon the number of boys in the building dwindled down to a precious few. But the owner did not change her ways. Although her income suffered greatly because of the empty rooms, she continued her harangues. Within a short time, the remaining boys moved out. All except one — Yosef Geffen. One morning as Yosef was coming home from *shul,* carrying his *tefillin* and a *sefer,* he noticed this nasty woman walking towards him. As soon as she saw him in the distance, she started to yell. "You must be crazy! How can you still stay in my building? You see that all the others boys have moved out — why do you insist on staying? Why not get out just like they did?"

Yosef paused for a moment and then said softly to the woman, "I stay here for your sake. I realize that you live alone and I fear that one night you might fall or become ill and call out for help and there would be no one to hear your cries. I understand that when you yell at us you are merely letting out your frustrations about being widowed and struggling to support yourself and your son. I therefore felt that it was proper for me to stay, just in case you might ever need help."

The woman's face turned ashen. This was not at all what she had expected to hear. She had imagined that his retort would be a sharp remark. She was so flabbergasted by the unexpected concern that she literally fell to her knees and, looking up at the yeshivah *bachur*, she pleaded, "Forgive me! Forgive me, young man! It never dawned on me that that was the reason you were staying. How kind and gracious of you."

The previously harsh-looking woman suddenly looked old, crestfallen and vulnerable. She walked away slowly, immersed in her thoughts. Later in the day she came to Yosef to apologize again. For days afterwards she never said anything but kind words to the *bachurim* she met. Slowly word got around that she was no longer as bitter and nasty as she had been, and *bachurim* started moving in again. Eventually all the rooms in the building were filled.

However, even though Yosef continued to live there, he would always use a side entrance, never once using the building's front door. For if he did, he risked the chance of meeting and inadvertently embarrassing the woman who, every time she would see him, would apologize shamefacedly again and again.

> Shlomo *HaMelech* wrote "מַעֲנֶה רַךְ יָשִׁיב חֵמָה — A soft reply repels anger" (*Mishlei* 15:1). Such softness takes strength — of character.

Available by Appointment Only

Mr. William (Zev) Sukenik, a highly regarded philanthropist and genuine *baal chessed* living in Kew Gardens, New York, was once called by R' Aharon Kotler for an appointment. R' Aharon, at the time, was chairman of the *Chinuch Atzmai* organization, and in that capacity was visiting people to solicit funds for the schools offering a Torah education to children in Israel.

Mr. Sukenik immediately understood the nature of the call; he received many of them throughout the day. Yet he certainly didn't want to trouble R' Aharon to come to his office. Thus, when R'

Aharon asked when he could come to see him, Mr. Sukenik said, "*Rosh Yeshivah,* I'll come to where you are. I don't want you to trouble yourself." And then, trying to convince the *Rosh Yeshivah,* he added, "Besides, the time that you would save by not coming here, you could use to make other calls."

However, R' Aharon wouldn't hear of it. He insisted on being the one to come and once again he asked Mr. Sukenik when he would be available.

Mr. Sukenik persisted in his attempt to dissuade R' Aharon, but his efforts were to no avail. Finally he said, "I have someone here in my office right now. Please give me your telephone number and I'll get back to you to let you know when I'm available."

R' Aharon gave him the number and hung up the phone. As soon as Mr. Sukenik's line cleared, he dialed the operator. He gave her the number which R' Aharon had given him, had it traced to the address from where it came, and immediately took a taxi to where R' Aharon was.

As he entered the room and walked towards the *Rosh Yeshivah,* he extended his hand, smiled and said, "I am the Mr. Sukenik you just called. I am now available."

☙ *Programmed for Life*

For more than fifty years, one man in Baltimore has served as Yeshivah Ner Yisrael's Chairman of the Board. His name is Harry K. (for Koppel, his Yiddish name) Wolpert, a man dedicated to the ideals and principles of Torah and *Yahadus* (Judaism). Mr. Wolpert enjoys retelling the following incident, for it had an incredible influence on the way he deals with people.

In 1929, R' Boruch Ber Leibowitz (1870-1941), the *Rosh Yeshivah* of the Kamenitzer Yeshivah in Russia, and his son-in-law, R' Reuvain Grozovsky (1896-1958), came to America to raise funds for their yeshivah. Among the cities they were to visit was Baltimore, where they were to be met by R' Koppel Wolpert, a former *talmid* of R' Boruch Ber's from when he had still been teaching in Slobodka.

The former *talmid* was ecstatic that his revered *rebbe* would be visiting his city. Mr. Wolpert, already married at the time, made sure that his home was tidy for the special guests, and on the day of R' Boruch Ber's and R' Reuvain's arrival, R' Koppel went to the train station to greet them.

He brought the *rabbanim* to his home, made them comfortable and offered them something to eat. R' Boruch Ber and Mr. Wolpert got into a conversation, and as they were talking they walked into the living room where Mrs. Wolpert had turned on the radio and was listening to an afternoon program. As Mr. Wolpert came into the living room he shut the radio so that he could hear what R' Boruch Ber was saying.

When he turned to continue his conversation, he saw that R' Boruch Ber had left the living room and seemed very disturbed. Mr. Wolpert walked towards his *rebbe*, and R' Boruch Ber said to him in a hushed but strong manner, "Koppel! *Vus is gevuren mit dir?* (What has become of you?)"

The young man didn't understand what his *rebbe* wanted. Perhaps he had seen something in the living room which he didn't like? "*Oy!*" R' Boruch Ber said. "Is that how you were trained in Slobodka?"

R' Boruch Ber was getting more perturbed with each passing moment, and soon he motioned for R' Reuvain to go out onto the terrace with him. Mr. Wolpert tried to apologize for whatever it might have been that was bothering his *rebbe*, but it was to no avail. R' Boruch Ber and R' Reuvain spoke privately for a few moments, and then R' Boruch Ber announced, "Koppel, we cannot stay in your home any longer."

The young man was flabbergasted. What had gone wrong?

R' Boruch Ber finally explained. "How could you have done that in front of me? How could you have shut off that radio when, just moments before, your wife had turned it on? How could you have been so insensitive? You embarrassed her in front of me. Now every time she sees me she will feel humiliated! How can I stay here another moment if I will be the cause of her feeling uncomfortable?"

R' Koppel was astounded. His *rebbe* continued. "Unless you go in and apologize, R' Reuvain and I will have to pick up and leave right now."

Mr. Wolpert says that he did go in to apologize, and the two *rabbanim* indeed stayed that afternoon. Now, close to sixty years later, the incredible concern for another person's feelings that was shown by his *rebbe* still remains vivid in his mind.

To R' Boruch Ber, a home in which there were *treife midos* (non-kosher conduct) was just as objectionable as a home in which there was *treife* meat, and just as he wouldn't remain where the food was *treif,* neither would he remain where the *midos* were *treif.*

◆§ *Whose Shoulders?*

R' Yisrael Salanter (1809-1883), founder of the *Mussar* (ethical teachings) Movement, was known for the extraordinary concern he showed his fellow man. His discourses often evolved around man's obligation, in all circumstances, to be considerate of others. He would say, "When one is performing the *mitzvah* of putting on his *tallis,* he should be careful not to knock out someone else's eyes when the *tzitzis* swing around as he wraps the *tallis* around his shoulders."

The following incident is classic R' Yisrael.

R' Yisrael was once attending a *seudas mitzvah* (festive meal served as part of a religious celebration). He made his way, with other assembled guests, to the water barrel to wash his hands ritually (*netilas yadayim*) before the meal. When his turn came, the people near him noticed that he was using the minimum amount of water necessary to perform the *mitzvah.* The water just barely covered his hands up to his wrists.

Those observing were quite surprised, for they knew R' Yisrael to be very scrupulous in his performance of *mitzvos*. Surely he should have used a good deal more water in order to be absolutely positive that his whole hand had been covered with water in accordance with *halachah*. After R' Yisrael recited the *HaMotzi* blessing and ate a piece of bread, someone hesitantly and respectfully asked him about his behavior.

R' Yisrael looked at them kindly and explained. "Can any of you tell me where this water that we have for washing came from?"

He answered his own question. "The water carrier brought it, and he carried it quite a distance from the well. If I use a lot of water, it will only mean that he will have to go out again and get more water for everyone else. It's true I would like to be scrupulous in the performance of the *mitzvah* of *netilas yadayim*, but I cannot do so at the expense of someone else! Thus I didn't use any more water than I really had to."

◆§ *Checks and Balances*

Chazal (the Talmudic sages) teach (*Eruvin* 65b) that there are three ways in which a man's character can be recognized: (1) בְּכוֹסוֹ — by [what he reveals after he has had] his cup [of wine]; (2) בְּכִיסוֹ — by [how he deals with] the money in] his pocketbook; and (3) וּבְכַעְסוֹ — and by [how he controls] his temper.

Mr. Moshe Daniels,* a successful businessman and philanthropist of note, was not a man of many words, but a quiet, dignified individual who revealed much about his personality in the way he spent his money. A unique attitude regarding money was displayed when he married off his children.

Mr. Daniels had many friends and acquaintances in both his business and social circles. When each of his children was about to be married, Mr. Daniels did not hesitate to invite many of his

* All the names in this story have been fictionalized.

friends, nor was he stingy with the provisions for the wedding festivities. However, before each wedding he calculated to the dollar exactly what the entire wedding would cost. Then he called his children together to decide which charities were credible and noteworthy. When they reached their conclusions, he (and they) proceeded to make out checks for donations to those charities until the sum equaled the exact amount he would spend on the wedding!

Similarly, as a *bar mitzvah* gift for his grandson, he opened a checking account for the boy. A day before the *bar mitzvah* he asked the boy to come to his office, where he had the child make out checks from his new bank account for *tzedakah.* In this way he trained the young lad for a future of contributing generously to charity.

However, it was in 1943 that Mr. Daniels performed a most extraordinary gesture. He was about to enter into a real-estate venture and wanted a certain *rav*, a noted *talmid chacham* of that era, to be his partner in this endeavor.

He called the *rav* and said, "R' Mayer, I am about to purchase a piece of property and I would like you to be a partner with me."

R' Mayer laughed and said, "R' Moshe, I have full faith in your business acumen, but I don't have a penny to invest with you. My financial condition is such that I barely make a living for myself and my family."

"That's not a problem," said Mr. Daniels, already prepared to answer this protest. "I will lend you the money!"

And that is exactly what he did. Mr. Daniels wrote out a check to R' Mayer for a significant amount of money. He then took it back from him as an investment. When the business venture skyrocketed and the 'partners' made their profit, the *rav* paid back the original loan.

This business partnership continues until this very day!

Part B:

Family Life

Blueprint

There is a Talmudic expression (*Kesubos* 67a), לְפוּם גַּמְלָא שִׁיחְנָא, "In accordance with the camel is the burden." In other words, the stronger the camel, the more its owner is able to load onto it. "This teaching," said R' Sholom Schwadron at a recent *drashah,* "goes hand-in-hand with another famous Talmudic phrase (*Yevamos* 121b), הַקָּדוֹשׁ בָּרוּךְ הוּא מְדַקְדֵּק עִם סְבִיבָיו כְּחוּט הַשַּׂעֲרָה, '*Hashem* is precise (in punishment) as a hair's breadth, with those (*tzaddikim*) around Him.' "

R' Sholom went on to explain, "If an individual has elevated himself spiritually to the level of being a *tzaddik*, then more is expected of him. If he violates certain principles, it stands to reason that *Hashem* is more demanding of him." [This holds true in a secular sense as well. An adult can be chastised if he spills red wine on an expensive white carpet, but one could hardly blame a toddler who does the same thing.]

But why would *Hashem* be so meticulous in the punishment of *tzaddikim*? Would not they, who have achieved a higher level of living, deserve special treatment?

To answer this, R' Sholom cited a thoughtful parable given by R' Yosef Chaim Sonnenfeld, the noted *Rav* of the Old City of Jerusalem.

R' Yosef Chaim explained that if a person decided to erect a fifty-foot-long building, but through some miscalculation he built the building three inches too short, it is no great catastrophe. For a building forty-nine feet and nine inches long would probably serve his purposes. However, if the architect drawing up the plans for that building would have made a mistake of three inches, it would have had a drastic effect on the size of the building, because on his plan each inch actually represents five feet. A mistake of three inches on the model would mean a mistake of fifteen feet in the finished building!

"It is the same with *tzaddikim,*" said R' Yosef Chaim. "They are *Hashem's* plan for the world. People look to *tzaddikim* for leadership, guidance and direction. If they, Heaven forbid, make errors, the ramifications of those errors, as they filter down to the public, could be catastrophic in a spiritual sense. Hence, just like the architect, *Hashem* must be precise and exact in his handling of *tzaddikim*, for they are the blueprint of life for their generation."

Parents and teachers, too, are the architects of their children's lives. The words or actions of parents or teachers may seem insignificant in their own eyes, but just as a builder reads a blueprint, so does a child read his parent or teacher, and what he observes is magnified in his mind tenfold. It behooves us to act accordingly.

R' Moshe Feinstein (1895-1986) once remarked, "Each morning, in the blessing before *Shema*, we ask *Hashem* to grant us understanding hearts, 'לִלְמֹד וּלְלַמֵּד, to learn and to teach.' Now, we know that everyone must devote time to learning the Torah, but not everyone is a teacher! Why do we ask 'to teach'?

"The answer," R' Moshe replied, "is that all of us indeed do teach — by our example. What we do and how we do it instructs others, especially our children, whether we realize it or not."

◆§ *Is My Father still Alive?*

The little ten-year-old boy's name was Matthew. In Hebrew it was Mattisyahu. But it didn't matter much what his name was, because few of the boys in his class ever called him anything. He was a sad, withdrawn child with very few friends, and he kept mostly to himself. But who could blame him? His father and mother had been divorced when he was but five years old. Since that time he never saw or heard from his father. His mother had remarried quickly, and Mattisyahu's stepfather had very little use for either him or his younger sister. Every night was torment, every school day an escape from the reality that was home. But in his mind Mattisyahu really couldn't escape.

He attended a yeshivah in Brooklyn only because his grandmother insisted that he get a Jewish education. His mother didn't care one way or the other. In yeshivah, he chose to sit in the back of the classroom. Each day, his *rebbe*, R' Yitzchak Silver,* would try desperately to draw Mattisyahu into the discussion. It never worked. He hardly ever listened in class; his mind was always wandering. It was no surprise that he did poorly on tests.

Every week, while telling the story of the *parshah*, R' Silver would pause in the middle of his narration to ask a question or two. When the week of *parshas Vayigash* (*Genesis* 44:18) arrived, R' Silver described the scene in an Egyptian palace, where the sons of Yaakov were being questioned by a man whom they knew was second-in-command to Pharaoh himself. What they did not know, however, was that their interrogator was their own brother Yosef, the same Yosef they had sold years earlier to the Ishmaelites.

R' Silver explained, "According to the Midrash, Yehudah, the spokesman for the brothers, warned Yosef that he and his brothers were beginning to lose patience, as their elderly father Yaakov was waiting back home for them. He argued that Shimon had already been taken prisoner, and now the Egyptians were expressing a desire to take Binyamin as well. Yehudah insisted that their saddened father, who had already lost one son years before, could not survive the loss of another son. He thus confronted Yosef with the possibility of war."

The class was entranced as the *rebbe* went on. "The Torah explains how Yosef could contain himself no longer. Seeing his brothers, whom he loved, tormented by the troubles he alone was putting them through, he quickly ordered all the Egyptians out of the room in which he and his brothers were speaking.

"Yosef then cried out," exclaimed R' Silver to the class, " 'אֲנִי יוֹסֵף, הַעוֹד אָבִי חָי — I am Yosef! Is my father (Yaakov) still alive?' " The class was stone silent as the students listened intently to hear what the brothers would reply. But R' Silver interrupted the story to ask a question.

"How could Yosef have asked such a question, 'Is my father still alive?' During the time that the brothers had appeared before him they kept repeating, over and over again, how their elderly father

---

* The name has been fictionalized by personal request.

Yaakov was waiting anxiously for them to return. Surely Yosef knew that Yaakov was alive!"

The class pondered the question. The brothers had indeed mentioned Yaakov's name so often — how could Yosef now ask, "Is my father still alive?"

R' Silver looked around the quiet class to see if anyone might attempt an answer or explanation. Suddenly he noticed that in the back of the room, Mattisyahu had raised his hand. R' Silver was shocked! He hadn't realized that Mattisyahu was even paying attention. The class turned around to see what their *rebbe* was staring at. Mattisyahu was raising his hand limply, waiting to say something.

"Yes, Mattisyahu," said R' Silver. "Do you have an answer to the question?"

The boy began to speak slowly, almost in a whisper. "I think I know what Yosef meant," he said.

"Would you like to tell the class?" R' Silver asked, hoping that the shy child would not change his mind. "Go right ahead," said the *rebbe* anxiously.

"Yosef really knew that Yaakov was alive," the young boy began. "The brothers told him that. But Yosef did not ask, 'Is your father still alive?' He asked, 'Is MY father still alive? Does he still think about ME? After all those years that I have been separated from him, does he still care about me? Does he still consider me his son?' " The boy swallowed painfully, and then added, "That's what Yosef meant when he asked, 'Is my father still alive?' "

Tears came to R' Silver's eyes as he understood something that perhaps the boys in the class were too young to comprehend. He realized sadly that Mattisyahu was not only talking about Yosef in Egypt. He was talking about the forsaken child that sat in the back of this very class. He was talking about himself.

Every child has feelings and sensitivities. Sometimes they can't be expressed verbally. Other times the words are there, serving as open windows to the child's thoughts. The perceptive parent or teacher sees these windows hidden behind veils. Gently and compassionately the curtain must be drawn aside so that the essence of the child can shine forth.

◆§ A Mother's Concern

The Talmud (*Berachos* 28b) describes the moving discussion that the students of R' Yochanan ben Zakai had with him shortly before he passed away. First he cried as he gave them a final perspective on life and death. They, in turn, beseeched him for a blessing by means of which they could live on without him.

But then the Talmud describes how, moments before his passing, R' Yochanan ben Zakai uttered a seemingly mundane command. "Remove the vessels [from the house] so that they do not become *tamei* (spiritually defiled by being under the same roof as a human corpse)."

Actually this was a remarkable command because it vividly indicated the concern R' Yochanan ben Zakai had, even in the last moments of his life, for the welfare of his students. Were the vessels to become defiled, some of them would have to be discarded while others would have to be ritually purified, a laborious effort that could be avoided with some advance planning. As he breathed his last precious breaths, R' Yochanan ben Zakai showed more concern for his students that he did for himself.

A more recent incident that occurred in Monsey, New York, displayed a similar extraordinary act of compassion and forethought by an individual close to death.

About twelve years ago, a young mother of a large family was stricken with a critical illness. She knew that she had but a few days left to live. What made matters even more excruciating for the family was the fact that her son was about to celebrate his *bar-mitzvah* shortly, a few days after *Rosh Hashanah.*

With each passing day life seemed to ebb from her. A few days before *Rosh Hashanah* she called her beloved son into her room and said to him, "Please do me a favor and put on your special *bar-mitzvah* suit. I'd like to see how handsome you will look in it."

The child was surprised by the request, but, realizing the seriousness of his mother's condition, he hastened to obey. A few minutes later he came back into her room wearing the brand-new suit he had never worn before. He stood proudly before his ailing mother so that she could see him this one time.

She couldn't help but shed tears as she visualized how wonderful it might have been to share the *simchah* with her family. The son, too, was moved to tears by this moment. After a few minutes the boy left the room.

Later that afternoon the young mother was visited by a friend, to whom she described what had gone on earlier in the day. The friend expressed surprise. "How could you have done that to your son?" she asked. "Didn't you think that such an experience might be too painful for him?"

"My intention was not for my own benefit," the mother replied, "I did it solely for my son. I wanted him to be able to wear his new suit for his *bar-mitzvah*. You see, an *avel* (mourner) may not put on new clothes, and had he not worn the suit at least once before, he would not be able to wear it for the *bar-mitzvah*, and I wanted him to have at least that."

This wonderful woman passed away a few days later, merely hours before *Rosh Hashanah*. However, this story, and others about her, live on in the memories of those who knew her.

Brotherly Love

The Kapishnitzer *Rebbe,* R' Avrohom Yehoshua Heschel (1887-1963), was known for his immense *ahavas Yisrael* (love of his fellow Jew). The concern he felt for every Jew with whom he came into contact was so extraordinary that he was revered by all who knew him. This was especially true of those individuals who *davened* (prayed) in his *shul* (synagogue) with him every day, for they had the daily opportunity to observe first-hand the *Rebbe's* regard for anyone with a problem.

The following story, retold by R' Lipa Geldwerth of Brooklyn, exhibits the *Rebbe's* concern for others and the cunning approach he used to bring a point home.

One winter morning the *Rebbe* traveled from his home in Boro Park to see one of the members of his daily *minyan* who owned an office in the diamond district — on 47th Street in Manhattan. The gentleman, whom we shall call R' Chatzkel,* had no idea that he was about to be visited by his *Rebbe.*

When the *Rebbe* came into the office he asked to see R' Chatzkel. The secretary summoned her boss, telling him through a private intercom system that the Kapishnitzer *Rebbe* was there to see him. She had often heard her employer speak with awe about his *Rebbe,* and she knew that he would be greatly surprised to see him in his office.

R' Chatzkel burst into the reception area and stood open mouthed when he saw the *Rebbe.* "Why did the *Rebbe* come here?" he asked, careful to speak to the *Rebbe* in the respectful third person. "I would have come to the *Rebbe* wherever he would have called me."

The *Rebbe* smiled gently and said, "It is I who need you; therefore, it was proper for me to come to you."

R' Chatzkel ushered the *Rebbe* into his private office, making sure that the *Rebbe* walked into the room first and was seated before he himself sat down. R' Chatzkel began again, "I am very embarrassed that the *Rebbe* felt it necessary to come here. I would surely have met the *Rebbe* in Brooklyn just to save him the bother. It must have been an inconvenience for the *Rebbe* to come all the way to Manhattan."

Again the *Rebbe* reassured R' Chatzkel, " No, no, it is I who needs something from you, and thus it is proper that I should come to visit you, and not vice versa. You needn't worry about my trouble coming here. The trip was fine."

"*Rebbe,*" R' Chatzkel said urgently, "please tell me, how I can be of assistance?"

The *Rebbe* began slowly, looking R' Chatzkel squarely in the eye. "R' Chatzkel, I have become aware of a family that is in desperate need of funds. The husband is out of a job; the wife must be home to care for their many children, and thus she cannot work for an income. Some of the children have been ill and there are

* The name has been fictionalized for obvious reasons.

considerable doctor bills to pay. Even food is hard to come by in that home these days. I need a significant amount of money for them."

"But," R' Chatzkel protested, "if that is all the *Rebbe* came for, the *Rebbe* could have called me on the phone and I surely would have responded."

"No," said the *Rebbe*, "this is a very important situation to me and so I felt that I had to approach you personally."

"Okay," said R' Chatzkel. "I will give as much money as the *Rebbe* requests. Just tell me how much I shall give!"

The *Rebbe* explained that the amount a person gives to charity is a personal decision that only the donor can make.

R' Chatzkel thought for a moment, then said, "May I give a check?"

"Of course," the *Rebbe* replied.

"To whom shall I make out the check?"

The *Rebbe* looked down at the floor for a moment, hesitated before he spoke, and then said quietly, "Write the check to your brother!"

Many of us have opened our hearts and extended helping hands to charitable causes, for which we — justifiably — receive public acclaim and accolade. Yet there are times when some of our relatives — even siblings — are in dire and desperate straits. These relatives cry out with unwitnessed tears and unspoken words, for they are too humiliated to approach us (or others) for help.

The Kapishnitzer *Rebbe* was teaching R' Chatzkel that it is a man's obligation to hear those unspoken pleas and witness those invisible tears. Each of us must see to it that those who are close to us are supported, even if there is little or no public recognition attached to such an act of *chessed.*

☙ *Tranquility Base*

The world-renowned Chofetz Chaim, R' Yisroel Meir (HaKohen) Kagan (1838-1933), had a *rebbe* who was not nearly as well known as he was. His *rebbe* was a saintly man from the town of Horodna, Lithuania, named R' Nachum Kaplan (1812-1879). Those who knew him referred to him lovingly as R' Nachum'ke. The Chofetz Chaim made it a point to observe carefully R' Nachum'ke's every action and deed, for he knew that anything that R' Nachum'ke ever did was done with forethought and good reason.

It happened one night during *Chanukah* that the Chofetz Chaim was in the home of R' Nachum'ke. The *zeman* (time) for lighting *Chanukah* candles came and the Chofetz Chaim waited for his *rebbe* to recite the blessings and light the candles, but R' Nachum'ke let the time pass and made no move to light the *menorah*. The Chofetz Chaim was a bit surprised that his *rebbe* would let the time slip by — but he didn't dare say anything.

More time elapsed, and still R' Nachum'ke went about his regular routine without saying anything about the lighting of the *Chanukah* candles. An hour went by and then another hour; still the *menorah* was not lit. The Chofetz Chaim simply could not understand his *rebbe's* inaction and apparent inattentiveness to this *mitzvah*.

Finally, deep into the night, there was a knock at the door. The Chofetz Chaim ran and opened it; it was R' Nachum'ke's wife. Almost immediately after she came in, R' Nachum'ke began his introductory prayers, recited the appropriate blessings and then lit the *Chanukah menorah*.

The Chofetz Chaim felt that there had to be a lesson here and so, once the flames were flickering, he respectfully asked his *rebbe* to explain to him why he had let so much time elapse before finally lighting his *menorah*.

R' Nachum'ke explained patiently to his beloved student. "The Talmud (*Shabbos* 23b) poses a question: What is the law if a man has money to use for only one candle on the Friday night of *Chanukah*? Should he spend it on a *Shabbos* candle and fulfill the *mitzvah* of lighting *Shabbos* candles, or rather spend the money on a candle for his *Chanukah menorah* and thereby fulfill the *mitzvah* of *Chanukah* candle-lighting?"

R' Nachum'ke continued. "The Talmud states unequivocally that one is obligated to spend the money for a *Shabbos* candle, the reason being that the *Shabbos* candle, aside from the *mitzvah* involved, adds to *shalom bayis* (peace and tranquility of the home). Thus a candle that fosters *shalom bayis* takes precedence even over the *mitzvah* of lighting a *Chanukah* candle." (See also *Orach Chaim* 678:1.)

"I have no doubt," continued R' Nachum'ke, "that had my wife come home and realized that I did not wait for her with the *Chanukah licht* (candles), she would unquestionably have been distraught. There would have been tension, and perhaps even anger on her part that I didn't show her the courtesy to wait until she returned. Thus I delayed and delayed until she came home."

"You see," added R' Nachum'ke, "the Talmud itself used *Chanukah* candles as a focal point to bring out the importance of *shalom bayis*. Should I then have taken these same *Chanukah* candles and through them caused a lack of *shalom bayis?* I had no choice but to let the ideal time for candle lighting pass, and wait until later to kindle them at a time that was still consistent with *halachah.*"

When R' Sholom Schwadron retells this story he adds an interesting insight. "*Shalom bayis* in this instance also meant that R' Nachum'ke didn't complain to his wife — when she finally arrived — that her lateness had caused him to wait so long to perform a *mitzvah*. He understood that to complain would have fostered ill will as well and minimized *shalom bayis.*"

☙ *Latecomer*

The following story was told by R' Sholom Schwadron, the *Maggid* of Jerusalem. The lesson he drew from this incident is one of which many of us, all too often, have to be reminded.

One of the grandchildren of the Chofetz Chaim was a *talmid* in the Yeshivah of Lakewood when its first *Rosh Yeshivah*, R' Aharon Kotler, was still alive. Aware of the young man's lineage, both R' Aharon and the *Mashgiach* of the yeshivah, R' Nosson Wachtfogel, יבל"ח, were proud to have him as one of the members of the Lakewood *Kollel*.

As time went on, though, R' Aharon and the *Mashgiach* noticed that many times the young man was late for morning *minyan*. On other occasions he even missed the *minyan* entirely. R' Aharon and R' Nosson were puzzled by the young man's behavior, and one day R' Nosson called him aside to discuss it.

"I'm surprised at how often you have been coming late to *minyan* recently," the *Mashgiach* began. "What would your *zaide* (grandfather) the Chofetz Chaim say about this?"

"I would love to be able to come on time," the young man replied respectfully. "But I know of a woman who has several children, and every morning as I am about to make my way to *minyan*, I hear her children crying. One needs a bottle, another needs to be sent to school, a third requires breakfast. There is no one else to help her, and so I feel it's my obligation to assist." ["Indeed," adds R' Sholom, "the Ari, *z'l*, says that it is proper for one to perform a *chessed* (a benevolent act) before one begins to *daven*."]

The young fellow continued, "At times I can still manage to make it to the *minyan* in the yeshivah, but other times I just have to find a later *minyan* elsewhere."

The *Mashgiach* was surprised and touched by the young man's obviously exemplary behavior. His sensitivity was fitting for a grandchild of the Chofetz Chaim. But at the same time he felt sorry for the poor woman. "Who is that woman?" asked the *Mashgiach*. "Is she widowed? Is she divorced? I too would like to assist."

"Oh no, *chas veshalom!*" exclaimed the young man. "The woman is my wife!"

"People often run to do *chessed,* and rightfully so," says R' Sholom, "for after all, King Solomon proclaims, 'רֹדֵף צְדָקָה וָחָסֶד, יִמְצָא חַיִּים צְדָקָה וְכָבוֹד — Those who run after charity and benevolence will find (that they receive from *Hashem*) life, charity and honor' (*Mishlei* 21:21).

"But I often ask," continues R' Sholom, "why do people find it necessary to run away from home to do favors? *Chessed* begins at home! There are so many daily opportunities for a husband, a wife, and even for siblings to perform kind and benevolent acts for each other. And yet sometimes the very same people, who take pride in their kindness and consideration towards others outside their doors, leave a lot to be desired of their actions behind closed doors. How often we forget that! That is, we perhaps forget, but the Chofetz Chaim's grandson didn't.

"By the way," R' Sholom reminds everyone once again with a smile, "the young man did not forgo *davening* with a *minyan* altogether. When he missed the yeshivah *minyan*, he made sure to attend another one somewhere else."

◆§ *Children's Children*

Being a *rav* in a small town, far from any city with a large Jewish population, is often a lonely and thankless job. True, there is much to accomplish, but the challenges which need to be overcome on the way to building a day school, solidifying a *minyan* of *shomrei Shabbos* (Sabbath observers), or convincing people to uphold and maintain standards of *kashrus* and family purity always seem to be uphill struggles. More often than not, a *rav* in an area with a limited number of Jewish inhabitants gets the feeling that the Jews he is dealing with are simply not on the same wave length as he is.

One such *rav* was R' Lipa Brenner, who had been inspired to enter the rabbinate by his mentor in Yeshiva Torah Vodaath, R' Shraga Feivel Mendlowitz (1886-1948). After a few years of serving as a rabbi and principal in a small town in New Jersey, R' Lipa was becoming exasperated. The local *baalei battim* (laymen) were not cooperating with him in his endeavors, and R' Lipa's accomplishments seemed to dim with every passing year. Meanwhile, to add to his dilemma, business opportunities beckoned from New York. Aside from the potential financial security that was so alluring, New York offered a variety of boys' and girls' yeshivos in which R' Lipa might finally have the opportunity to provide his children with the *chinuch* (education) that he felt was proper and essential.

In a quandary as to whether or not to leave the rabbinate, he decided to travel to *Eretz Yisrael* and seek the advice of the Vizhnitzer *Rebbe*, R' Chaim Mayer Hager (1888-1972). R' Lipa obtained his tickets and a passport, and made the trip. However, upon his arrival he was informed that the *Rebbe* was preparing to leave for Lugano, Switzerland, and would receive no more visitors before his departure. So R' Lipa followed him to Switzerland.

In Lugano, R' Lipa made his way to where the *Rebbe* was staying. He waited his turn to see the *Rebbe* and, when he was finally ushered in, the *Rebbe* asked R' Lipa to sit beside him at his table. Seated across the table was another *rav* from Tel Aviv. After a few moments the *rebbetzin* came in with a glass of hot tea for her husband. Before she could even put the tea on the table, the *Rebbe* gently admonished her and said, "Please bring two more glasses of tea. We are three *rabbanim* here about to have a discussion."

R' Lipa was astounded. The *Rebbe* had referred to him as a *rav*, and talked of him as though he were a peer. R' Lipa trembled as he realized the significance of the title the Vizhnitzer *Rebbe* had inadvertently bestowed on him. But perhaps it wasn't inadvertent? Did the *Rebbe* know that he was thinking of leaving the rabbinate? R' Lipa never bothered to find out. Then and there he resolved his own conflict. He would retain his position as *rav*.

❀ ❀ ❀

That winter, back in New Jersey, R' Lipa received a call from the head of a nearby children's foster home. The woman told him that five Jewish boys had been placed in her care. "School registration is coming up soon, and I feel that the boys should be given some background in Jewish culture," she said. "I am Jewish, although not religious," she continued, somewhat apologetically, "and I just can't see sending these five children to a regular public school." She asked

R' Lipa if he could find places for the boys in his day school. "At least in a Jewish environment they would get to know something about their heritage." She went on to explain that the foster home could not pay any tuition because its budget covered only room and board. The children in the home were supposed to attend public school, which was free. As if to reinforce her point, she then added, "And don't think for a moment that any of these children's parents left us any money for parochial schools!"

R' Lipa realized that this was an opportunity to perform spiritual *hatzalas nefashos* (the saving of lives). Tuition at the time was one thousand dollars per child, but maybe if he spoke to the members of the Board of Directors they would be willing to foot the bill for these children. He tried, but had no luck. As a matter of fact, the Board members were totally opposed to his idea. "Our school is not a charity organization," one of them said. "If neither the parents of the children nor the foster home will contribute at all towards their tuition, then we won't accept them. Finished."

The young *rav* was incensed. True, it wouldn't be easy for the school to absorb the cost of educating additional boys, but it was the attitude of the Board members that enraged him. "They shouldn't be pushing away problems," he thought, "they should be tackling them head on!"

R' Lipa thought about the situation for a day and then came back to the Board with his mind made up. "I won't allow these boys to fall by the wayside," he declared. "If the director of the foster home was considerate enough to contact us, it would be a *chillul Hashem* (disgrace of *Hashem's* Name) not to respond affirmatively to her suggestion. I will consider these children as my own and assume responsibility for paying their tuition." The Board members were stunned but silent, and the next day the five boys were enrolled in the town's Hebrew Day School.

R' Lipa had no idea from where he would get the money. Already he was raising funds for the *shul*, the school, the *mikveh* and the *chevra kaddisha*. But he persisted in his search, all the while taking a special interest in these children.

One day he made an appointment with a wealthy woman who headed a prestigious store downtown. She hadn't been known for her charity in the past, but he felt that perhaps the plight of these five boys would awaken within her a sense of sympathy. Miraculously it did, and by the time R' Lipa walked out of her office he had with him a check for five thousand dollars — the amount necessary to cover the entire year's tuition bill for the boys.

That night R' Lipa asked himself countless times, "What if I wouldn't have gone to the Vizhnitzer *Rebbe?* What if I would have left the rabbinate?" He was thankful, grateful, and humbled by the day's events.

❦ ❦ ❦

The school year progressed as the boys advanced, each at his own pace. At year's end one of the five was reunited with his family, two remained in the day school, and two brothers, having made significant strides in their studies, were encouraged by R' Lipa and another teacher to enter fine yeshivos in New York.

The next year R' Lipa left New Jersey and eventually lost contact with the people there.

❦ ❦ ❦

More than two decades later, R' Lipa was visiting in the Mattersdorf section of Jerusalem. It was *Shabbos* afternoon and dozens of children were playing in the streets, which are cordoned off until nightfall. Suddenly a bearded young man came running over to R' Lipa, yelling, "*Rebbe*! !" R' Lipa turned around, but did not recognize anyone. "*Rebbe,*" the young man said, smiling, "you are R' Brenner, aren't you? You probably don't recognize me anymore. I went to your school back in New Jersey more than twenty years ago. Come with me," the young man said warmly. "I want to introduce you to your grandchildren."

The young man took R' Lipa by the hand and brought him to where his wife was watching their children play. "כָּל הַמְלַמֵּד בֶּן חֲבֵרוֹ תּוֹרָה מַעֲלֶה עָלָיו הַכָּתוּב כְּאִלּוּ יְלָדוֹ — Anyone who teaches Torah to a child of his friend, it's as though he gave birth to him," said the young man, citing the Talmudic text (*Sanhedrin* 19b). "Thus, if I am your child, these are your grandchildren."

The young man was indeed one of the five from the foster home in New Jersey. R' Lipa had seen to it that he attend the Mirrer Yeshiva in New York, and from there the young man went on to become an outstanding *talmid chacham.* R' Lipa had all but forgotten him, but the young man had remembered. The face of his mentor had been etched in the child's memory forever.

☙§ *Imperfections*

There is a Yiddish expression, "A person must know the fifth *Shulchan Aruch.*" Actually the *Shulchan Aruch* (*Code of Jewish Law*) is divided into four sections. The reference to the 'fifth *Shulchan Aruch*' alludes to a special perception and ingenuity which allows a person to apply to practical cases everything that is found in the four divisions of the *Shulchan Aruch.*

The following incident was recalled by R' Yaakov Eisen of Montreal about his late father, R' Sholom Eisen (1917-1988), a noted *dayan* (rabbinical judge) in Jerusalem. It depicts the *dayan's* sensitivity as he viewed a situation in its totality, and reached a conclusion which, on the surface, seemed unrelated to the original question.

R' Eisen was known as one of the great experts in determining the *kashrus* of a *lulav* and *esrog.* Before the holiday of *Sukkos,* hundreds of people would come to his home, seeking his counsel as to whether or not to purchase the particular *esrog* or *lulav* they had chosen for themselves.

It happened that a young man came to R' Eisen a few days before *Yom Tov* with what he thought was a magnificent esrog. At the gentleman's request, R' Eisen began to examine the *esrog* very carefully for any imperfections — discolorations, punctures or growths — that could invalidate the *esrog.*

After a few moments, the *Rav* looked up and said to the young man, "This *esrog* is not for someone like you."

The young man was startled. He had studied the complicated laws of the Four Species, and had spent considerable time searching for an *esrog* that he thought was perfect. Why did the *Rav* feel that it wasn't fit for someone of his caliber?

"Is there a *she'eilah* (religious question) regarding this *esrog*?" the young man asked respectfully. "I thought it fulfilled all requirements."

Instead of answering the question, R' Eisen asked one. "Tell me," he said to this young man whom he had never met before, "What do you do?"

"I study in *kollel* here in Jerusalem," the fellow answered.

"Do they pay you there?" the *rav* asked.

"Yes, of course," came the reply.

"What amount?"

The young man told the *Rav* the amount of his weekly paycheck, which was actually a very minimal amount of money.

"How much do they want for this *esrog*?" the *rav* inquired.

The young man stated an astronomical figure.

"That's what I thought," said the *Rav*. "You are right, the *esrog* is truly magnificent. However, if you would follow my advice, you would buy an *esrog* that is much cheaper, and with the balance of the money that you were going to spend, buy your wife a dress for *Yom Tov*. That would truly be *kavod Yom Tov* (honoring the holiday)!"

Part C:

Coming Home

The Captain

A little boy was once playing alone on a beach when a man walked up to him and said, "Young man, why are you playing here by yourself? The other children are all playing on the other side of the beach. Why don't you go there and join them?"

"That's okay," replied the little boy. "I am playing here because I am waiting for a boat to pass by so I can wave my flag to the captain."

"But there are no boats allowed in these waters," said the man. "This is not water for small boats. There is only one huge ocean liner that goes by out there in the water. So why don't you just go back with the other children."

"No — that's exactly the ship I am waiting for!" the boy said eagerly. "I am waiting so that I can wave my flag to the captain of that ocean liner. Then he will wave a flag back to me."

"That's silly," said the man. "The captain of that big ship is a very important person. I doubt that he can even see you from that distance. In fact, I can't imagine why he would be looking in this direction altogether!"

"Oh, I know that not only will the captain be looking for me — I know he will even wave back to me," the child said confidently.

"How can you be so sure?" the man wondered.

The boy looked up at the man and said simply, "Because the captain is my father!"

Each of us is a cherished child to the Captain of the world, *Hashem* — the Father of *Klal Yisrael. Hashem,* the Navigator of the universe, looks towards us expecting us to 'wave' our flag, a feat which we accomplish by our study of Torah and the performance of *mitzvos.* If we do indeed make our presence known in this manner, *Hashem* will surely acknowledge us in return, for a father responds warmly to a beloved and obedient child.

Tears at the Kosel

Although one fleeting moment of inspiration can become a life's treasure, an individual hardly ever knows in advance what place, person or event will suddenly touch his or her heart. In this touching episode — retold by R' Shmuel Dishon, *Mashgiach* of the Stoliner Yeshivah in Brooklyn — it is the spontaneous reaction that affects both the participants in the story and all who hear it.

During the third day of the Six Day War in 1967, Israeli soldiers finally burst through into the Old City of Jerusalem and were able to fight their way to the area of the *Kosel HaMaaravi* (the Western Wall).

As soldiers both old and young fell upon the wall they wept with emotion, all the while kissing and caressing with awe the last remaining segment of the *Beis HaMikdash* (the Holy Temple). This, in large part, was what they had been fighting for, this holy place to which Jews had not been allowed to come for close to two decades. Now they, at the high cost of many soldiers killed and wounded, had captured it from the enemy's hands. The picture of those anxious weeping soldiers at the *Kosel* is etched forever in the minds of those who saw it first hand.

Standing back from those huddled close to the *Kosel*, were two soldiers who came from a non-religious *kibbutz*. They had no religious background whatsoever, and thus the holiness and significance of the place was lost on them. They looked around, overwhelmed by emptiness, and then suddenly one of them began to cry uncontrollably.

The second soldier, surprised by this sudden outburst, turned to the first and said, "לָמָה אַתָּה בּוֹכֶה — Why are you crying?"

The first soldier looked up as tears rolled down his cheeks and replied sadly, "אֲנִי בּוֹכֶה עַל מַה שֶׁאֲנִי לֹא בּוֹכֶה — I cry because I don't know what there is to cry about."

The Jewish heart yearns to be close to *Hashem*. Sometimes, though, layers of materialism and secularism become an iron shield that seem impenetrable. There comes a moment, though, when *der pintele Yid,* the tiny speck of Jewish pride inherent in all of us, cries out and pierces through any and all barriers. It is a moment of opportunity for those who are fortunate to hear it. It behooves them to be attentive and responsive, for that special moment, once lost, is gone forever.

◆§ *Sasha*

On a trip to *Eretz Yisrael* in 1987 I had the *zechus* to meet an incredible young man named Sasha, who had just come from Russia. He had arrived in Israel only four months earlier, and was living with his parents and brother temporarily in a *Merkaz Klitah* (absorption center) in Jerusalem. We sat and talked for more than an hour, and the story he told was absolutely spellbinding. He spoke in almost flawless Hebrew. I couldn't help but wonder where and how in the Soviet Union he learned to speak the language so fluently. However he did it, I am convinced that it was merely the least of his astonishing accomplishments. This is his amazing story.

Ever since Sasha was a little boy, he remembered that in the springtime his father would bring home this strange-looking food, telling his children that it was the family tradition to eat this thing called *matzah* at this time of year.

One year when Sasha was eighteen and the flowers of spring were beginning to blossom, Sasha's father told him to go to the *synagoga* to pick up *matzah* for the family. Sasha made his way to the *shul* in Moscow, where he met for the first time a gentleman named R' Arye Katzin. He asked R' Arye where he could purchase *matzah.*

"Do you know why you eat *matzah?*" asked R' Arye. "Not really," replied Sasha. "My father told me that it was a family tradition to eat it during this time of the year."

Sasha remembers that the family used to eat the *matzah* together with bread — or even pork. It never occurred to him that it might have any religious significance.

"Sasha, many years ago the Jews were freed from bondage in Egypt and this freedom is commemorated by our eating this type of food," R' Arye tried to explain. Sasha was unimpressed. "Sasha," R' Arye exclaimed, "you are a Jew and you must always remember that!" The two of them got into a conversation and R' Arye invited Sasha to come back and meet with him again. A few weeks later he did.

Slowly and patiently R' Arye began to teach Sasha about *Yiddishkeit*. One day R' Arye decided to broach a delicate topic. He prefaced his remarks by saying that there was a *mitzvah* that Jews had performed throughout their history, regardless of any trying circumstances or ensuing consequences. The *mitzvah* was *bris milah*, ritual circumcision. Sasha, who was uncircumcised at the time, listened, but was hesitant to undergo 'elective' surgery at his age. But then R' Arye told him about the verse (*Yechezkel* 16:6) recited at each *bris*, "Sasha, always remember, you may think that you are wallowing in your blood, but it is 'בְּדָמַיִךְ חֲיִי' — through your blood [that will be drawn at your *bris* that] you will live.' " That made an impression.

Sasha went home in the evening with the expression 'Through your blood you will live' ringing in his ears. After a few days he agreed to have a *bris*. Quietly and secretly, so that the Soviet authorities would not become aware of it, arrangements were made and the *bris* was performed.

Sasha began to attend synagogue functions more often, and as he was an accomplished musician he was asked to entertain at a *Purim chagigah* (celebration). A few weeks later, R' Arye arranged for a *Lag B'Omer* picnic to take place. Once again Sasha played music for those who attended — but that night he received visitors. It was the KGB, the Soviet secret police. They wanted a list of the Jews who had attended the *Lag B'Omer* picnic that afternoon.

Sasha couldn't believe their request. Did they think that he was going to become an informer? He refused to furnish even one name. The authorities told him, "Sasha, in a few weeks you will be getting your induction letter from the Army. We can see to it that you get sent to the musicians' brigade, so that you will never have to serve in the front lines."

Sasha would have loved to play music in the Russian Army, but he wouldn't do so at the expense of other Jews. He had no strong religious commitments, but to hurt another Jew by informing was simply out of the question.

Sure enough, a few weeks later he got his induction letter and was assigned to regular basic training. Before he left for the Army, R' Arye gave him a *siddur* and told him, "Keep this with you at all times, and make sure to use it every day. At least say the verse of *Shema Yisrael.*"

For a little while Sasha did use the *siddur* occasionally, but then his use of it slackened off. However, the more Sasha became familiar with the other soldiers in his barracks, the more disenchanted with them he became. His disenchantment first began at meals. When food was served at the table the soldiers attacked it like animals. Soviet soldiers who had already been enlisted for more than a year felt they had seniority, so they grabbed food and supplies away from the newcomers. Many of these same soldiers were people that Sasha had known in secular grade school, and he was shocked to see how beastly they had become. They drank vodka regularly; they cursed; they shouted; they were immoral; and worst of all, they hated the few Jews who were among them.

Sasha began to realize that he could not and would not live his life as they lived theirs. They represented the lowest form of mankind. He had thought that his fellow soldiers would be gentlemen, but he saw how wrong he had been. Sasha was sickened by their behavior, and that drew him closer to the four other Jewish soldiers in his brigade. On his days off he would now spend a little more time meeting with some of the young Jews he came to know through R' Arye Katzin in Moscow.

No Soviet soldier loved Jews, but the biggest anti-Semite of them all was a huge bear of a man named Dmitri, from the Ukraine. He stood six feet four inches tall, and towered over everyone. He personally ridiculed and pestered the Jews mercilessly. It made no difference to him whether a Jewish soldier was one who tried to find favor in the eyes of the other soldiers, or if he was the quiet, book-reading, minding-his-own-business type. Dmitri despised all Jews, and he and his followers let them know this.

One day, as Sasha was walking in a barracks hallway, he thought he heard the sounds of a struggle coming from one of the rooms. As he opened the door he saw that Dmitri, the enormous one, was on top of one of the Jewish soldiers and about to lay him out with a punch. All Sasha could see of Dmitri was his huge back. Instinctively Sasha, no small fellow himself, ran towards the men and, with a flying tackle, grabbed Dmitri around his huge waist and dragged him off the helpless Jew.

Both Sasha and Dmitri got up from the floor. Sasha backed up against the door through which he had come, and was convinced that he was in for a brawl. Instead, he says, something happened that changed his life forever. Dmitri was perhaps too shocked and stunned to fight. He began to yell at Sasha in a voice that was animal-like. Sasha says that the veins in Dmitri's neck were bulging like taut ropes of iron. Dmitri's eyes were as wide as doorknobs. He shouted, he threatened, he cursed, and then he said, "I will see to it that you will wallow in your blood!" And then Dmitri stalked out of the room.

Sasha was stunned. He had heard that expression, "Wallow in your blood," someplace, sometime before. Previously that very expression had touched his heart — and then he remembered! R' Arye Katzin had told him a few months before that, "You may think that you are wallowing in your blood, but it is through your blood that you will live," by his having a *bris milah*. Sasha was suddenly ecstatic. He knew in his heart that it could not have been incidental that this low, evil person, this *rasha* (wicked man), should have used an expression similar to the one which a *tzaddik* had used.

Sasha ran wildly to his room in confused ecstasy. "*Hashem*," he said to himself, "show me a sign that you're here!" He ran to his closet where he had his *siddur* hidden and took it out. He opened it at random and there, on the page before him, was the verse of *Shema Yisrael* in bold letters! That was the Hebrew sentence he was most familiar with. *No, it couldn't be,* he thought. It had to be purely coincidental that the sentence which had given strength to Jews for thousands of years should just appear at this moment when he had wanted a sign from Heaven. He closed the *siddur* and opened it again to a different section. He couldn't believe his eyes. There it was again — the verse of *Shema Yisrael.* "This is impossible," he muttered to himself. He closed the *siddur* and opened it near the end of the book, and there it was again — the verse of *Shema Yisrael*! [Sasha did not realize it at the time, but he had opened the *siddur* first to *Shacharis,* then to *Maariv,* and then to *Maariv* for *Shabbos* night, which was printed near the end of the *siddur.*]

Overcome with emotion he began to cry. And through tear-filled eyes he recited the *Shema* as he had never said it before and then with great fervor he recited the verses of *Tehillim* (20:2), "יַעַנְךָ ה׳ בְּיוֹם צָרָה — May *Hashem* answer you on the day of distress."

Sasha was simply exuberant. He couldn't wait for his next day off to meet his Jewish friends back in Moscow. He was now ready to make a full commitment to *Yiddishkeit.* A few days later he had his usual Sunday off, and he told his friends in Moscow what had transpired. He now expressed his interest in learning as much as he could about Torah and the observance of *mitzvos.* He took back with him his first pair of *tzitzis,* which he wore secretly under his Russian Army uniform.

He told his Moscow friends that he wished to participate in the next Jewish holiday. He wanted to be an integral part of the Jewish people. He asked R' Arye what festive day was coming up next, and was surprised by the answer. Of all things, it was a day of fasting! *Taanis Esther* (the Fast of Esther, the day before *Purim*) would be in two weeks, on a Tuesday. Sasha said he would make sure to be back for it.

Sasha's next problem was to get off in mid-week. It is simply unheard of for a soldier in the Soviet Army to be off duty any day except Sunday. But Sasha knew that to fast in the Army, watching all the food being slopped all over the table at mealtimes, would be an impossibility. Besides that, it would be obvious that he wasn't eating.

As *Taanis Esther* approached, Sasha pleaded with the officer in charge that he be allowed this once to take off a day in the middle of the week. He claimed that his family was getting together for an important function. For some reason that Sasha cannot figure out until this very day, the officer looked aside this time and granted Sasha the rare permission to take off on a Tuesday.

He spent the entire day of *Taanis Esther* in the company of R' Arye in Moscow. He said the proper *Slichos* (special repentance prayers for that day), fasted, and tried to learn as much as he could about the history and significance of *Purim*, the holiday occurring on the morrow. "It is the day when the Jews were saved from the descendants of Amalek," said R' Arye. Sasha heard the story of Haman and his evil plot that backfired.

At night Sasha heard the *Megillah* being read, and then rushed back to the Army barracks. As he made his way to his room, he found a crowd of soldiers waiting for him. "Where have you been?" they all seemed to be shouting at once. "You can't believe what went on here today! Where in the world were you? It's a miracle you weren't here today!"

They were all talking at once and it took a few moments for Sasha to comprehend what they were telling him. Finally he understood.

It seems that on that very day, Dmitri, who had meanwhile been discharged from the Army, came back with a group of friends looking for Sasha. They were wild with rage and drunk beyond control. They were out to kill Sasha and avenge what he had done to Dmitri two weeks before. They brandished weapons and conducted a room-to-room search for Sasha. Dmitri and his cohorts never found him because he was then in Moscow, commemorating the day on which Jews had been spared from the descendants of Amalek.

Sasha understood that now he, too, had been spared. He smiled with confidence and heaved a sigh of relief. Quietly he thanked *Hashem*. It was a *Purim* he would always remember.

An Ember Ablaze

There is a famous Yiddish expression: *der pintele Yid.* This refers to the tiny spark of pride in *Yiddishkeit* that remains with a Jew regardless of how far he has strayed from the ways of his forefathers. One never knows when that spark can suddenly be ignited into a roaring flame of commitment. However, one thing is certain: as long as a Jew breathes, the spark of his *Yiddishkeit* flickers, even if its glow has been dimmed by years of neglect and disregard.

In this extraordinary story, which R' Sholom Schwadron heard from R' Yaakov Kaminetzky (1892-1986), we witness one such hidden ember erupt in a blaze.

In Russia in 1919, the followers of the Bolshevik Revolution, led by Vladimir Lenin, struggled against the group known as the *Petlyureftzas,* led by the vicious anti-Semite Simon Petlyura. Each group struggled to establish its sole rulership, particularly in the Ukraine. First the Bolsheviks would storm into a town, killing and injuring people with abandon as they sought to take over the local government. Then the *Petlyureftzas* would battle with the Bolsheviks and try to oust them from power. If they were successful, they, in turn, made sure to execute all those who had resisted them.

This vicious cycle of fighting and killing continued, and the Jews were always caught in the middle. If the Bolsheviks were the ones in control, they would seek out some Jews of the town, blame them for the existing problems in the city, and put them to death. Then, when the *Petlyureftzas* overpowered the Bolsheviks, they too made the Jews the culprits, claiming that they had sided with the opposition. So regardless of which faction ruled, the Jews stood to lose as they were tortured and killed by whoever was in power.

It happened one time that the *Petlyureftzas* stormed a particular city and took control. They laid waste to building after building, after which they rounded up the people in the city to announce new ordinances and decrees. Among their decrees was one ordering that the Jews of the area were to be brought at once to the center of the town — where they would be shot in full view of the townsfolk.

Protest as they did, the Jews were helpless, for the rest of the townsfolk knew that if they didn't bring the Jews to be killed, they themselves would be shot instead. As quickly as they could be found, the Jews were dragged to an open square outside a courthouse, where a *Petlyureftza* revolutionary leader was shouting about the importance of being loyal to the incoming government.

As he continued to rant and rave, the police lined up the Jews who had been forcefully brought there. Soldiers with rifles took their positions opposite them. A huge crowd gathered as the revolutionary leader announced that the Jews were about to be killed for treason. "We are making an example of these people for all of you to see, so that you will not follow in their ways," the leader said.

The crowd grew nervously silent as the Chief of Police barked at the soldiers to ready their rifles. He instructed them to fire at the count of three. "One!" he yelled. "Two!" Just as he was about to yell "Three!" a man jumped from the crowd and pierced the silence as he screamed out, "Wait! I too am a Jew! If you kill them, you have to kill me as well!"

The crowd was shocked, for the man who had run out in front of the rifles was none other than the town pharmacist. He was loved and admired by all, and until then everyone had taken him to be a gentile. He had never given anyone even the slightest hint that he might be Jewish. People knew that he never distinguished at all between kosher and non-kosher food; his drug store was always open, even on *Yom Kippur;* and not once was he ever seen in a *shul.* He was considered to be among the most prominent people of the community, a man whom almost everyone had depended on at one time or another for medical advice and reliable medications.

Quickly a tremendous argument broke out among the townspeople. Many argued that the pharmacist was too valuable a person to the community to be killed, while just as many turned on him and argued that if indeed he was a Jew, then he deserved to be put to death just like the rest of them.

Pandemonium erupted as people screamed and shoved each other. Within moments the arguments had turned into fisticuffs, and the *Petlyureftzas* saw that unless they risked their own lives there was no way they would be able to restore order that day.

The soldiers and their leader, badly outnumbered, had no choice but to leave the courthouse area, vowing they would be back another day. A few days later, however, the Bolsheviks took over and the *Petlyureftzas* themselves ran for their lives. But those Jews, so perilously close to death just a few days before, were spared. And only because the tiny spark of *Yiddishkeit — der pintele Yid* — suddenly erupted in a man who, at the risk of losing his life, wanted more than anything else to be counted with his brothers.

◆§ *Verdict*

One of the primary objectives of *Rosh Hashanah* is for every Jew to proclaim and understand that *Hashem* is indeed the King and Ruler of the entire universe. It is for this reason that we make numerous references in our *Rosh Hashanah* prayers to the sovereignty of *Hashem*. We say הַמֶּלֶךְ הַקָּדוֹשׁ — The Holy King — in every *Shemoneh Esrei* from *Rosh Hashanah* until *Yom Kippur,* and in the *Mussaf* prayers of *Rosh Hashanah* we cite ten different scriptural verses proclaiming that *Hashem* is King.

The feelings of fright that can overcome an individual on this day are overwhelming, for *Rosh Hashanah* is the day of judgment on which *Hashem* decides what will be in store for every person during the upcoming year. In this well-known episode we can almost feel the intensity with which R' Aharon Karliner (1736-1772) experienced this day.

It is customary throughout the world for the *Baal Shacharis* on *Rosh Hashanah* (the one who leads the congregation in the morning prayers, after the recital of the *Pesukei D'Zimrah* — Verses of Praise) to begin by chanting a moving melody that builds up to a crescendo, at which point he proclaims with resonance, "*HaMelech*! (The King!)"

One *Rosh Hashanah* as R' Aharon, the Karliner *Rebbe,* approached the *amud* to lead the *Shacharis* prayers, he chanted the word *"HaMelech,"* and promptly fainted. The people of the *shul* immediately ran to him to revive him, and the *davening* continued. Afterwards people asked the *Rebbe*, "What was it that caused you to faint?"

The Karliner *Rebbe* replied, "I thought of a Talmudic teaching. The *Gemara* (*Gittin* 56a) describes how R' Yochanan ben Zakai appeared before the Roman general Aspasyanus (Vespasian) to plead on behalf of his fellow Jews. R' Yochanan ben Zakai greeted the general by saying, 'Peace to you, O king! Peace to you, O king!'

"Aspasyanus, surprised by this accolade, exclaimed, 'If I am indeed the king (and not merely a general), then how is it that you have not come to me until now?'

"That is what I thought of," said the *Rebbe*, still visibly shaken. "If *Hashem* is indeed the King, then why haven't I come to him (with repentance) until now?"

It is a question that each of us can ask ourselves every day of the year.

A Question of Merit

The Talmud states "בְּמָקוֹם שֶׁבַּעֲלֵי תְשׁוּבָה עוֹמְדִים אֵין צַדִּיקִים גְּמוּרִים יְכוֹלִים לַעֲמוֹד — In the place where the repentants stand, even the totally righteous are unable to stand." This is so due to the trials and tribulations which the *baalei teshuvah* (repentants) have to overcome in the process of becoming religious (see *Rashi, Sanhedrin* 89a). The following incident illuminates an interesting insight from an "insider's" point of view.

R' Yaakov Galinsky, a noted orator in Israel, was once asked to address a group of *baalei teshuvah* in Bnei Brak. In the audience was a writer from the secular Israeli newspaper, *Maariv*. Although he was not religious, the writer had come to the *drashah* (speech) in order to interview some of the assembled people and get their views on the new way of life they had chosen.

After the *drashah*, the writer approached one of the *baalei teshuvah,* a man in his thirties, and asked him, "Who will get more merit in *Olam Haba* (the World to Come): you (who have come back to authentic Judaism), or the children here in Bnei Brak (who have been religious all their lives)?"

At that moment R' Yaakov happened to be walking by and overheard the question. He stopped and stood near the two, wanting to hear what the reply would be. He was sure the man would cite the well-known Talmudic teaching (*Sanhedrin* 89a) which implies that *baalei teshuvah* are regarded as being on a higher level than even those who have been righteous all their lives, thus according them more merit in the World to Come. However, what the gentleman actually replied startled R' Yaakov.

"The boys here in Bnei Brak will surely get more reward than I will," said the man with confidence.

"But why is that?" asked the writer.

"I am one who is compelled," the *baal teshuvah* replied. "I have seen the outside world and I know it is one of emptiness, vanity and falsehoods. I was thus compelled to come to the truth, which is the practice of authentic Judaism. These children, though, still think there is a world of attraction out there — and yet they cling to their beliefs!"

◆§ *Tearing Away*

Throughout the Jewish world today a silent revolution is going on. Thousands of Jews, be they in Russia, Israel, Europe or America, who until now had no commitment to authentic Judaism, are now coming home to the practice of Torah and *mitzvos* with a vibrancy that is contagious. The following two stories — the first of which took place recently, the second incident decades ago — put this sweeping revolution into a provocative perspective.

One day, as R' Yaakov Galinsky was giving a *shiur* (Torah lecture) in his yeshivah in Chadera, Israel, he received a message that the local Chief of Police wanted to see him at Police

Headquarters. When he walked into the office, a man sitting next to the Police Chief, not wearing a *yarmulke* or any other head covering, became visibly angry and began to verbally attack R' Galinsky. The man was yelling so loud and talking so fast, all the while ridiculing and deriding religious people, that R' Galinsky could not imagine why he was summoned there.

Finally the Chief of Police got the gentleman to settle down, and then in a somewhat calmer tone the man explained what it was that was bothering him. "You are brainwashing my son!" the man exclaimed to R' Galinsky. "My son is in your yeshivah, conducting himself in a religious manner, totally against the way his mother and I have raised him. You have done such a job on him that now he won't leave your place, and it's all because of your influence. I demand that you send him out of the yeshivah and back home!"

R' Galinsky was taken aback, for he knew very well that the boy had entered the yeshivah of his own free will. Over the previous summer this boy had become friendly with the son of the *shochet* (ritual slaughterer) in Rosh Pinah, and the *shochet's* son had encouraged him to try learning in a yeshivah. Now the boy was happy and thrilled to be among religious friends. R' Galinsky tried to explain to anyone who would listen that the boy could leave whenever he so desired, but that he was content in the yeshivah and was staying there of his own free choice.

The angry father would not believe the *rav's* words. He kept yelling that his son had been brainwashed and was being confined in the yeshivah against his will.

The Chief of Police tried to calm things down, and soon the *rav* got into a more pleasant conversation with the irate father. The gentleman explained that he had come to Israel from Europe more than fifty years ago, had entered a *kibbutz* and led a 'free' life — not like the life that his late father, a Sokolover *chassid*, had led in Europe. "I want my son to follow my ways," the father now stormed, as his anger simmered once again.

"But he is!" retorted R' Galinsky. "You rebelled against your father and now your son, like you, is rebelling against *his* father!"

❧ ❧ ❧

When R' Galinsky retells this incident he recounts another one — in a more serious vein — that took place many years earlier in Bnei Brak. In 1950 a *bachur* from a totally non-religious *kibbutz* entered the Ponevezher Yeshivah in Bnei Brak. It seems that after great introspection he had decided to leave his irreligious Shomer HaTza'ir *kibbutz* to come learn in a yeshivah.

The Chazon Ish, R' Avrohom Karelitz (1878-1953), summoned R' Galinsky and asked him to keep an eye on this *bachur* and try to be a source of encouragement to him. This was not the first boy who had left a *kibbutz* to come to Ponevezh, and the trickle of boys trying to become religious was now turning into a thin but steady stream.

R' Galinsky took the liberty to ask the Chazon Ish, "Why do you suppose so many children are now coming back to *Yiddishkeit*, leaving behind them the ways of their non-committed parents?"

The Chazon Ish's answer took R' Yaakov by surprise. "The generation that became non-religious," observed the Chazon Ish, "came from parents that were religious. These religious parents saw what was happening to their children but, for whatever reasons, they could not stop them. They cried lonely, bitter tears, they prayed, they fasted, but it was too late to stem the tide. But *Hashem* does not forget a Jewish tear. If those tears of sincerity did not help to save their own children, they have helped for the grandchildren and, in some cases, great-grandchildren. That's the reason why these children come back to *Yiddishkeit* today — because *Hashem* doesn't forget Jewish tears."

◆§ *Bon Voyage*

R' Sholom Schwadron enjoys retelling this short but powerful anecdote about a *tallis*. He heard it cited in the name of the Bialystoker *Maggid*, R' Myrim Hillel Rappaport (1870-1963). Some say that the story was first told by the Minsker *Maggid*, R' Binyomin Shakovitsky (1863-1938). Either way, when a *maggid* delivers this lesson about priorities, it usually leaves his audience thunderstruck.

The Bialystoker *Maggid* told how he was once walking in the street when he heard a faint cry coming from inside a building. The cry was continuous and he wondered why no one seemed to be paying attention to it. He decided to see what it was all about.

He walked into the building from where the cry was coming. As he entered he could hear the weeping getting louder. At once he realized that the sounds were coming from somewhere on the second floor.

He ran upstairs and saw that a door to an apartment had been left open. The cry was coming from inside that apartment. After knocking on the door and not getting a reply he walked into the apartment and began to look around. No one was there. But still he could hear the wailing. He walked from room to room and soon realized that the sounds were coming from inside a closet.

He opened the closet door and saw that it was a *tallis* that was crying! The *maggid*, quite taken aback, looked down at the *tallis* and said, *"Tallis'l, tallis'l,* why are you crying?"

The *tallis*, looking forlorn, said, "My owner and his family have all left for their summer vacation. They took their clothing, their food and furniture, but they left me here alone, forsaken and forgotten."

The Bialystoker *Maggid* smiled at the *tallis* and said thoughtfully, *"Tallis'l, tallis'l,* don't feel bad. There will come a time when your owner will take a long trip — and you will be the only thing he will take along!"*

The *tallis,* to the Bialystoker *Maggid,* represented everything that is spiritual in this world. It is that, and not material things, that man 'takes along' with him after he has lived his prescribed years on this earth.

"How wise then is the man," says R' Sholom, "who enhances his spiritual life in this world so that he has ample 'baggage' to take along with him on his final voyage!"

* There is an almost universal Jewish custom to bury a man in the *tallis* he wore while he was alive.

◆§ *Trip and Fall*

R' Yaakov Galinsky recently recounted a short incident involving the Chofetz Chaim, which contains a potent message. The perspective drawn from this story might make a person think twice before he speaks once.

The Chofetz Chaim once walked into a *shul* outside of Radin. As the people were about to begin *davening,* he couldn't help but overhear how certain individuals were ridiculing the town simpleton. This poor fellow was usually the subject of much derision, and it upset the Chofetz Chaim.

He approached one of the people making snide comments and asked, "Why do you joke about that unfortunate man?"

"He is really silly," came the reply. "Can you imagine — he told us that he just got back from Aisheshuk (a big city more than twenty miles from Radin), and all he brought back was some *tabak* (strong sharp snuff). Isn't it foolish to make such a long trip and come back with so little?"

The Chofetz Chaim peered gently at the individual who was speaking and said, "My dear one, you should be concerned about yourself instead. Your *neshamah* (soul) came from Heaven and made a much longer trip down here to this earth. If you continue in your ways, then after 120 years, when your *neshamah* returns to Heaven, it will bring back a lot less than this fellow did!"

◆§ *Down to Earth*

The Ramban (1195-1270), in his famous letter known as the *Iggeres HaRamban,* implores his son to refrain from ever getting angry. Anger, he points out, is the root of much evil, causing a person to become additionally engulfed in the heated flames of numerous sins. [One is more apt to slander, become haughty, and misjudge others while enveloped in wrath.] Rather, says the Ramban, a person should humbly think of where he came from and where he will go at the end of his days (see *Pirkei Avos* 3:1). Those sobering thoughts will cause him to withdraw his anger and act with humility.

R' Yissachar Frand, a noted Torah scholar and lecturer in Baltimore, recently described an incident that took place in the time of R' Chaim Volozhiner (1749-1821), which aptly emphasizes some of the futility of anger.

Two people had a violent argument about a piece of property. The property under discussion was adjacent to both their fields, and each of them claimed that the property was rightfully his. Neither would hear of a compromise, and neither gave much credence to the arguments of the other.

Finally they decided to seek the counsel of R' Chaim Volozhiner. R' Chaim listened to their arguments and told them that he wanted to go with them to see the property first-hand; perhaps that would help him understand their individual points of view.

Together with R' Chaim, the two gentlemen went to the field in question. R' Chaim studied the layout of the land and its boundaries, and then listened once again as each of the men emphatically claimed the property was his.

Suddenly R' Chaim bent down and placed his ear to the soil. The two gentlemen were astounded. "What are you doing there on the ground?" one of them asked.

"I have heard your points of view about this piece of property," answered R' Chaim, "but now I would like to hear what the ground has to say for itself."

The two men thought that R' Chaim was joking, and so in a humorous tone one said to him, "All right, so do indeed tell us — what does the ground say?"

R' Chaim smiled at them and said, "The ground finds it hard to understand the anger and short-sightedness of both of you. It says, 'This one claims that I belong to him, then the other one claims that no, I belong to him. The truth, though, is that eventually *they* will both belong to *me*!' "

A sobering thought for humility and compromise.

Recently I had the opportunity to spend a *Shabbos* in Detroit, Michigan. It was my first trip to the "Motor City," and that *Shabbos* happened to be an eventful one. There was a *shalom zachar* Friday night, a *bris* as well as an *aufruf* on *Shabbos* morning, and a gala *Melaveh Malkah* for a new *cheder* (children's school) on *Shabbos* night. The local Jewish community seemed to be going from one *simchah* to another.

At the *shalom zachar* Friday evening, the conversation veered to the status and standards of *Yiddishkeit* in Detroit decades ago. The grandfather of the new infant, a native Detroiter, recounted an incident of long ago that changed the face of the city forever.

Many years ago, around the year 1915, a woman named Mrs. Bessie Cohen decided that she wanted an authentic Torah education for her sons. There were no yeshivah-type schools to speak of, and so she decided to have a man brought from New York to enhance *Yiddishkeit* in Detroit. She figured that her children would need an energetic man, deeply committed to Torah and *mitzvos*, who would teach them and set an example for others. Towards this end she imported her nephew from New York named Herschel Cohen, known for his boundless energy, his *yiras Shamayim*, and his adherence to *mitzvos*. She hoped that he would move to their city and help *Yiddishkeit* grow.

R' Herschel was married at the time and had five young children, but Mrs. Cohen assured him that she would augment his income as a carpenter if he would serve as a tutor and role model for her teen-aged sons, his younger cousins.

On the day of his arrival, Mr. Cohen was met at the train station by his two cousins, Wolf and Isadore Cohen. It was already late in the afternoon, and the younger Cohens decided they would take R' Herschel to the Magen Avraham *shul* on Farnsworth Street, where they would *daven Minchah* (the afternoon service) and *Maariv*. It would be as good a place as any for R' Herschel to get a taste of what *Yiddishkeit* in Detroit was all about.

The younger Cohen men were proud of both their *shul* and the many people who came there to learn and study before *Minchah.* As they opened the doors to the *shul* and the sound of Torah reverberated throughout the hallway, they said to their cousin, obviously trying to impress him, "You see, Detroit is a little Vilna."

Mr. Cohen was not easily impressed. After all, Vilna, the capital of Lithuania, was noted for its Torah scholarship. "Let me first look around and then I will tell you if it's a little Vilna."

The people soon began to *daven Minchah,* and afterwards Wolf and Isadore went over to R' Herschel to get his appraisal. They didn't even have to say a word to him, for as soon as they approached he said with certainty, "This is very far from being a little Vilna."

The two were surprised and taken aback by the strong conviction with which he stated his evaluation, but then the wise R' Herschel explained. "I don't see any young people here — I don't see any children!"

The younger Cohens realized that R' Herschel was right. The future of a nation is dependent on its youth. R' Herschel, as an outsider, could perhaps see the bleak panorama of the "forest" while those living there could merely see the few blossoming "trees." Mr. Herschel Cohen moved to Detroit and helped change *Yiddishkeit* there forever by teaching children and inspiring all those with whom he came in contact. His prize pupils, Isadore and Wolf Cohen, eventually became the first presidents of the first yeshivah day school, Beis Yehudah, in Detroit.

How much did the city change?

The same *Shabbos* that I was in Detroit, I *davened Minchah* in the Bnei Avraham *shul* on Ten Mile Road. The *gabbai* there honored me with *hagbah* (the honor of lifting the Torah after it has been read), and as I sat holding the *Sefer Torah* afterwards, I overheard a conversation behind me between a young boy and his father.

The boy, a student in a local yeshivah, was wearing his

immaculate new black hat, which led me to believe that he had recently become a *bar mitzvah.*

"Dad," the boy said. "I would like to wear a *gartel* (belt worn by some individuals during *davening* — see *Orach Chaim* 92:2)."

The father did not seem pleased, and said, "But I don't wear a *gartel*. Why should you wear one?"

The boy did not relent. "But *Zeide* (Grandfather) wore a *gartel*!"

"Yes," said the father, "but that was when *Zeide* was older."

"How old was *Zeide* when he started wearing a *gartel?*" the boy asked inquisitively.

"I think he was in his early forties," the father replied.

The eager young child looked up at his father and said, ever so respectfully, "But then, Dad, maybe it's time *you* wore a *gartel.*"

I could not help but think how the tables had turned. Decades earlier, R' Herschel Cohen saw no Jewish future in Detroit because *Yiddishkeit* cannot exist without the zest and enthusiasm of children and young folk. Now, more than seventy years later, after schools, *shuls,* a Bais Yaakov and a *kollel* had been established, the youth in Detroit was a vibrant force seeking to enhance its adherence to *mitzvos,* not shying away from religious responsibility.

Before our very eyes we are witnessing an enthusiastic change evolving. Throughout America and Europe, all across Israel and even in Russia, there is a resurgence of Torah study and *mitzvah* observance that is unprecedented.

In the very last verse in *Neviim* (Prophets) the prophet Malachi (*Malachi* 3:24) states that in the time of *Mashiach:* "וְהֵשִׁיב לֵב אָבוֹת עַל בָּנִים — The heart of parents will be brought back [to *Hashem*] through the acts of their children" (see *Rashi* to this verse).

May the children of *Klal Yisrael* be an inspiration to their parents as these same parents encourage and become role models for their children — so that together we may witness the coming of *Mashiach* in our day.

Part D:

Jewish Observance

❧ *Royal Rescue*

This story about R' Zalman Grossman, the central figure in "Request of a Lifetime" (page 42), also revolves around the unusual approach R' Zalman had in his loving observance of *Shabbos*. As explained before, R' Zalman never slept on *Shabbos*. Instead, from sunset on Friday evening until darkness on Saturday night, he was totally involved with the holiness of *Shabbos*. For the duration of the *Shabbos* he was either learning *mishnayos*, singing *zemiros*, praying or partaking of the *Shabbos* meals. As impoverished as he was, once a week R' Zalman was a stately king who relished his every moment with the queen that was *Shabbos* (see *Shabbos* 119a).

In the year 1912, R' Zalman, leaving his family behind in *Eretz Yisrael*, had come to America to find a job by means of which to support his family back home. He opened an office in the Lower East Side of Manhattan on behalf of Yeshivah Ohel Moshe in Israel, and from there organized a group of men who would travel throughout the United States to raise money for the yeshivah. They, in turn, would send the accumulated funds to the home office in the East Side, and R' Zalman would forward the money to Israel.

The office, located on the second floor of a two-story office building, contained four small rooms. In the back room there was a little table, a chair and, along the wall, a bed. These, along with a small refrigerator, were the sole furnishings of R' Zalman's home. He lived there quietly, hardly ever going to anyone else's home to eat, for throughout his stay in America he neither drank milk nor ate meat. [He would use only dairy products that were *cholov Yisrael*, which was difficult to obtain in those days in New York, and he only would eat meat slaughtered by his own *shochtim*.]

One Friday night, as he was lovingly engrossed in his observance of *Shabbos*, alone in his room, he began to recite the *Kiddush* with great emotion. Suddenly he felt an excruciating pain in his side. It was of such intensity that the cup of wine in his hand dropped to the floor and he crumpled in a heap right where he stood. The paralyzing pain prevented him from getting up to reach a phone and call a doctor. He yelled out for help, but as he was in an office building where no one else lived, and it was already well after business hours, no one heard his cries. He lapsed into semi-consciousness, lying moaning beside his *Shabbos* table.

❦ ❦ ❦

One of the *meshulachim* (collectors of funds) who worked for R' Zalman was a certain R' Nachum, who had also come from *Eretz Yisrael*. R' Nachum had just completed a trip out of town, and was spending *Shabbos* with some relatives in Manhattan. He had arrived a short while before *Shabbos*, and had called R' Zalman to let him know that he had returned to New York. As a result of his hectic trip and the frantic rush, his nerves were on edge and he was unable to fall asleep after the *Shabbos* meal. He therefore decided to go for a short walk and then return home to sleep. He began walking through the streets of Manhattan, immersed in thoughts about all that had occurred to him over the past week. Then he began to think about the weekly *parshah* and the *drashos* that he used to hear every week in *Eretz Yisrael*. He walked on and on, and after half an hour he realized he was lost.

R' Nachum tried to retrace his steps but it was impossible. After asking a few people for directions, he was surprised to learn that he was actually much closer to his office in the Lower East Side than to the house in which he was staying for *Shabbos*. By now he was already quite tired and he remembered that R' Zalman, who lived at the office, didn't sleep on *Shabbos*. *Why not go to the office?* he thought to himself. He could spend the night with R' Zalman in song and learning and then, if he wanted to sleep, he could use R' Zalman's bed, for it wasn't going to be occupied that Friday night anyway.

It was already late at night by the time he made his way to the office building. He walked up the stairs and knocked softly. He was surprised when there was no answer. He knocked louder. Still nothing. He couldn't understand. He knew that R' Zalman was in town for *Shabbos* and that he was surely up even at this late hour.

He put his ear to the door with the hope of being able to hear something. It was then that he heard the low groaning and moaning sounds coming from within the apartment. "R' Zalman!" he called out. "R' Zalman! What's going on in there?" But there was no answer. R' Nachum became frightened. He banged louder — but there was still no response. He bolted down the stairs, ran outside, and looked up and down the street. A police car was coming his way! He flagged down the car and together with the officers ran back up the stairs. When the policemen heard the anguished moans coming from inside, they smashed the door with their billy clubs and entered.

Once inside they ran to the back room, where they found R' Zalman lying on the floor and writhing in pain. He did not even recognize R' Nachum. The policemen picked him up and rushed him to the hospital, where an emergency appendectomy was performed. R' Nachum stayed up all night in the dimly lit waiting room, waiting for news about his close friend, R' Zalman. When the surgery was finally over, the doctor came out and told R' Nachum, "If you and the police had found your friend an hour later, he probably would not be alive at this moment."

Years later, when R' Zalman was back in Israel, he would tell this story to his children and then say, "The Ibn Ezra wrote in a song that we sing every *Shabbos*, 'כִּי אֶשְׁמְרָה שַׁבָּת קֵל יִשְׁמְרֵנִי — Because I watch over *Shabbos*, G-d will watch over me.' Only because R' Nachum knew that I stay up all night long with the holy *Shabbos* did he even think to come to me that night. Otherwise, as it was so late, he would surely not have come to visit me. But I observed *Shabbos* with special care and thus *Hashem*, in his graciousness, watched over me and saved me."

Shabbos Rest

"Who is wise? He who learns from every man" (*Pirkei Avos* 4:1). As simple as this teaching sounds, it is often difficult to implement. One who feels he has reached a certain level of maturity and understanding may find it difficult to admit that he can learn something from someone who admittedly is far below his own level of knowledge. Yet truly great people, who have a constant thirst for truth and knowledge, do not let groundless barriers impede their progress. They will learn from anyone — even from little children.

This beautiful episode was told by R' Sholom Schwadron:

One *Shabbos* afternoon, after he had finished eating the *Shabbos* meal, the Tshebiner *Rav* (R' Dov Berish Weidenfeld, 1879-1965) went to lie down for a while. He had been resting only a short time when he heard a knock at the door. He decided to disregard it because he was truly exhausted. But the knocking on the door was persistent.

He thought to himself, "Maybe it's an emergency. Whoever is there is not going away. Perhaps I should get up to see who it is." And so, tired as he was, he got out of bed and went to the door. When he opened it, he saw that it was a little nine-year-old boy holding a *Gemara*. (Most areas in Jerusalem are within the confines of an *eiruv*, thus allowing the child to carry on *Shabbos*.)

"*Gut Shabbos*," the *Rav* said. "What is it that you want?"

The little boy looked up at this great sage and said, "I just finished *Hamafkid* (the third chapter of tractate *Bava Metzia*), and I would like that the *Rav* should give me a *farher* (test)."

The elderly *Rav* asked the boy to come in and sat down with him at the dining room table. "My child, I will listen to you say the *Gemara*," said the *Rav*, "but I would just like to explain something to you first. If you come to a *Rav's* house on a *Shabbos* afternoon, and you knock on the door and there is no answer, and you knock again and still there is no answer, then you have to think that perhaps the *Rav* might have been somewhat tired and gone to rest for a little while."

The little boy's face turned pale as he looked up at the Tshebiner *Rav* and said, with purity and innocence, "I never thought that a *Rav* sleeps on *Shabbos*."

The child's comprehension of what a *Rav* is was such that he was positive that a man as holy as a *Rav* would, on a *Shabbos* afternoon, either be totally engrossed in Torah study or else busy answering people's *she'eilos* (religious questions). Sleeping was for mere mortals, not *rabbanim*. The Tshebiner *Rav* was so taken aback by this child's perception of a *Rav* that from then on he never slept again on a *Shabbos* afternoon!

Flat on His Face

The Talmud (*Berachos* 28b) notes that a nineteenth blessing was added to our daily *Shemoneh Esrei* during the time of Rabban Gamliel II, after the destruction of the Second Temple. (The term *Shemoneh Esrei* means "eighteen," and indeed the original *Shemoneh Esrei* consisted of eighteen blessings; see *Megillah* 17b.) With the additional blessing we pray three times a day that *Hashem* spare us from the influence of heretics and non-believers and from the devious plans of slanderers and informers.

The following story, told by R' Eliezer Ginsburg of Brooklyn, is an example of one such demented informer.

In the town of Luban, Russia, where R' Moshe Feinstein (1895-1986) was the *Rav*, there was a *moser*, an informer, who did great harm to his fellow Jews. He would report to government officials any wrongdoings in the community; he made up stories about Jews he didn't like, so that they would have to pay higher taxes and be subject to beatings by the police.

Because the Russian authorities hated the Jews, the *moser* himself was safe because the officials considered him their friend. On the other hand — if he were to be harmed, the Jews would be held accountable. Thus he was treated carefully — even to the point of being able to get merchandise from Jews at a lower price than the general public — because everyone feared to get on his bad side.

It happened that this *moser* became very ill and realized that he was about to die. He demanded that the *Chevra Kaddisha* (burial society) be brought to his home, for he wished to speak to them. They were summoned at once.

Once they were in his home he told them that he had a desire that he wanted fulfilled. When he died he wanted to be buried face down! The members of the *Chevra* couldn't believe their ears. They had never heard such a ridiculous request and besides — it was against Jewish law to bury anyone that way! (See *Yoreh Deah* 362:2, and *Or HaChaim, Bereishis* 23:3.) They didn't try to convince him to change his mind, for they knew he would just argue relentlessly. They left his home without making any commitments to him.

A few days later he died. The *Chevra Kaddisha* went to ask R' Moshe a *she'eilah.* They were in a quandary, for on one hand they were familiar with the Talmudic teaching (*Gittin* 14b) that "מִצְוָה לְקַיֵּם דִּבְרֵי הַמֵּת — It is an obligation to fulfill the words of one who is about to die," and so perhaps they were obligated to fulfill the *moser's* request to be buried face down. On the other hand, the informer's request was against Jewish law and practice.

R' Moshe replied that the obligation to fulfill a man's final request in such a situation is only binding if the request is within the confines of *halachah.* A request such as this one — to be buried face down — is clearly a violation of Jewish law, and so it must not be obeyed. The *Chevra Kaddisha* thus buried him in the conventional way, as they would anyone else: face up.

A few weeks after the funeral, a group of Russian officials came to the *Chevra Kaddisha* and demanded that the grave of the *moser* be opened. The *Chevra* protested, claiming that this was against Jewish law. Once a person was laid to rest, his body was not to be tampered with in any way, save if it was being moved to *Eretz Yisrael.*

The officials threatened to send the *Chevra* members to Siberia if they didn't comply. They simply were not going to take "no" for an answer. And so, hesitantly, the *Chevra* opened the grave of the informer. The Russians peered in, looked at the dead man's remains, and began to leave. Unable to contain his curiosity, one of the members of the *Chevra* asked them, "Tell me, what were you looking for?"

The Russian glared back at the man and said, "We received a letter from our friend saying that he knew how much you Jews hated him, and that he was sure you would do something nasty to him, such as burying him upside down. We just wanted to be sure that you hadn't done that."

One can only imagine how much grief R' Moshe spared his fellow Jews by his strict adherence to the *halachah.*

Housing Project

The complex of homes known as Battei Orenstein, located near the Geulah section in Jerusalem, was built over a hundred years ago by a wealthy Jew, a Boyaner *chassid* by the name of R' Dov Ber Orenstein. Recently, R' Sholom Schwadron retold the fascinating story of how this housing development came to be built.

R' Dov Ber Orenstein was a generous man with a caring heart. His open hand was always extended to all who were not as financially secure as he was. One day a certain R' Zorach approached him and asked R' Dov Ber for help out of a desperate situation. He had no funds at all, said R' Zorach, but had to marry off a daughter. Furthermore, he saw no way of raising the necessary funds. R' Dov Ber agreed to help the poor man and gave him a fantastic sum of money. R' Zorach couldn't thank the wealthy man enough. "I just ask that you invite me to the wedding," said R' Dov Ber.

More than a year passed before the wedding could be held. The family of the *chassan* also had financial difficulties, and until they raised their share of the funds needed to provide the new couple with the basic necessities to set up a home, more than twelve months had passed. Finally, though, a wedding date was announced and friends and relatives were invited.

On the evening of the wedding, just a little while before the *chuppah* was to begin, R' Zorach, the father of the bride, suddenly remembered that he had forgotten to invite R' Orenstein, the wealthy man who had given him so much money more than a year ago. As soon as he recalled R' Dov Ber's request that he be invited to the wedding, R' Zorach approached his future son-in-law, the groom, and explained that he had to leave for a little while to go and invite R' Dov Ber personally. It was bad enough that he had forgotten to extend the promised invitation, he explained, but now, moments before the *chuppah*, to send an emissary with an invitation would surely be an insult. He had to go himself. The groom fully understood the importance of keeping this promise and insisted on coming along. As other guests heard of the situation they decided they could not allow the *chassan* and the father of the *kallah* to go by themselves, and thus a group of people accompanied them to the home of R' Dov Ber to invite him to the wedding.

As they came close to R' Dov Ber's home, they were surprised to find that the gate in front of the house was locked. It certainly wasn't late at night, and everyone knew that the Orenstein home was always open to wayfarers and friends. Despite his age, the *kallah's* father climbed over the fence to get to the front door, closely followed by the *chassan* (new suit and all) and those who had accompanied them. To their surprise, the front door, too, was locked. They knocked but there was no answer. *Something must be wrong here*, they thought. They quickly rushed around to the back and found the rear door open. The men entered the home quietly, and as they made their way into the dining area they saw both R' Dov Ber and his wife bound and gagged, lying on the floor. "What's going on?" the *chassan* shouted.

Suddenly three men dashed past the wedding group, ran outside and disappeared into the darkness. Instead of chasing the fleeing intruders, R' Zorach and the *chassan* went to untie the elderly couple and set them free. The others who had come along with them looked around and noticed that silver and other valuables had been stacked high in the kitchen. They had entered during an attempted robbery, and the would-be robbers were making their final search for any valuables they might have missed when the group came in through the back entrance.

Once the Orensteins recovered from their initial fright and began to calm down a bit, they were convinced to go join the wedding festivities. At the wedding, R' Dov Ber repeated over and over again how fortunate he was to have been saved. "I feel as if *Hashem* has given me a new lease on life," he kept saying. "It's as if I am now living on borrowed time. I must find an appropriate way to show my gratitude."

A few days after the incident, R' Dov Ber began to think of an appropriate way to display his thankfulness to *Hashem* for saving him from the robbers. He realized that his life had been spared as a direct result of the help he had given R' Zorach in marrying off his daughter. He therefore decided that his thankfulness to *Hashem* would best be shown by his doing an act of kindness for young couples about to be married. "Since marriage represents the building of a home by the new couple, I will build a housing development for people who cannot afford apartments on their own." And so R' Dov Ber had these homes built. For years afterwards, any young couple who could not afford to move into quarters on their own would move into one of the Battei Orenstein — rent free — until they could afford the money to buy an apartment of their own. R' Dov Ber also had a *mikveh* built near the premises, and both the housing development and the *mikveh* are known by the Orenstein name until this very day.

And all because a man kept his promise!

☙ *Lost and Found*

The *Tosefta* (*Peah* 3:13) relates a story about a pious man who was gathering bundles of wheat on his farm. Inadvertently, he forgot to collect one of them and it remained lying outdoors. When he realized later that he had forgotten a bundle, he became ecstatic. He ordered that the bundle be left in the field (so that poor people could take from it) and instructed his son to have sacrifices brought on his behalf to the *Beis HaMikdash* in Jerusalem.

The surprised son asked his father, "Why such joy that you want sacrifices brought?"

The father explained to his son that it is not often that one gets the opportunity to perform the *mitzvah* of *shikchah* (leaving a forgotten bundle in the field — see *Devarim* 24:19). Thus his sudden 'good fortune,' which allowed him to fulfill this *mitzvah,* gave him cause to rejoice and give thanks to *Hashem* through sacrifices. (One cannot plan to perform the *mitzvah* of *shikchah,* for it is impossible to plan to forget something.)

Pious Jews view their performance of every *mitzvah* as a privilege, not a burden. The minutes or even hours involved in doing a *mitzvah* are moments to be treasured. It is for this reason that many Jews offer the prayer 'הִנְנִי מוּכָן וּמְזוּמָן — Behold, I am ready and prepared to perform . . .' before they perform a *mitzvah,* to emphasize their preparedness and joy at what they have a chance to do.

R' Lipa Geldwerth of Brooklyn witnessed just such a spontaneous burst of joy from one of the *gedolim* in our time, the Steipler *Gaon,* R' Yaakov Yisrael Kanievsky (1899-1985), when he realized that he could perform (what was for him) a rare *mitzvah*.

When R' Lipa was studying in *Eretz Yisrael,* he made it a point to visit the Steipler at his home in Bnei Brak to seek advice and counsel. The Steipler, who made few public appearances, would spend most of the day learning in his home on Rechov Rashbam and then, during specified hours, would see the people who were lined up outside his door. He saw literally hundreds of people every week.

One time as R' Lipa spoke to the Steipler, the Steipler noticed that he was carrying a rare *sefer, Kochav M'Yaakov,* written by R' Lipa's great-grandfather, the Rimaliver *Rav,* R' Yaakov Weidenfeld (1840-1894).

The Steipler's eyes lit up. "You know," he said, "I have been searching for years for this wonderful *sefer,* but no one that I know seems to have it. Do you perchance know where I can buy a copy of this precious *sefer*?"

"Here, please take mine," R' Lipa offered. "I am a descendant of the *Kochav M'Yaakov* and I can surely get a replacement for myself through the family."

"Chas veshalom! שׂוֹנֵא מַתָּנֹת יִחְיֶה — He who hates gifts will live long (*Mishlei* 15:27)," the Steipler retorted as he quoted the famous verse. Having no other choice, R' Lipa told the Steipler where he thought he could purchase it.

A few weeks and a few hundred visitors later, R' Lipa returned to the Steipler Gaon. Once again he was carrying the *sefer Kochav M'Yaakov*. The Steipler didn't recognize R' Lipa, but when he noticed the *sefer* he was carrying, he praised it as he had a few weeks earlier. When it became obvious to R' Lipa that the Steipler had not yet had the opportunity to purchase the *sefer* for himself, he once again offered it to him, explaining that as a family member of the *Kochav M'Yaakov* he could easily get another one. Once again the Steipler refused to accept it unless he could pay for it with an exchange of *sefarim* that he himself had written. The Steipler began piling up his own works, and said humbly, "For the value of what's written in that *sefer*, and for the fact that it's printed on American [superior] paper, here are these as equal payment." R' Lipa counted eight *sefarim!*

Then the Steipler asked R' Lipa whether he had cousins in Israel who were also from the family of the *Kochav M'Yaakov*. "Yes," said R' Lipa, curious as to why the Steipler would be interested.

"A descendant of the *Kochav M'Yaakov* was here a few weeks ago," the Steipler exclaimed, "and left something behind. Wait right here!"

The elderly *Rav* got up from his chair, rushed into the next room, and came back carrying something in a brown paper bag that had some writing on it. The Steipler removed the item — a brown scarf — from the bag, and said, "He lost this when he was here."

R' Lipa was stunned. He had lost his brown scarf a few weeks ago, but had no idea where he had left it. R' Lipa nodded and said, "That is my scarf. It was I who was here, but I didn't remember that I forgot it here. I'm truly sorry for troubling the *Rav*."

"Now," said the *Gaon*, beaming, "I have a rare opportunity to fulfill a *mitzvah* that I hardly get a chance to fulfill, the *mitzvah* of *hashavas aveidah* (returning a lost object).

"You see," the great *Gaon* continued, "I am confined here to this room most of the day. I am rarely in the streets. Where would I get the opportunity to find a lost item? But you, *Baruch Hashem* (blessed is G-d), gave me the opportunity."

The Steipler paused, then with great fervor said aloud, "הִנְנִי מוּכָן וּמְזוּמָן לְקַיֵּם מִצְוַת עֲשֵׂה שֶׁל הַשָׁבַת אֲבֵידָה — Behold, I am ready and prepared to fulfill the positive commandment of returning a lost item."

He then gave R' Lipa his brown scarf and a bright smile.

R' Lipa also has the bag in which the scarf was kept all those weeks. On the outside is written in the Steipler's own handwriting, "Tuesday night, *parshas Tetzaveh.* Item inside that may possibly belong to a descendant of the *Kochav M'Yaakov.*"

⸎ *The Real Thing*

The prophet *Yeshaya* (29:13) cried out that *Hashem* was upset with the Jewish nation, for although they seemingly paid sincere homage to Him in speech, their hearts were far from being totally devoted to *Torah* and *mitzvos. Hashem* said, "וַתְּהִי יִרְאָתָם אֹתִי מִצְוַת אֲנָשִׁים מְלֻמָּדָה, *their fear of Me is merely habitual.*"

Indeed many people distort, in their own minds, the reality of their own behavior. They rationalize that their words or actions are nothing but sincere but actually they are fooling themselves. In this story, told by R' Ṣhlomo Teitelbaum of Kew Gardens, New York, one comes to appreciate the unyielding honesty, self-analysis and introspection of the Satmar *Rav,* R' Yoel Teitelbaum (1887-1979).

As the *Rav* and *Rebbe* of a large community, the Satmar *Rav* had many opportunities to attend *simchos.* It happened one time that the *Rebbe* attended a wedding at which there was a *badchan* (jester). When a *badchan* is in attendance the guests gather around him and, to the enjoyment of all, he sings or mimics — in beautiful melody — lyrics interspersed with verses of *Tanach* and phrases of *Chazal*, regarding the families, marriage in general or the people present.

At this particular wedding the *badchan* asked the Satmar *Rav* if he would mind if he imitated him. To have imitated the *Rav* without permission, especially in his presence, would have been disrespectful. The *Rav* however smiled and gave his consent.

The *badchan* began impersonating the *Rav's davening*. The Satmar *Rav's* high-pitched voice and *tefillos* on such special days as *Hoshana Rabbah* were legendary. The *badchan's* gestures and voice were amazingly similar to the Satmar's. The people roared with laughter and delight. The *Rav* though watched the *badchan* carefully and soon began crying. The *badchan* felt terrible.

When he finished his routine, the *badchan* approached the *Rav* and began to apologize. "*Rebbe*," he said, "I feel terrible that I upset you. I am truly sorry."

"Don't feel bad," the *Rav* said. "It is not your fault."

"So then why were you crying?" the concerned *badchan* asked.

"When you were imitating me, you were doing it so exactly, that it sounded just the way I sound. It suddenly occurred to me that if a stranger could imitate me so well, then maybe at times when I myself am *davening* I am merely imitating myself!"

There are times when each of us prays with great intent. But what about the rest of the time? Do we merely mimic the motions of prayer we did the day before and the day before that? It was this haunting question that caused the Satmar *Rav* to cry, because to him the jester's act was no laughing matter.

◆§ *A Prayer in Kiev*

A number of years ago I was called to perform a *bris* on twin boys. After I had finished the *bris* on the older child and was preparing to do the *bris* on the younger child, a *rav* who had just returned from Russia told the assembled guests a fascinating story about an event that he had witnessed first hand.

The story gave those who heard it a new perspective on the upcoming *bris*.

In the Soviet Union it is illegal to have a *bris* performed on a Jewish child. If the authorities learn that a family has had their child ritually circumcised, they could remove the father of the child from his job, jail him, or even send him to Siberia. Thus it came as quite a shock to this *rav* when one morning, in a Russian synagogue in Kiev, a gentleman came over to him and whispered in his ear, "Do you want to be present at a *bris milah?*"

The *rav* nodded in the affirmative and was then told that after leaving the synagogue he should walk two blocks, make a left turn, go down one more block and, at the first alley, make a right turn and look for a lit candle in the window of one of the apartments. "That's the sign that a *bris* is to take place there," the Russian man said quietly.*

After he had finished his *Shacharis* prayers, the *rav* walked out of the synagogue alone and followed the exact directions he had been given. Sure enough, once he entered the alleyway he could see a candle burning in the window of a second-floor apartment. He made his way into the building, walked up the stairs, and knocked on the door.

He recognized some of the people as those he had seen in the synagogue earlier. The *mohel* was already there, and the chairs for the *sandak* (the gentleman who holds the child during the *bris*) and Elijah the prophet, who according to the *Midrash* (*Pirkei D'Rabbi Eliezer* 29) attends every *bris*, had already been set up. Soon the infant was brought in and the *bris* was performed. The *rav* couldn't help but notice that the people there were not familiar with any of the prayers that were being recited, and so he thought he would be

---

* In times of religious persecution, Jews could not make public announcements regarding a *bris*. Instead, they would use covert signals (such as placing candles in the window during day-light hours) to inform their coreligionists that a religious rite was to take place there. (See *Sanhedrin* 32b with *Rashi* and *Tosafos;* see also *Bris Milah,* Mesorah Publications, p. 75.)

helpful and explain the procedures and their meanings to the assembled guests.

He did his explaining in Yiddish, a language which he spoke fluently and which was understood by most of the people there.

"When the baby came in," the *rav* began, "the *mohel* loudly exclaimed, '*Baruch haba!*' which means, 'Blessed is the one who has come!' " He went on to explain the significance of the Chair of Elijah, and the meaning of the blessing that the *mohel* had recited and of the one which the father had been instructed to repeat.

He explained why the child was given his name at a *bris*. Then the *rav* began to explain the phrase that everyone said out loud at the conclusion of the *bris* prayers, 'כְּשֵׁם שֶׁנִּכְנַס לַבְּרִית כֵּן יִכָּנֵס לְתוֹרָה וּלְחוּפָּה וּלְמַעֲשִׂים טוֹבִים — Just as he (the child) has entered into the covenant, so may he enter into the (study of) Torah, the marriage canopy, and (the performance of) good deeds.'

As the *rav* spoke he noticed a commotion in the back. People were obviously upset about something, and they were rumbling to each other in Russian and pointing at the *rav*. He realized that he had said something that bothered them, but he could not figure out what it might be. He walked slowly towards the back of the room and said to the men there, in Yiddish, "You all seem troubled. What did I say that makes you so upset?"

They looked at him sternly and said, "*Rebbe*, you think you have given us a blessing, but in reality you have just cursed us."

"What are you all talking about?" he asked incredulously. "I merely translated the prayers of the *bris*."

"Yes," they replied, "but for us that's a curse. You said that just as the child was entered into his *bris*, so too shall it be with his Torah, *chuppah*, and good deeds. Do you really think that we want to continue having to perform *mitzvos* like this, in secret, in fear of the authorities? Do you think we want to stay here in Russia and be forced to study in secret? We want to get out of here and go to either Israel or America where we can practice our *Yiddishkeit* openly, without any apprehension at all!"

The *rav* was left speechless and amazed that a *tefillah* written by *Chazal* as a supplication for good things could be twisted so horribly by people in a very unfortunate situation. He tried to console the downtrodden people and vowed to do anything in his power to hasten their release from the Soviet Union.

Now, months later, as he stood in a country where one was free to perform any *mitzvos* that he wished, the *rav* reflected on what had occurred in Russia. Still deeply moved, he said, "That incident made me realize how grateful we, here in the free world, have to be. We can perform *mitzvos* openly and joyfully participate in the *simchos* which *Hashem* allows us to celebrate. Thus, as we have been blessed with these opportunities, we have the responsibility to perform all *mitzvos* with great enthusiasm and happiness."

The *bris* on the second of the twins was performed with an enhanced appreciation for much that we take for granted.

☙ *Of a Badge and Courage*

At the West Point Military Academy in upstate New York there are few Jewish cadets. Hospital and medical staff there do not include many Jewish personnel, either. Yet a number of years ago, a sequence of events which took place at the Academy led to a thrilling moment of *kiddush Hashem* (sanctification of G-d), and illustrated to the generals and all the other officers the eternal truths of the teachings of *Chazal* (the Talmudic sages).

Michelle Dobin,* wife of the only Jewish dentist at West Point, had great trouble conceiving a child. Now, after ten long and anxious years, she finally gave birth to a baby boy on a *Shabbos* afternoon. Both she and her husband were thrilled, and throughout the next day people came by the maternity floor to offer their congratulations.

Among those who visited the new mother was a dear and close

---

* The names of the West Point personnel in this story have been fictionalized.

friend, Sarah Lerner, wife of the Chief of Neurology, Doctor Rafael Lerner. Mrs. Lerner and Mrs. Dobin shared a somewhat painful common bond, for Mrs. Lerner also had not been able to have children for the past six years. Mrs. Lerner had a six-year-old son, Eli, but since his birth she had borne no other children.

When all other visitors had left the room, Mrs. Lerner warmly extended a *mazel tov* to her friend and then said excitedly, "Well, now it's time to plan the *bris*."

Mrs. Dobin's demeanor suddenly became cold. She looked at Mrs. Lerner with contempt and said, "Sarah, you know that I am not religious like you. I'm not planning to have a *bris*."

"What does being religious have to do with anything?" Mrs. Lerner asked in surprise. "A *bris* is the first *mitzvah* in a child's life and, regardless of what your own personal degree of observance is, your child is entitled to have his life as a Jew begin properly."

However, her words did not move her friend. The two women parried and argued but each remained adamant in her conviction. Finally in exasperation Mrs. Lerner said, "Is this how you show gratitude to G-d after He granted you a healthy son?"

❧ ❧ ❧

That evening at home, Mrs. Lerner related her afternoon's conversation to her husband, Rafael. Mrs. Lerner — who drove her son, Eli, one hundred twenty miles round trip every day from West Point to Spring Valley, New York, so that he could attend a religious kindergarten — was determined that the new, innocent child of her friend would have his *bris*. "Speak to her husband," she urged Dr. Lerner. "He is a friend of yours. Maybe he will listen."

Dr. Lerner tried to explain to his wife that he had already broached the topic to Dr. Dobin but he, like his wife, was against having a *bris* for his son. "Besides," said Dr. Lerner, "why is it your concern? It's their child. Let them do as they see fit."

But Mrs. Lerner would not give up, and throughout the week she pleaded, cajoled and begged both Dr. and Mrs. Dobin to allow their son to have his proper *bris*. The Dobins had agreed to have a doctor circumcise their child, but that was obviously not good enough for Mrs. Lerner. She insisted that the *bris* had to be done by a *mohel*. "The

Dobins and everyone else here at West Point have to know that a *bris* is a religious occasion, not a medical procedure," she kept repeating.

Dr. Lerner tried once again to convince the obstinate parents about the importance of a *bris*. Finally, on Thursday afternoon, the new parents consented. The Lerners were given the job of locating a *mohel*. However, they were instructed that the *mohel* would have to agree to two conditions: first, that a doctor be allowed to stand alongside him to make sure that he performed the *bris* in a manner that was medically acceptable, and second, that he not insist on a celebration afterwards. The Lerners assured them that both terms would be met.

Thursday night Dr. Lerner contacted a *mohel* and arrangements were hastily made for him to come to West Point for *Shabbos*.

None of the medical staff or Army personnel could remember ever witnessing a *bris* at West Point. This *bris* could have been a very festive occasion, but the new parents insisted on keeping it very low key.

On Friday, when the *mohel* came to bring his instruments to the home where the *bris* would take place, the new mother would not let him into the house, for she refused to even see him. He had to leave his instruments on the front doorstep for her to bring inside later. On *Shabbos*, the day of the *bris*, the mother of the new baby refused to talk to the *mohel;* he had to give the father the instructions that he usually gives to the mother. The *bris* was performed uneventfully, with a doctor in attendance. A small amount of food was served, but the atmosphere was cold and damp just like the weather outside. Mrs. Lerner, who had arranged the *bris*, thought to herself sorrowfully, *If only I could have been the one making the bris at West Point . . .*

That *Shabbos* the Lerners *davened* as they did every week — in their living room. So that their six-year-old Eli would become familiar with the procedures of an Orthodox *shul*, they arranged their small living room like a *shul*, a number of chairs separated by a *mechitzah*. Dr. Lerner and any male *Shabbos* guests (usually an uncle or a brother-in-law, and on this *Shabbos*, the *mohel*) would sit in the 'men's section' while Mrs. Lerner and any women guests (usually a grandmother or a sister, and for this *Shabbos,* the *mohel's* wife) would sit in the 'women's section.' Dr. Lerner had built a little *amud* (lectern) from where he would serve as *chazzan,* and a little *bimah* (platform) from where he would read the portion of the week with the proper *neginah* (tones), but without reciting the *brachos,* from a small (paper) *Sefer Torah.* The Lerners went through all this effort so that their son would be familiar with everything that any other religious six-year-old boy saw every week in his own *shul.* (This went on for two years!) After *Shabbos* the *mohel,* inspired by the dedication and commitment of both Dr. Lerner and his wife, thought to himself, *If only they could have been the people making a bris at West Point . . .*

Months went by and the memory of the *bris* began to fade. It had been an experience for the *mohel,* perhaps a once-in-a-lifetime experience. Winter turned to spring and then almost ten months to the day since he had been in West Point, the *mohel* received a call from an excited Dr. Lerner. "Would you be willing to come back to West Point for another *bris?*" he asked. "Who are the parents this time?" the *mohel* inquired hesitantly.

"My wife and I!" exclaimed Dr. Lerner ecstatically. Incredibly, and to the surprise of her own doctors, Mrs. Lerner had conceived and gave birth to a healthy boy!

Unbelievable? Not really.

The *Midrash* (*Bamidbar Rabbah* 14:2) notes that *Hashem* says, "מִי הִקְדִּימַנִי וַאֲשַׁלֵּם — He who has preceded me will be compensated (*Iyov* 41:3)." To those who give charity even though they have no money, and to those who participate in and perform *bris milah* even though they have no children, *Hashem* says, "They have performed the *mitzvah* even though I did not give them anything to perform it with. Therefore, I must now pay them back with money (in the case of charity) and children (in the case of *bris milah*)."

Thus less than a year after Mrs. Lerner had seen to it that another woman's child had his *bris, Hashem* had blessed her with her own son, and had given her the opportunity to fulfill the *mitzvah* another time.

On the day of this *bris,* held in the West Point Officers' Club, the sun shone brightly and the flowers sparkled brilliantly in their spring colors. The entire hospital staff, more than one hundred officers, colonels and lieutenants, along with the Commanding General of West Point, gathered for the festive occasion. Smartly attired in his Army uniform, Major (Dr.) Rafael Lerner stood at attention together with his fellow officers as R' Moshe Tendler from Monsey, New York, spoke the following words:

> Here at West Point, one can have an appreciation of what *bris milah,* ritual circumcision, symbolizes. Every cadet, every officer, must always wear the badge of his Army, as an indication of his loyalty to the Military of his country which he serves so faithfully. For Jews, beginning with the Patriarch Abraham, a *bris* has been the badge and symbol of our commitment to G-d, our Master General, that we will serve him dutifully and loyally. Today we affix this badge on the newest soldier amongst us.

The little boy was named David — as was the author of *Tehillim* (*Psalms*) — because his parents considered him a living song of testimony and praise of *Hashem's* miracles.

> Those two *brissim* at West Point were among the most extraordinary I have ever performed as a *mohel.*

◆§ *False Tears*

R' Chatzkel Levenstein (1885-1974), the world-renowned *mashgiach* of the Ponevezher Yeshivah in Bnei Brak, Israel, was known for his fiery talks and the strong demands of honesty and integrity he made on all his students. A man of great emotion and intensity, he awed the people who came into contact with him.

The following story, heard from both R' Sholom Schwadron and R' Eliezer Ginsburg of Brooklyn, is a striking example of R' Chatzkel's fierce honesty.

In 1952, R' Chatzkel's nine-year-old grandson, Tzvi Yehudah, who lived in America [and who had been named for R' Chatzkel's father, R' Yehudah] became critically ill. Needless to say, family members both in America and in Israel were saddened and worried. Unfortunately, one Friday night the child passed away.

After *Shabbos*, not wanting to break the news to R' Chatzkel suddenly, the family in America sent a telegram to a very close acquaintance of R' Chatzkel, R' Nachum Pertzovitz (1922-1986) of the Mirrer Yeshivah in Jerusalem, informing him of the sad news. They reasoned that he would best know how to relay the sad message. On Sunday, R' Nachum went to R' Chatzkel to tell him the news.

R' Nachum walked into the room where R' Chatzkel was sitting, and with a drawn face and downcast eyes he said, almost inaudibly, "We received information from America."

"About the child?" R' Chatzkel asked.

R' Nachum nodded. R' Chatzkel said, "I know already."

"How?" asked R' Nachum incredulously.

"Friday night I had a dream that my late father and another man buried the child, wrapped in the cover of a *Sefer Torah!*"

R' Nachum was speechless. After a short while, the two saddened sages tearfully resumed speaking. As they talked, a young man entered to speak to R' Chatzkel. That particular Sunday was the *shloshim* (the thirtieth day since the passing) of the Slobodka *Rosh Yeshivah*, R' Isaac Sher (1875-1952). A huge crowd was expected to gather at the Slobodka Yeshivah, not far from R' Chatzkel's home, to listen to the eulogies which would be delivered in R' Isaac's honor.

"When does the *Mashgiach* wish to go to the *hesped* (eulogy)?" the man asked.

"I can't speak there today," R' Chatzkel replied softly.

The young man was surprised. "But the *tzetlach* (public notices) all say that you are one of the speakers," the fellow politely protested.

R' Chatzkel looked up at the man and explained. "I know that if I speak about the passing of R' Isaac it will awaken in me a sadness that I personally feel about my late grandson. I will surely be moved to tears, but the people in attendance will think they are tears shed because of R' Isaac's passing. I know, however, that they will be for my grandson, and I do not wish to shed false tears!"

Aside from everything else that is startling in this story is the aspect commented on in an essay on אֱמֶת (*truth*) by the *Orchos Tzaddikim*. He writes, "Those who train themselves, so that all their thoughts [during the day] are truthful, are shown visions (dreams) at night that are truthful as well." Thus R' Chatzkel, who was so brutally honest with himself, saw in his Friday-night dream the reality of his grandson's situation, even before anyone told him about it.

◆§ *A Cry for Shabbos*

One year, on the occasion of the Chofetz Chaim's *yahrzeit*, a *rav* in Miami lectured on the life and accomplishments of the Chofetz Chaim. He mentioned the many *sefarim* the great Torah sage had authored, both in *halachah* and in *mussar*. He described his sterling character, and recounted numerous stories that stood out in his mind depicting the Chofetz Chaim's deep concern for his fellow Jew.

There was one story the *rav* had wanted to tell, but he was troubled, for he only knew part of it. As he stood at the lectern, he thought for a moment and then decided that he would tell it anyway. He rationalized that even an unfinished story about the Chofetz Chaim would certainly have a message.

He began to relate an incident about a *bachur* in the Chofetz Chaim's yeshivah in Radin, who was found smoking a cigarette on *Shabbos*. Some students in the yeshivah had caught him in this act of desecrating the holy day, and ran to tell the *rebbeim* of the yeshivah. It was decided that the boy should be expelled. However, when the Chofetz Chaim heard of this he asked that the *bachur* be brought to his home.

At this point, the *rav* recounting the story interrupted the narrative and said, "I don't know what the Chofetz Chaim said to the boy. I only know that they were together for only a few moments. I would give anything to know what he said to the youngster, for I am told that the boy never desecrated the *Shabbos* again. How wonderful it would be if we could relay that message — whatever it was — to others, to encourage them in their *shmiras Shabbos*, and get the same results!"

The *rav* then continued with his lecture.

After the speech, the hall emptied of everyone except for one old man. This gentleman remained in his seat, alone with his thoughts. From the distance it seemed he was trembling, as if he was either crying or suffering from chills. The *rav* walked over to the elderly gentleman, sat down beside him and asked, "Is anything wrong?"

"How did you know that story of the cigarette on *Shabbos?*" the man said by way of response. He did not look up, and was obviously still shaken and upset.

"I really don't know," answered the *rav*. "I heard it a while ago. I don't even remember who told it to me."

The old man looked up at the *rav*, somewhat embarrassed. "I was that *bachur*," he said softly. The *rav* — who just moments ago had delivered an articulate speech, and from whom words usually flowed so easily — was now speechless.

He was startled by the coincidence of his having told this anecdote on just the particular evening when this particular gentleman happened to be in the audience. He knew it was illogical, but in his mind the boy in the story had remained a teenager forever. It just didn't seem plausible that the old man next to him and the defiant child in Radin could be one and the same. Yet the *rav* was anxious to know what had happened between the boy and the Chofetz Chaim. But at this moment he could not bring himself to ask.

The *rav* wisely let the man recover from the impact of the event, as it appeared to have hit him once again. The two sat quietly for a few moments, and then the gentleman said, "I'll tell you what happened, but let's go outside."

The old man seemed to need air. The traumatic event of years ago had suddenly begun to envelop him again. Today had suddenly become yesterday, and in the transition he was overwhelmed.

As the two walked together, the old man explained. "This incident occurred in the 1920s, when the Chofetz Chaim was in his eighties. I was terrified to have to go into his house and face him. But when I did go into his home, I looked around with disbelief at the poverty in which he lived. It was unimaginable to me that a man of his stature would be satisfied to live in such surroundings.

"Suddenly he was in the room where I was waiting. He was remarkably short. At that time I was a teenager and he only came up to my shoulders. He took my hand and clasped it tenderly in both of his. He brought my hand in his own clasped hands up to his face, and when I looked into his soft face, his eyes were closed for a moment. When he opened them, they were filled with tears.

"He said to me in a hushed voice full of pain and astonishment, '*Shabbos* . . .' and then he started to cry! He was now holding both my hands in his, and he repeated with astonishment, '*Shabbos* . . . *hailiger* (holy) *Shabbos!*'

"My heart started pounding and I became more frightened than I had been before. Though he held my hands loosely, I felt as if I were tied by chains of iron.

"Tears streamed down his face and one of them rolled onto my hand. I thought it would bore a hole right through my skin. When I think of those tears today I can still feel their heat. I can't describe how awful it felt to know that I had made the great *tzaddik* cry. But in his rebuke — which consisted only of those words — I felt that he was not angry, but rather sad and disappointed with me for having personally betrayed his confidence. He seemed frightened of the consequences of my actions."

The old man became silent, lost in a river of thoughts.

The young boy never forgave himself for having caused the old *tzaddik* such torment, and now, an old man himself, he caressed the hand that bore the invisible scar of a precious tear. It had become his permanent reminder to observe *Shabbos* for the rest of his life.

Counterforce

The following episode took place in the 1920's outside a *shul* in the famous Chatzar Strauss (Strauss Courtyard) in Jerusalem. The apartments in that area were built by the philan- thropist, Mr. Shmuel Strauss (father-in-law of the noted activist and President of Agudath Israel, R' Yaakov Rosenheim). He designated them for *baalei mussar* of note, especially for the world-renowned *talmidim* of R' Yisrael Salanter (1810-1883). Such *tzaddikim* as R' Itzele Peterburger (1837-1907) and R' Naftoli Amsterdam, giants in the *Mussar* Movement, and others hers resided in those apartments when they were first established.

This story was told by R' Simcha Zisel Broide, who today is the *Rosh Yeshivah* of the Chevron Yeshivah in Jerusalem.

One particular morning, when R' Simcha Zisel was a young boy of twelve, he was making his way with his father to the *shul* in the Strauss Courtyard to *daven Shacharis.* As he approached the building, he noticed that there had been fresh *tzetlach* put up the night before on one of the walls adjacent to the *shul.* Standing and reading one of the new posters carefully was the well-respected and elderly *tzaddik,* R' Hirsch Weisfisch. R' Hirsch and his group of friends were known as the *Yakirei Yerushalayim* (the precious ones of Jerusalem) because of their piety and adherence to Torah and *mitzvos.*

R' Hirsch seemed to be concentrating intently on the information printed in the loud, bold typeface. And since he was nearsighted, his face was almost up against the poster. As he finished reading, he took out a pencil and a piece of paper, made a few notes, and then walked into the *shul*.

The little boy and his father were somewhat surprised at the intense interest that R' Hirsch had shown in the poster. Was there a special *shiur* (lecture) being given? Had someone important died and was there going to be a *hesped?* Was a particular *tzaddik* coming to town, and was someone making a *kabbalas panim* (welcoming reception) for him?

The boy and his father were curious and decided to read the

poster as well. The more they read, however, the more shocked they became. The poster proclaimed that a movie would be shown that night in the city of Jericho, and that it would be followed by moonlight dancing. Boys and girls were invited to attend.

R' Simcha Zisel and his father read and reread the poster two or three times to see if there could possibly be anything there that would have interested R' Hirsch. R' Hirsch was known to be a holy man who seemed almost always to be totally immersed in *avodas* (service of) *Hashem* through learning, *davening*, or the performance of *mitzvos*. R' Simcha Zisel's father shook his head in disbelief and then made his way into the *shul*, confused and puzzled.

In the little anteroom of the *shul*, R' Hirsch was washing his hands before entering the main sanctuary to *daven*. R' Simcha Zisel's father went over to R' Hirsch and questioned him. "What connection could you possibly have to the events described in that poster? Why were you so interested in what was written there?"

R' Hirsch smiled wistfully at both the father and his young son. He could understand their dismay. "You know," he said softly, "recently, *nebach* (unfortunately), they have begun a terrible thing here in Israel. They have begun showing movies. It is the work of the Satan, the *yeitzer hara* (evil inclination), that boys and girls should come together there, and talk and act in ways not becoming to Jewish children. The atmosphere is spiritual poison."

He continued. "When the first movie came out, a group of friends and I decided that at the same time the Satan is doing his work, we in turn will counterbalance that with holy work and service to *Hashem*. And so every time a movie is shown, my friends and I have a *mishmar* (vigil) in which we study Torah uninterrupted, so as to be a counterforce of sanctity against the evil that is going on. When I came to *shul* I noticed that a new sign was up, with a new time for the movies. Tonight is my night for learning, so I wanted to know exactly how long I should keep my *mishmar*. I wrote it down to make sure I wouldn't forget!"

R' Simcha Zisel has repeated this story dozens of times and each time with a new reverence for the saintly R' Hirsch whom he was privileged to know in his formative years.

◆§ *It's No Bother*

A number of years ago, R' Avrohom Kabalkin, a noted Torah scholar in Jerusalem, was traveling in England. When he came to the home of R' Mordechai Miller, dean of the Gateshead Women's Teachers Seminary, R' Miller went out of his way to make R' Kabalkin feel comfortable. R' Kabalkin was embarrassed by R' Miller's efforts and said to him, "Please don't trouble yourself that much; I've merely come for a short visit with you."

R' Miller replied, "I think I ought to tell you this story."

There was once a fellow who was traveling through Poland. Late one evening he came into the town of Brisk and began to seek lodgings for the night. Wherever he went he found that all the lights were shut, and he was reluctant to knock on a door and perhaps wake the people inside. To make matters worse, he soon realized that there was no inn to be found, either.

As he continued to walk through the dark and quiet streets he noticed a house with lights on, in the distance. He made his way towards the house, peered into the window and saw an older man poring over some *sefarim,* deeply engrossed in his studies.

With hesitation, he knocked softly on the door, and soon the elderly man came out to greet him. The traveler apologized for disturbing him, and explained that he needed a place to stay overnight.

"Of course, of course," the elderly man said, as he warmly invited the traveler into his home. In no time at all, the host poured his visitor a hot drink, put out some food, and went to prepare a bed for the man. The traveler now had an opportunity to look around the house, and he suddenly realized that he was in the home of none other than the Brisker *Rav*, R' Chaim Soloveitchik (1853-1918).

Full of misgivings, the traveler approached the *Rav* and said to him, "Please, please, don't trouble yourself. I am sorry that I am such a bother to you. Just show me where I can sleep, and I will take care of the rest myself."

R' Chaim paid little attention to the man's protests, and continued his attempts to make the man feel as comfortable as possible. The next morning, R' Chaim and his guest went together to *shul* for *Shacharis*.

It was a Thursday morning and the *gabbai* (attendant) in *shul*, noticing that there was a new face present, decided to honor the guest with an *aliyah*. However, right before the Torah reading was to begin, R' Chaim walked over to the *gabbai* and said to him softly, "Please give the guest *hagbah* (the honor of raising the Torah at the conclusion of its being read)."

The *gabbai* was surprised, because usually the *Rav* did not get involved in the selection of the *aliyos* — but of course he heeded the *Rav's* request. After the reading was concluded and the *Kaddish* recited, the *gabbai* approached the guest and asked him to raise the Torah.

The guest made his way to the *bimah* (central platform) and placed his hands on the *atzei chaim* (wooden handles of the Torah Scroll). As the guest was about to lift the Torah, R' Chaim, who had made his way to the *bimah*, said to him softly, "Please, please don't trouble yourself!"

The gentleman smiled as he understood the full intent of R' Chaim's words.

After hearing this story, R' Kabalkin graciously accepted R' Miller's hospitality.

Cents of Value

At a convention of Agudath Israel of America, R' Avrohom Yaakov Pam spoke about today's financial opportunities and obligations of our people, who live in a society that is collectively as wealthy as any Jewish generation since the time of the second *Beis HaMikdash* (Holy Temple). R' Pam stressed that we must put special emphasis on the expression in *Shema*, "וְאָהַבְתָּ אֵת ה׳ . . . וּבְכָל מְאֹדֶךָ — You shall love Hashem ... and with all your money" (*Devarim* 6:5, see *Rashi*).

Throughout our history the truly committed Jew has always declared that he was ready to risk his life for *Yiddishkeit* as he recites: "וְאָהַבְתָּ אֵת ה׳ אֱלֹקֶיךָ בְּכָל לְבָבְךָ וּבְכָל נַפְשְׁךָ — You shall love *Hashem,* your G-d, with all your heart, (and) with all your soul . . ." All too often, under tragic and dire circumstances, Jews were challenged to prove that commitment.

Today, though, in most areas where Jews live, life-threatening situations hardly present themselves. Rather, in societies where man is obsessed with the accumulation of massive wealth, a major test of the committed Jew is whether he can withstand the secular influence of trying to build a financial empire instead of using his money (not only his *maaser* [tithe] money) for Torah causes and charity. How one uses his money has become a yardstick showing how an individual values Torah and *mitzvos*.

In this light, the story that was recently told by R' Sholom Schwadron about the Berditchever *Rav,* R' Levi Yitzchak of Berditchev (1740-1809), is most illuminating.

One *Yom Kippur* night, as the huge crowd in the Berditchever *shul* waited for the *chazzan* to begin the *Kol Nidrei* prayer that would inaugurate the holiest day of the year, the Berditchever *Rav* motioned to the *chazzan,* requesting him to delay for a while. R' Levi Yitzchak was not yet prepared for the *chazzan* to start saying the solemn prayer.

The people assembled in the *shul* were somber and silent as they waited for the *Rav* to give the signal to begin, but he was immersed in deep thought. The minutes passed slowly as people whispered among themselves, wondering why the *Rav* would cause a delay right before *Kol Nidrei*.

Soon R' Levi Yitzchak turned to his *shammas* (attendant) and asked, "Is Muttel from the neighboring town of Zhitomer here?" The *shammas* let his eyes pass over the assembled crowd and saw, off to a side, the plain, simple Jew, Muttel.

"Yes," the *shammas* reported, as all looked on. "Muttel is present."

"Ask him to come up here," R' Levi Yitzchak requested. Muttel was escorted to the *Rav*, who began to question him at once. "Tell me, don't you live on land owned by the *paritz* (gentile landowner) Vladik?"

"Yes," said the surprised Muttel. He hadn't realized that the *Rav* knew that. Then the *Rav* asked, "Doesn't your *paritz* own a dog?"

"Yes, *Rebbe*," answered Muttel, not having the slightest idea why the *Rav* needed to know this information right now, on *Yom Kippur* eve, just moments before *Kol Nidrei*.

"Do you by any chance know how much he paid for that dog?" the *Rav* wanted to know.

"I most certainly do," Muttel said proudly. "The *paritz* paid four hundred rubles for that dog. He said that it had a pedigree and was a rare breed of dog, and he bragged to everyone how much he paid for that hound."

Muttel remembered that just about everyone who heard about the fantastic sum the *paritz* had paid for the dog thought it was ridiculous. No one, however, dared say anything to him because all were dependent on his good graces throughout the year.

R' Levi Yitzchak, though, was thrilled. "Four hundred rubles! That's wonderful." The *Rav* thanked Muttel for his help, then motioned to the *chazzan* to begin *Kol Nidrei*.

Those who had overheard the conversation were bewildered and confused. What could be so important about how much the *paritz* paid for a dog, and why would it make the *Rav* content just at that moment?

Later, after the *davening* had ended, a group of people gathered around the Berditchever *Rav*, inquiring about his discussion with Muttel.

The Berditchever explained. "You see, an incident happened this past year that troubled me. A *melamed* (tutor) came to our town from a distant city. He had accumulated many debts back home, and therefore he came to tutor children in order to earn a reasonable amount of money. His plan was to return home, pay his debts, and still have money remaining for his family's daily living expenses. He was here for almost a year. He earned the money that he needed, and then began his trip home.

"On the way home, he stopped overnight at an inn. Until that point he had always kept his money in a bag that he held securely with him at all times. However, on this fateful night he was not careful enough, and as he slept, the bag with all his hard-earned money was stolen. When he awoke in the morning and realized that his money was gone, he began to scream and cry, but it was to no avail. No one claimed to have seen any robbers; no one had seen any strangers carrying his bag of money. The poor man was devastated. A whole year's effort was wasted!

"However, staying overnight at that same inn was this *paritz* of Muttel's. When he awoke in the morning, he heard the crying and wailing. He inquired as to what had happened. When he was told the story he approached the *melamed* to find out exactly what had occurred. He became very impressed with the *melamed* and, right then and there, gave him from his own pocket a sum that equaled the amount that had been stolen from him — four hundred rubles."

The Berditchever continued. "As we were about to start *Kol Nidrei* earlier, I thought about that incident, and it worried me. Here we are standing before *Hashem,* Who we hope will look at us with favor throughout the coming year. But how could *Hashem* view us favorably? Who amongst us did such an unusual act of *chessed* this past year? If a gentile could do such a wonderful act, what does that say for *Hashem's* people who should be expected to do deeds of even greater kindness and consideration — not less?

"Then I remembered about the dog. I knew that the *paritz* had spent a great deal of money for the dog, but I didn't know how much. When I found out that he gave away four hundred rubles for something as unreasonable as a pet — not even a watchdog — that showed me that four hundred rubles didn't have much value to him. Thus, while it's true that the act to the *melamed* was one of kindness, it wasn't obviously one of great sacrifice. If a man can spend that sum on a dog, then money does not mean that much to him."

"This," says R' Sholom, "is how we should look at ourselves when we take pride in the fact that we have spent a hundred dollars for an *esrog,* gave a two-hundred-dollar *tzedakah* donation, or spent four hundred dollars on a pair of *tefillin*.

True, these are noble acts. But these acts are all relative. For if a man spends twice as much on a stereo system as he does on his *tefillin,* or if he spends three times as much for a camera as he does for an *esrog,* then the money he has 'sacrificed' for the *mitzvah* is not the 'sacrifice' he would like to believe it is." As one spends freely for the material objects he desires, so too must he be willing to spend freely as well for spiritual objects, i.e., *mitzvos* and charity.

A Cry at Midnight

The Talmud (*Berachos* 3b) describes how, during the reign of King David, as the hour of midnight approached, a north wind would waft through the king's open window and gently strum the strings of a harp that hung above his bed. The gentle musical notes would awaken King David, and from that moment on he would spend the rest of the night, until dawn, engrossed in prayer and praise to *Hashem.* In the loneliness of the night, while the rest of the world slept, King David poured his heart out in supplication to his Creator.

One cannot help but be reminded of that nightly episode, and the intensity of King David's prayers, as one listens to this touching story which was told by R' Yaakov Teitelbaum (1899-1968), who heard it directly from the young girl to whom it happened.

Mrs. Rina Turkel was the daughter of one of the *gedolei hador* (great Torah sages) of his time, R' Yaakov Weidenfeld, the Rimaliver *Rav,* author of the famous *Kochav M'Yaakov.* (Her brother, R' Dov Berish Weidenfeld [1879-1965], became world famous as the Tshebiner *Rav.*)

When she was but a little girl of four, Rina developed an unsightly rash beneath her eyes and across her cheeks. No medications seemed to help; no ointments managed to dim the dark red blotches. Her parents took her from doctor to doctor, until finally one particular doctor said that he was sure of the cause of the rash.

"This is not a regular skin rash," he said confidently. "This rash occurs for only one reason. This child cries continuously, and her constant tears are causing this outbreak on her skin."

The *Kochav M'Yaakov* and his wife were surprised by the doctor's words. "But this can't be!" the parents protested. "She is a very happy and playful child. She hardly ever cries!"

"Let us call her in," said the doctor. The little girl was brought into the room and the doctor addressed her gently, "I believe that you have this rash because you cry a great deal. Tell me, dear, do you cry a lot?"

Although the little girl was taken aback by the question, she told the truth. "Yes, yes," she stammered. "I do cry — every night."

"Every night?" the parents wondered aloud.

"Yes. When I hear my father crying it scares me, and so I cry too."

The father took his little daughter on his lap and held her tightly. "My precious child, my precious child," he repeated apologetically. "I had no idea you could hear me."

It seems that every night the *Kochav M'Yaakov* would spend hours and hours deeply engrossed in Torah study. When he finished, he would take out his *Tehillim* and recite, with great fervor, the psalms that King David had written long ago. The *Tehillim*, along with the *Tikkun Chatzos* (midnight prayers mourning the loss of the *Beis HaMikdash*), would so stir R' Yaakov that he would cry uncontrollably in the loneliness of the night. His study room was adjacent to the little girl's bedroom, and as her father began to sob she would awaken, become convinced that something was terribly wrong, and cry along with him until she fell asleep again!

That night her parents moved her to a room on the other side of the house, and within days the rash disappeared.

☙ A New Line

Ask someone what it means to be an observant Jew, and he will undoubtedly tell you that it means observing *Shabbos*, keeping the laws of *kashrus,* being mindful of prayers and attentive to studying Torah.

This famous story involving R' Yisroel (Lipkin) Salanter (1810-1883) merits retelling, for it sheds new light on the definition of the term 'observant Jew.'

A young man known for his sincerity and piety came to R' Yisroel to discuss a matter that was disturbing him. The young man was a *shochet* (ritual slaughterer) in a town, and most of the meat supply for the townsfolk came from his *shechitah.*

"*Rebbe,*" he began, "the responsibility that I have is too great for me to handle. So many different problems come up that require my decisions, and I feel woefully inadequate to have so many people in town relying on me. Aside from the fact that my *chalef* (knife) has to be checked constantly so that it doesn't have even the slightest nick along its blade, there is the checking of the animals' lungs for *sirchos* (lesions or adhesions), which is no simple matter. Additionally, there is the personal moral battle that I have when I must decide that an animal might be *treif* (not acceptable according to *halachic* standards), when that ruling might cause the owner a substantial financial loss. I simply want to be an observant Jew, and here I have so many pitfalls to avoid — with opportunities for failure constantly staring me in the face. I want to quit my job as a *shochet* and *bodek* (examiner)."

"What would you like to do instead?" R' Yisroel asked the distraught young man.

"I would like to go into business and be a simple businessman, without all that responsibility."

R' Yisroel thought for a moment and then said to the young man, "Tell me, do you have *semichah* (rabbinical ordination)?"

"Yes," came the reply.

"Do you have years of experience as a *shochet?*" R' Yisroel asked.

"Yes, quite a few years of experience, as a matter of fact," the fellow responded.

"Did you study at all before the *bechinah* (test) for *semichah?*" R' Yisroel continued.

"Why, of course!" the fellow answered, surprised by the question. He had studied diligently for months.

"And it goes without saying that you have *kabbalah* (acceptance) for *shechitah*, isn't that correct?" asked R' Yisroel.

"Yes, *Rebbe*," the young man answered, puzzled as to what R' Yisroel was trying to bring out.

"Now," said R' Yisroel, "have you ever studied the laws of *Choshen Mishpat* in the *Shulchan Aruch?* Are you familiar with the laws of partnerships, the laws of sales, or the laws of property damage?"

"No, not really," the young man answered, taken aback by the question.

"So explain to me," said R' Yisroel, "if in a profession which you have studied, taken tests, and have years of experience, you still feel inadequate and are afraid that you are violating Torah or rabbinic laws and are thus not 'observant,' should you not have even more trepidation in entering the field of business, for which you have not studied? It is an area fraught with the danger of violating countless Torah laws. Unless you studied the laws of *Choshen Mishpat* in advance, would you not be woefully non-observant by taking another man's money unlawfully? How can you hope to be considered an observant Jew if you enter the business world without proper preparation?"

> When R' Sholom Schwadron tells this story he adds, somewhat whimsically, "That's why the *velt* (world) says *hilchos ribis* (the laws on interest and usury), which are obvious financial matters, are included in the section of *Yoreh Deah* which deals with, among other things, permitted and forbidden foods. It's to teach us that *treife* money is just as prohibited as *treife* meat."

R' Mordechai Gifter, *Rosh Yeshivah* of Telshe Yeshiva in Cleveland, recently recounted that he related this episode during a *mussar* (ethics) lecture to a group of businessmen. A year later, two business partners who had attended the lecture met him at a wedding and told him, "The day we heard your lecture, we began a *seder* (regular study session) to study the laws of *Choshen Mishpat*. It is now a year later, and we're shocked almost every day by how many Torah and rabbinic laws we had been violating all these years, albeit unknowingly."

R' Gifter comments, "R' Yisroel's message to the young *shochet* more than a hundred years ago is as relevant today as it ever was — and maybe even more so."

◆§ *The Honor and the Glory*

The Talmud (*Makkos* 22b) criticizes those who merely give honor to a *Sefer Torah* itself (by rising in its presence) but don't show reverence to those who learn and observe its tenets. The display of *kavod haTorah* (respect for those who study Torah) reflects not only on those who receive this respect, but also on those who bestow it.

R' Simcha Zisel Broide, the *Rosh Yeshivah* of Yeshivas Chevron in Israel, related an incident that portrayed *kavod haTorah* in its fullest sense.

When R' Arye Leib HaKohen Heller (1745?-1812) was but a young man of eighteen years, he authored the classic *sefer Shev Shematisa*. This young, highly regarded Torah scholar went on to write the classic scholarly commentary *Ketzos HaChoshen* on *Shulchan Aruch Choshen Mishpat* (the volume of the *Code of Jewish Law* which deals with financial matters). It was when he had his manuscript for the *Ketzos* complete that this episode took place.

R' Arye Leib sought to get a letter of *haskamah* (approbation) from the world-renowned *gaon* of the era, the author of *Yeshuas Yaakov*, R' Yaakov Meshulem Orenstein (d. 1839). He traveled to the town where the *Yeshuas Yaakov* lived, went to the *Rav's* home, and presented him with the manuscript. R' Arye Leib asked the

Yeshuas Yaakov if he would be so kind as to look over the manuscript and, if he deemed the Torah thoughts therein worthy, to write a letter of *haskamah*.

As *Rav* of his town, the *Yeshuas Yaakov* was exceptionally busy. He told R' Arye Leib to wait in a nearby inn for a few days, during which time he would try to read the manuscript and get back to him.

A few days went by and R' Arye Leib still hadn't heard from the *Rav*. One afternoon he heard music outside. He couldn't imagine why anyone would be playing music in the middle of the day. He looked out his window and saw throngs of people marching behind a *chuppah* (canopy). *A wedding?* he wondered. If so, then he had better go outside and participate in bringing joy to the bride and groom. However, as he was about to leave the inn, he saw that a crowd had gathered outside the door.

As he stepped outside the crowd parted to let him go through. He looked around in surprise. He wasn't the *chassan* (groom) — why were they making way for him? Then he looked down the street and could hardly believe his eyes. There, under the *chuppah* and marching towards him, was the *Yeshuas Yaakov*, flanked by the judges of the Jewish rabbinical court. In his hands, the *Yeshuas Yaakov* was holding the pages of the manuscript that R' Arye Leib had given him just a few days ago.

Because the *Rav* was so impressed by what he had read, he treated the words of Torah that R' Arye had written as though they were a *Sefer Torah* itself. Thus he, along with the members of his community, marched as people would at a *Hachnasas Sefer Torah* (the ushering in of a new *Sefer Torah* to a synagogue) to honor those precious words of Torah by escorting them to their rightful ark — the ark of their author.

◆§ *A Promise Fulfilled*

One of *Hashem's* greatest gifts to man is the power of speech. However, because the act of talking (for most of us) is almost effortless, we tend to abuse the privilege. Quite often we express ourselves without much forethought, and this sometimes results in another person's feelings being hurt. At other times we say things with good intentions, yet shortly afterwards put out of mind that which we have said, and thus make no attempt to keep our word.

The following incident reveals how a great Torah scholar valued his every word.

R' Sholom Eisen (1917-1988), a former *dayan* (judge) in one of Jerusalem's most prestigious courts, was also known as one of the world's experts on the *kashrus* (worthiness) of an *esrog* and *lulav*. Every year, during the days before *Sukkos*, hundreds of people, including friends and casual acquaintances, would wend their way through the narrow alleys of Meah Shearim and then up the long stairway to his home, just to have R' Eisen examine their *esrogim* and *lulavim* and comment on their beauty and form. Many people wouldn't buy an *esrog* or *lulav* unless R' Eisen had assured them that it was perfect in every aspect. The *rav* thus came to know countless people from all walks of life.

When his son Yaakov reached the age of *bar-mitzvah*, the family made a *seudas mitzvah* in the boy's honor. Seated around the head table were the most distinguished *rabbanim* of Jerusalem. That is, all of them were there except one, R' Isser Zalman Meltzer (1870-1953), the *Rosh Yeshivah* of the world-renowned Yeshivas Eitz Chaim.

As the *seudah* progressed, R' Eisen looked around and realized that R' Isser Zalman, who was considered to be one of the *gedolim* of his time, was missing. *How did it happen that he isn't here?* thought R' Eisen. Suddenly he remembered: he had simply forgotten to invite R' Isser Zalman! Knowing as many people as he did, and having so many obligations, extending this invitation had slipped his mind.

He decided to rectify the situation immediately and was about to ask someone to go at once to R' Isser Zalman's house and invite him. But just as he turned towards the back of the room, he saw that R' Isser Zalman had entered. R' Eisen ran towards the door to greet the esteemed *rav*. Excitedly, R' Eisen said, "I'm so glad that you came, but I . . ." Before he could finish his sentence or even start his apology, R' Isser Zalman said, "I had to come tonight."

"You had to come?" R' Eisen asked in surprise.

"Yes," said R' Isser Zalman. "I had to fulfill a promise I made to you thirteen years ago. You may not remember, but when this *bar-mitzvah* boy was born, you informed me about his *bris*. At that time I wasn't feeling well and I told you that I couldn't attend but that I'd make sure to come to his *bar-mitzvah*, and thus tonight I had to keep my promise!"

To a *gadol*, a word is a commitment.

◆§ *Saved!*

Mrs. Chedva Silverfarb, a noted teacher and lecturer for women in Bnei Brak, Israel, recently recounted this story on her trip to America. Her listeners were left awe struck, because the lesson inherent in this episode is applicable to so many so often.

In the Feingold* home in Ashdod, Israel, mixed emotions reigned. There was great joy because the oldest daughter had just become engaged, yet at the same time the parents — particularly the father, R' Usher Feingold — were in a constant state of worry. They realized that very little money was available to pay for either the upcoming wedding or for their share of the cost of an apartment for the new couple.

Mr. Feingold traveled throughout Israel and even to the United States to raise money. In addition, because his neighbors and friends understood his difficult situation, they too began to raise money on behalf of the Feingold daughter, who had been a classmate of many of their own daughters.

Finally a date was set for the wedding. Invitations were sent out,

* The names and cities in this story have been fictionalized.

and on the appointed night friends and relatives came to the well-known catering hall where the wedding was to take place.

This particular catering hall has many rooms of various sizes so that different functions can be held simultaneously. As people enter the establishment they are directed by signs to the ballroom in which the event they are attending is being celebrated.

When the Feingold guests read the sign indicating their particular ballroom, they were quite surprised. The wedding was taking place in the largest ballroom. When they walked into the ballroom they were shocked! The room was decorated with opulent magnificence. The floral arrangements were stunning, the tableware elegant, and a seven-piece band was already playing. Was this what people had raised money for?

The meal was a seven-course dinner, the portions were huge, and photographers seemed to be everywhere. The people at the wedding were highly offended. The Feingolds had always portrayed themselves as poor people, and now they were spending not only beyond their means, but enough to pay for three weddings! Surely the money that Mr. Feingold and others had raised could have been put to better use! It could have been given to the young couple! Aside from that, *rabbanim* had recently been speaking out against ostentatious weddings, encouraging people not to make lavish affairs, because that might compel others of more modest means to imitate or duplicate them. And here the Feingolds had taken money from others, and they used it like this? How dare they spend so much money — especially other people's money — for one night? Wasn't any of it being saved for the *chassan* and *kallah?*

The matter was so distasteful that it was all people talked about at the wedding. Of course, no one had the audacity to say anything directly to the Feingolds, but the *kallah's* parents couldn't help but sense a touch of resentment and disfavor in the air.

For the *Sheva Berachos* (the festive meals that take place during the first week of marriage) on *Shabbos*, the family once again gathered in the same hall, and once again were served lavishly. The people who had been invited left the hall dismayed and displeased.

When the week of the *Sheva Berachos* was over and the Feingolds resumed their regular routine back in Ashdod, they detected an undercurrent of dissatisfaction with them that permeated almost every conversation. In *shul*, in the markets, and in the streets, eyes were raised and noses were turned up as the comments of jealousy and distrust, subtle at first, became more obvious.

Finally the Feingolds could stand it no longer, and one Friday night after the *Shabbos seudah* (meal), Mr. Feingold went to see the *rav* in his community, R' Elya Weiss.

"I would like to talk to you about the wedding," R' Usher began. "I can't help but notice how much resentment there is against us ever since that night, but I would like to explain."

The *rav* was eager to listen because he, too, had been wondering what had gone on. R' Usher began. "When I first came with my wife and daughter to the hall to discuss prices and fix a date, we spoke with the owner's wife. We got into a discussion and suddenly she looked up at me and asked, 'Do you by any chance have any Feingold relatives that lived in Germany?' I was taken aback by the question, because I didn't think anyone knew us from the small town we came from. 'Yes,' I told her, 'we do come from Germany.'

"She asked if we knew a Leo Feingold and when I told her he was my father her face suddenly paled. I thought she would start to cry. She stood up and asked, 'You are Leo Feingold's son?' Before I could answer, tears welled up in her eyes as she exclaimed, 'I am alive today only because of your father! He hid my family and me and saved us from the Nazis. My whole family owes their lives to your father!'

"I could not believe what I was hearing," R' Usher told R' Weiss. He went on to detail how she told him that since the war she had always wanted to meet her saviors but had never come across them. Now that she was fortunate enough to meet close family members, she wanted to do something special for them. "She insisted that she would make us a beautiful wedding," R' Usher explained, "but we tried to talk her out of it. She wouldn't listen. We tried to tell her that we are not at all wealthy people, but she felt that this was a way for her to show us her gratitude and that of her family.

"When we came to the hall that night," continued R' Usher, "we were as shocked as everyone else. I couldn't say anything to anyone because our benefactor had asked that her present remain a secret.

However, when I saw the attitudes of many of our friends, both at the wedding and at the *Sheva Berachos*, and then later here in Ashdod, I went to her and requested permission to reveal the truth about how we came to have such a lavish affair. I now ask of you," R' Usher pleaded, "please let the people know the truth."

The next morning, after the reading of the Torah, R' Weiss, from the *bimah*, told the whole story to his congregation. Once again the people were surprised, but this time at themselves. All those who had spoken disparagingly suddenly realized that in reality they had not had all the facts, even though, at the time, they were sure they did.

How many times does that happen to us?

☙ *Short Cuts*

On *Shavuos*, the holiday which commemorates *Hashem's* giving His people the Torah, R' Shmuel Blech of Lakewood, New Jersey, told his congregants an unusual parable. As improbable as the following parable may be, the lesson therein is all too applicable in many people's lives.

A small community wished to have a *Sefer Torah* written for its synagogue. The people got together, raised the necessary funds and hired a *sofer* (scribe) to do the writing. After many, many months the job was completed, and the townspeople began to plan a day of celebration for when the Torah would be brought to their synagogue.

As part of the festivities, the *Rav* of the community was going to drape the *Sefer Torah* with a beautiful *mantel* (covering). The women in the town were each asked to make a *mantel* for the new *Sefer Torah*. They would all eventually be used on different occasions; however, the nicest one would be used to enwrap the Torah on the day that it would be brought through the streets under a *chuppah*, accompanied by the entire congregation, to the synagogue.

The women worked feverishly, each trying to weave and sew the most magnificent covering. The day of the celebration finally came, and the *Rav* and the *Rosh Hakahal* (leader of the community) were asked to choose which of the coverings they deemed the most beautiful.

All the coverings were spread across a wide table, and one was more gorgeous than the next. After examining each one carefully, the *Rav* and the *Rosh Hakahal* both agreed that the purple one with the multicolored embroidery that depicted Mount Sinai was the most suitable one.

The elderly woman who had made it was thrilled beyond words. She felt that her arduous work had been worthwhile, for now she would have the honor of having her handiwork bedeck the new *Sefer Torah*. Her family shared in her pride.

The Torah was brought outside to the waiting crowd, and the *Rav* picked up the beautiful covering made by the elderly woman and began to slip it over the Torah. But it wouldn't fit! He tried to tug it, pull it and yank it, but it was simply too short. The people were surprised, but the woman who had made it was aghast. How could she have made it so small? Her pride quickly turned to humiliation.

The *Rav* and the *Rosh Hakahal* conferred for a few moments and then agreed that they would have to choose another covering. When their decision became obvious, the elderly woman ran up to them and cried out, "Wait, I have an idea! You can still use my covering!"

"And how do you suppose that could be done?" asked the *Rav*.

"It's very simple," answered the woman. "Just cut the Torah down to size, and it will surely fit!"

❦ ❦ ❦

After telling this parable, R' Blech continued on with this message. "Surely all of us would agree that the woman's suggestion was ludicrous. Yet how many of us, in our daily lives, do exactly what that woman proposed to do?

"We each have a certain life style that we feel is suitable for ourselves. At times, though, what we may perceive as desirable and important is in violation of Torah or Rabbinic law. What we *should* do is readjust our priorities. However, what many try to do, instead, is find a way to bend the law, and perhaps even 'cut down' one aspect of Torah, so that the Torah will seem to suit our desires — when actually we should be seeing to it that our lives fit the criteria of the Torah."

☙ *Downhill*

In his classic *sefer Nefesh HaChaim* (2:12), R' Chaim Volozhiner (1749-1821) gives us a thoughtful parable that offers a new perspective on a familiar topic. (See also *Mishnas Rav Aharon* by R' Aharon Kotler, Vol. 3, p. 16.)

A father and son were walking down a steep mountain. The child, in his exuberance, wished to run ahead, but the father cautioned the child that there were thorny bushes, protruding rocks and dangerous cliffs below. He encouraged his son to walk along with him slowly.

But the child persisted and ran ahead. Soon, to the father's dismay, the boy tripped and fell and went rolling down the mountain. With each fall and bump that the lad took, the father winced in pain and cried out in anguish, as though the accident were happening to himself.

Finally the child came to a rest at the bottom of the mountain and the father slowly and carefully made his way down towards his son. He told the child that he would have to take him to the hospital.

At the hospital a doctor carefully checked the child and said that a number of bones had indeed been fractured. He would have to set the bones back in place and put the broken limbs in casts.

The child cried out as the doctor moved the broken bones to align them so that they would heal properly. As the child cried out the father once again felt his anguish, and winced with compassion for his child.

"However," says R' Chaim Volozhiner, "although the father felt pain for his child both when he fell and then again when his bones were being set, the pain of the accident was surely more disturbing. For at least in the hospital the father knew that what was being done was for the child's benefit, in order for him to heal properly.

"It is the same with our Father in Heaven," says R' Chaim. "At times He must punish some of His people for sins they have committed. Surely He feels a Jew's pain when the Jew has to undergo suffering. However, it was even more painful for *Hashem* when that person first had the accident — when he stumbled and committed a sin. An 'accident' of transgression causes *Hashem* to wince (so to speak) in pain. The 'healing' that comes afterwards, although painful and inevitable, is actually for the person's own benefit."

◆§ *Time and Life*

R' Sholom Schwadron, the *Maggid* of Yerushalayim, and R' Elya Lopian (1872-1970), the *Mashgiach* of the yeshivah in Kfar Chassidim, were once going together to collect funds for a family in need. As they were walking near the Geulah section in Jerusalem, R' Elya paused for a moment, leaned on his cane and said, "R' Sholom, the *Gemara* (*Bava Basra* 9a) says 'גָּדוֹל הַמְּעַשֶּׂה יוֹתֵר מִן הָעוֹשֶׂה — Those who cause others to do (the *mitzvah* of giving charity) are greater even than those who do (give charity) themselves.' Do you know why?"

R' Sholom understood that R' Elya had something to say on the matter, and so he waited quietly for him to answer his own question.

After a pause R' Elya continued. "Firstly, the one who gives is doing merely for himself [he alone gets merit in the World to Come], while one who causes others to give is doing for others [seeing to it that they also get merit in the World to Come].

"Secondly, the one who gives, receives praise, while one who causes others to give, receives abuse.

"And thirdly, the one who gives, gives merely of his money,

while one who causes others to give, gives of his time — and time is life."

R' Sholom says that both he and R' Elya continued on their way with renewed enthusiasm.

A Step Ahead

When R' Sholom Schwadron told me the preceding story, it brought to mind another episode which, in a completely different way, underscores the link between time and life.

Chazal (Talmudic Sages) note (*Shabbos* 31a) that when a person appears before the Heavenly Court on Judgment Day, he will be asked a series of questions regarding his behavior in this world. One of the questions will be, "קָבַעְתָּ עִתִּים לַתּוֹרָה? — Did you set aside time for (the study of) Torah?"

Some commentaries stress the specific word in the question "קָבַעְתָּ — Did you set aside?" It is not sufficient for one to learn Torah "whenever he has a chance," for that leaves him with the option and excuse of saying, "I just didn't have the time." Rather, a person must schedule himself so that he learns Torah on a regular basis (and, according to some, for a specific amount of time) every day. Only then will he be able to answer the aforementioned question in the affirmative.

For a young *kollel* fellow, being prepared to answer this question in the affirmative became the difference between life and death.

As a child, Nachum* was the victim of a serious bus accident in which he almost lost his life. Using the miracles of modern medicine, doctors were able to revive him, but his leg was so badly injured that life-threatening infections set in and his physicians had no choice but to amputate part of his leg from the knee down. Nachum was then fitted with an artificial leg.

* The name has been fictionalized by personal request.

As time passed, Nachum grew to be an exceptional *masmid* (student diligent in his Torah studies), and went on to become a highly regarded *talmid chacham*. Eventually he became part of the *kollel* in the Telshe Yeshivah in Wickliffe, Ohio, where he continued his studies. He never let his handicap become an excuse for lateness or failure to attend *seder* (set time for study).

While in the *kollel*, in 1977, Nachum began to have serious problems with the artificial leg. Every step he took caused him great pain, and soon he found that he could barely hobble along. He called his prosthetist (one who works with artificial parts of the body) and made an appointment for an hour that would allow him to leave the yeshivah after morning *seder*, get to the medical office, spend time with the doctor getting a new limb measured and fitted, and return before the afternoon *seder* began.

He drove to Broadway in downtown Cleveland, and hobbled in agony from the parking lot into the office. Once inside, he was surprised to see a group of people sitting in the waiting room. It had been his impression that he would be whisked right in to see the doctor, enabling him to get back on time. However, with the number of people ahead of him, there was no way he would see the prosthetist for at least another hour.

Nachum waited patiently. He took out a *sefer* and began to read. After fifteen minutes he checked his watch. If the doctor didn't see him shortly, he would have to make a decision: either wait for the prosthetist and miss part of the afternoon *seder*, or reschedule his appointment for another time, and continue to suffer his miserable pain.

Another ten minutes passed, and Nachum became distraught. He considered calling his *chavrusa* (study partner) to tell him that he was detained, but soon discarded the thought. Instead, he rose from his seat slowly, and painfully made his way out of the waiting room in the direction of the examining rooms, which were situated at the end of a long corridor.

He met his doctor coming towards him. Nachum began to explain that he simply could not wait any longer and that he would have to return to yeshivah and come back to the office another time.

Suddenly there was a thunderous crash in the waiting room.

Pandemonium broke loose as terrified people screamed in pain and horror. A car had come smashing through the wall of the waiting room, stopping short against a wall of filing cabinets. The driver lay slumped over the wheel in total shock over what had just occurred. Somehow, as he had been trying to park in the lot adjacent to the office, the accelerator of the car had jammed and the car was propelled onto the sidewalk and through the wall of the building, tearing into the prosthetist's office.

All around Nachum confusion and commotion reigned. After a few minutes Nachum suddenly began to tremble as he realized, with a jolt, that the people who had been sitting on either side of the chair that he had just vacated, were fatally injured.

> Nachum's life was spared, because he was conscientious about his scheduled time for learning. In this instance, time meant life.

⸎ Color Schemes

A *melamed* (teacher) of young yeshivah students (who wishes to remain anonymous) was once donating blood in a local hospital. As he lay there with his arm outstretched, hooked up to the tubes that were drawing his blood, a man approached him and said in a defiant tone, "I see you are a rabbi. Let me ask you a question."

The *melamed* realized he could not sidestep this confrontation, as he was attached to an array of medical equipment. He therefore accepted the challenge head on and replied, "Go right ahead and ask."

"Tell me," the man said brazenly, "what difference is it to G-d if a Jew wears clothes made of wool and linen? I know Jews are prohibited from wearing clothes of that mixture (*shatnez;* see *Devarim* 22:11) — but why does it matter? I can understand precepts like honoring parents or giving charity, but not that other kind of law for which there is no explanation. You explain it to me."

From his years of experience dealing with *talmidim,* the *melamed* knew that this man wasn't interested merely in an answer as to why a Jew cannot wear *shatnez*. He knew the man was troubled by more than he had shown on the surface. The man needed an answer that would be broad in scope, but simultaneously geared specifically to his question. The *melamed* thought for a moment and then told him the following parable he had once heard from R' Eli Teitelbaum of Yeshiva Torah Temimah in Brooklyn, creator of the Dial-a-Daf and Dial-a-Shiur programs.

"Let me tell you a story," the *melamed* began patiently.

> There was once a king who, aside from everything else, was a great artist. He had ten children and he wished that at least one of them would follow in his footsteps and become an artist. But not one of them was interested. That is — not one of them except his youngest son. He had observed his father's great love for painting and expressed interest in studying it as well. The king was thrilled.
>
> He hired a famous artist to give his child lessons and promised the artist huge amounts of money and gifts if he would be successful. Two weeks later, the artist came to the king, forlorn. "I am so sorry to tell you, Your Majesty," the artist said sadly, "but your son is color blind. There is simply no way I can teach him to paint."
>
> The king was heart broken. Finally he had a child who was interested in painting, but the boy couldn't tell red from green or blue from gray! In desperation the king announced that whoever could somehow teach his son to paint and overcome this terrible handicap would be given great rewards for the rest of his life. Very few even offered their services because they knew the situation was hopeless. However, one artist in a small town far from the palace contacted the king and assured him that he could teach his son to paint and draw. The king assured the artist about the rewards awaiting him if he could accomplish this feat.
>
> For three months the artist worked with the young prince. At the end of that time the boy came to the palace and announced that he was ready to display his artistic

talents. The king was overjoyed. He called together his family and advisers, set up an easel for the child's canvas, and the prince began to paint.

To everyone's amazement, he splashed a color here, a color there, dabbing colors in a pattern that at first seemed incoherent; but then, as the picture began to emerge, they were astonished to see that indeed it was a very fine painting! The king and his followers cheered wildly. The next day the people were again assembled to watch as the young lad splashed colors here and there with no apparent order, and somehow the result was brilliant again.

This went on for days and no one could figure out how he did this. Actually, the artist who had taught the young prince to draw had not done much except teach the child to paint by number. He had prepared for the child countless sketches with outlines that were too faint to discern from a distance. Each section of every drawing had a number written on it that corresponded to a number on one of the cans of paint set up before the child. Thus, by matching the numbers and making sure to stay within the hardly visible lines, the boy appeared to be producing masterpieces.

One day the child decided that he was indeed a great artist after all, and didn't need his teacher's assistance. Thus when his father, the king, placed another easel in place, the boy did not follow the numbers that had been indicated for him, but rather chose the colors he wanted at random. The people watching were shocked as the result emerged: a disastrous mixture of frantic scribbles!

By this time, the man listening to the *melamed's* parable was completely spell bound. The *melamed* continued. "You see, when G-d gave the Jews six hundred thirteen *mitzvos*, he chose each one so that it accomplished a certain goal for man, both physically and spiritually. The precept of Sabbath observance cannot accomplish what the precept of *shatnez* can, and thus both of them are necessary. We ourselves can't be sure about the purpose of any of the *mitzvos*, and so we are like the little child who must paint by number. If we fill in every space properly, the total result will be a thing of beauty. However, if we choose our precepts at random, observing only those we think we understand, we can end up like that young boy who, choosing only those colors he himself wanted, wound up with disaster."

By this time, the medical equipment had been removed from the *melamed's* arm, and he was getting up to leave. The man he had spoken with was in awe of this simple parable and its magnificent teaching. He accompanied the *melamed* out of the room, through the hospital corridors, into the elevator and right to his car. They shook hands warmly and the man said, "I know that some day you will be a great Rabbi. May G-d bless our Jewish people with others like you."

Some time later, this same *melamed* was preparing a lesson for his class. He came across the following *Midrash* (*Shemos Rabbah* 35:6): "When *Hashem* told Moshe *Rabbeinu* to make the upright beams for the *Mishkan* in the desert, Moshe wasn't sure that he could build them properly. *Hashem* reassured Moshe and said to him, 'You just follow the patterns that I showed you [in a vision] — blue, purple and scarlet. [There is no need for you to innovate. Just] work with the materials you have and it will [turn out fine and] be acceptable to Me."

The *melamed* read and reread the *Midrash* with fascination. What he had told the man at the hospital as a parable had actually occurred thousands of years earlier with the building of the *Mishkan*. That afternoon he told his *talmidim*, "From Moshe *Rabbeinu* until today, our role is to follow the patterns. The Master Artist of the universe has drawn for us — for all circumstances — the perfect outline for life."

☙ Know Thyself

The following story was told by R' Reuvain Grozovsky (1887-1958), the *Rosh Yeshivah* of Beth Medrash Elyon in Monsey, New York. The story took place in Lithuania and is a classic lesson in a man's honest evaluation of his own emotions.

R' Zev* was a wealthy man who was known for his compassion to others. Although he was a tough businessman, he would make it a point to help those who were less fortunate than he. Thus people were constantly calling on him for favors and seeking to borrow money from him.

One day, a certain R' Shimon called to ask him for a sizable loan. R' Shimon had a dubious reputation at best. He had reneged on loans in the past, and people knew that he wasn't a safe bet. Yet R' Zev figured that if no one else would lend R' Shimon money, perhaps he should. He knew he was taking a chance but thought that surely R' Shimon, realizing that few people if any would be willing to lend him anything, would certainly show his appreciation to R' Zev by paying back the loan on time. Thus, he lent R' Shimon the requested amount.

However, R' Zev was wrong. Not only did R' Shimon not repay the loan on time, but he let much time elapse, and did not even have the decency to let R' Zev know that he would be late with payment. More than two years passed after the loan was due, and then R' Zev finally approached R' Shimon for the money. R' Shimon denied ever having received the money. R' Zev was flabbergasted!

"How can you deny that I lent you money, when you know good and well that I was the only one willing to take a chance on you and give you a large sum when you needed it?" cried R' Zev.

"I don't know what you are talking about," R' Shimon said calmly. "I have no money now — I am bankrupt — and besides, you never gave me anything."

R' Zev was enraged and he took R' Shimon to a *din Torah*

---

* The names in this story have been fictionalized.

(religious court). The *dayanim* (judges) ruled that R' Shimon would have to swear that he never received any money — and then he would be free. R' Zev couldn't imagine that R' Shimon would have the audacity to perjure himself. But R' Shimon did, falsely swearing that he had not accepted the loan that R' Zev claimed he had.

When R' Zev heard this, he lost his self-control completely. He started to yell at R' Shimon in front of the *dayanim.* "I don't care about the money, but how can you swear falsely? Don't you realize that you are violating one of the Ten Commandments? You ought to be ashamed of yourself! You are a disgrace to all Jews! Forget the money — you are a shameful sinner!" R' Zev then stalked out of the room.

For months R' Zev would become furious whenever the topic was brought up. And every time he would say the same thing. "I don't care about the money, but how could a self-respecting Jew have sworn falsely?"

Years went by, and people forgot about the incident. Although R' Zev and R' Shimon continued to live in the same neighborhood, no one gave the matter much thought. Then one *Shabbos* morning, R' Zev walked up to the *bimah* (the central platform in *shul*). "I have an announcement to make," he began. "A number of years ago I had an incident with R' Shimon. After the ruling of the *dayanim*, I criticized R' Shimon severely to many of my friends and spoke evil of him. Just as I defamed him in public I wish to ask his forgiveness in public. I am sorry for all that I said, and I beg your forgiveness, R' Shimon."

The crowd in *shul* was stunned to silence. But suddenly everyone started talking at once. The *rav* ordered the *chazzan* to begin the *Mussaf* prayers, before the whole *shul* would erupt into a cacophony of irrepressible noise.

After *davening,* people ran over to R' Zev and asked him what had prompted him, after all these years, to make this public apology. He then told the following story.

"This past week, I was traveling on business through a town far away from here. In one of my dealings a fellow told me about a *din Torah* which was coming up, and he asked me whether I wished to come to the court to listen to the case and its ruling. I had time on my hands and so I said I would go. As I sat and listened to the case, I realized that the case was exactly like the one I had brought against R' Shimon years ago.

"A man, who everyone knew had borrowed money from a wealthy individual (he had himself told them), was now denying that he had ever borrowed it. The *dayanim* ruled that the man had to swear that he had not borrowed the money, and then he would be free from paying anything. No one there thought he would swear, but he did. I sat in court and watched it all happen and it didn't faze me. I left the courtroom without saying a word.

"As I was traveling home, a thought occurred to me. That man had sworn falsely — he had violated one of the Ten Commandments — and yet I did not utter even one word to him. As a matter of fact, it didn't even bother me that he had lied so blatantly. But why not? Had he not violated the same law that I thought R' Shimon had violated years ago? And if yes, why did it bother me when R' Shimon did it and not the other fellow? It could only be that it was my money that was involved here and not there. And if that's the case, then that which I had been saying all along, "It's not the money, but how can a man swear falsely?" just wasn't true. It was not the sin that bothered me, but my own cash. And for that I had no right to besmirch R' Shimon as I did. I realized in that small town, long after our own case, that I was deluding myself into thinking that I was being righteous in standing up for the *kavod* (honor) of *Hashem*. But now I realize that I was worried about myself and my pocket, nothing more. That's why I apologized publicly."

☙ *Account Settled*

Throughout his career in public life, R' Shlomo Lorincz, a former member of the Israeli Knesset (Parliament) from the Agudath Israel Party, had almost daily contact with many of the *Gedolei Torah* living in Israel. He is fortunate to have been very close with the Brisker *Rav* (R' Velvel Soloveitchik, 1887-1959).

R' Lorincz marvels at the foresight and concern displayed in this episode.

One afternoon, when R' Lorincz came to the home of the Brisker *Rav* in Jerusalem, he noticed that the *Rav* seemed somewhat upset.

"Is everything all right?" R' Lorincz asked. "You seem disturbed today."

"Yes, you are right," replied the Brisker *Rav*. "Something is indeed troubling me. You know that I support a group of *yunger leit* (young married men) in my *kollel*, and every month I make sure to pay them on *Rosh Chodesh* (the first of the month). I have always made it my business to have the money that I need two weeks before the start of the month. However, now it's less than a week until *Rosh Chodesh* and I still don't have the money for those fellows — and they depend on me."

"How much are you missing?" asked R' Lorincz.

"A thousand *shekalim*," came the reply.

R' Lorincz thought for a few moments, then took out his checkbook and wrote a check for the entire amount. "I know how much these *talmidim* mean to you," he said, as he gave the check to the *Rav*.

"Can you afford such a steep amount?" the *Rav* asked.

"Well, not really," answered R' Lorincz. "But I thought that a hundred of that thousand would be from me, while the rest I would raise from others."

The Brisker *Rav* was overjoyed and relieved that he could now pay the *yunger leit* on time.

Weeks went by and when R' Lorincz checked on the amount of money he still had in his bank account, he was surprised to see that an extra thousand *shekalim* were being credited to him. He didn't say anything about it at the time, for he assumed that the bank would soon correct the error.

However, when months had gone by and it was almost a year since he had given the *Rav* the check, and the thousand *shekalim* were still in his account, R' Lorincz returned to the Brisker *Rav*.

"I've noticed that the check which I gave the *Rav* almost a year ago has not been cashed," R' Lorincz stated. "Is there a reason for that?"

"Tell me," replied the Brisker *Rav*, "did you ever raise any of the other nine hundred *shekalim* you said you were going to raise?"

"Truthfully — not," responded R' Lorincz. "After I left your home that day, having seen how much joy it gave you that you finally had the money for the *kollel* fellows, I decided that I would undertake to donate the entire amount myself."

"That's what I thought would happen," said the Brisker *Rav*. "It occurred to me that you might not raise the money. However, as you yourself told me that you couldn't afford to give me more than one hundred *shekalim* of your own, I was not allowed to take any more from you than the hundred. It is for that reason that I never used the check."

The *Rav* then opened a drawer from which he removed an envelope with the check, and returned it to R' Lorincz.

Taking something from someone who can't afford it is wrong, even if it's given with a smile. How much more so if it's accompanied by a frown!

☙ *The Last of the Lions*

Shortly after World War I, R' Avrohom Kalmanowitz (1891-1965), the *Rav* of Rockov, Poland, was appointed by the Mirrer Yeshivah to be its president. From that day on, until the last day of his life, he carried the financial burden of the yeshivah. Interestingly, when R' Kalmanowitz was later selected as *Rav* for the town of Tiktin (where many years earlier the great Torah sage, the Maharsha, R' Shmuel Eliezer Eidels [1555-1631], was *Rav*), he stipulated that he must be allowed to travel on behalf of the Mirrer Yeshivah for a specific number of months each year.

At the beginning of World War II, R' Kalmanowitz and his family were able to emigrate from Europe to America. The

Mirrer Yeshivah, though, under the threat of Soviet persecution, could only escape from Mir to Vilna. This would prove to be only a temporary move, because soon the Soviets would swallow Vilna as well. Realizing this, R' Kalmanowitz, through his American contacts, tried desperately to obtain passports for the yeshivah *bachurim* (students) and staff members of Mir so that they could escape the impending danger. The fees for getting passports in Communist countries suddenly tripled, and so R' Kalmanowitz, now traveling throughout America, had to raise these funds, in addition to the day-to-day operating budget of the yeshivah.

It was during this period that some of the Mirrer *bachurim*, along with their *roshei yeshivah*, were able to get out of the Russian clutches and set up temporary quarters in Shanghai, China — the only city to which they could escape.

One winter day R' Kalmanowitz arrived in Baltimore, where he stayed at the home of R' Eliezer Beinish Friedlander. Throughout the cold and blustery afternoon he visited a number of individuals, telling them of the plight of the *talmidim*, and pleading for funds on their behalf.

The next morning he was to be in Washington, D.C., where he would meet with members of Congress to procure documents that would allow the Mir *talmidim* in Shanghai to come to America. A heavy snow began to fall in Baltimore. Quickly this developed into a raging snowstorm that paralyzed the city. All traffic stopped, and people sought shelter indoors as the city became immobilized.

The train that R' Kalmanowitz was to take from Baltimore to Washington was not leaving until nine o'clock the next morning. However, at four o'clock in the morning, R' Friedlander heard the front door of his house open and he thought he heard R' Kalmanowitz leaving. He ran to see if that was indeed the case, and sure enough, R' Kalmanowitz was already out the door.

R' Friedlander called out, "R' Avrohom, where are you going? It's the middle of the night!"

R' Kalmanowitz turned around and said, "I can't take a chance. Taxis are not running and I might not make it to the station in time later on to catch the train, so I decided to walk to the station now instead."

As the two *rabbanim* stood in the street, engrossed in this conversation, R' Friedlander suddenly realized that R' Kalmanowitz did not even have rubbers or boots!

Why did R' Kalmanowitz feel that it was imperative for him to go just then? Even if he didn't make the first train in the morning, he certainly would have caught the train in the afternoon!

Years later, he explained why he had such a tireless and almost impatient devotion to the Mirrer Yeshivah.

"There is a *Midrash Tanchuma* (*Noach* 9, see also *Rashi* on *Bereishis* 7:23)," began R' Kalmanowitz, "that relates how the lion in the ark took a swipe at Noach because Noach was late with his meal. That blow caused Noach to limp even after he left the ark. But why," asked R' Kalmanowitz, "did Noach deserve such a punishment? He must have been so exhausted and so pressed for time — for he was responsible for feeding all of the animals in the ark, each with their individual eating schedules and habits! What would have been so terrible if he would have fed the lion a half hour later? What was all the hurry about?

"The answer is," continued the *Rav*, "because the lion in Noach's ark was the last lion in the universe! If that lion had died, then there would have been no more of that species left." R' Kalmanowitz paused for a moment as he reflected on his work in the past. "It was the same with the *talmidim* of Mir. Many of them who were able to be with the yeshivah were in Shanghai, but they were poverty stricken and starving. If I didn't see to it that they survived, then that would have been the end of the Mirrer Yeshivah. This was the last of that breed of *talmidim*. How dare I rest? That's why I pressed on as I did."

In reality R' Kalmanowitz himself was a legendary lion, as he battled politicians and government officials relentlessly until countless Mirrer *talmidim* were saved by being brought to American shores.

Chazal (Talmudic sages) teach: "כָּל הַמְקַיֵּם נֶפֶשׁ אַחַת מִיִּשְׂרָאֵל מַעֲלֶה עָלָיו הַכָּתוּב כְּאִלוּ קִיֵּם עוֹלָם מָלֵא — Whoever preserves (even) a single Jewish life is considered by Scripture as if he had preserved an entire world'' (*Sanhedrin* 37a). One can hardly imagine the Heavenly reward for an individual whose tireless efforts saved so many.

Aside from everything else he accomplished, R' Kalmanowitz established the Mirrer Yeshivah Central Institute in Brooklyn and became its *Rosh Yeshivah,* a position he held until he passed away.

Guards of Honor

The *Zohar Chadash* (*Shir HaShirim*) writes that the word יִשְׂרָאֵל (Israel) is an acrostic of the words יֵשׁ שִׁשִּׁים רִבּוֹא אוֹתִיּוֹת לַתּוֹרָה (There are 600,000 letters in the Torah).

The number of men who left Egypt and subsequently received the Torah was 600,000. Thus each of them — and therefore each one of us as descendants of those 600,000 — is represented by one letter in the Torah. R' Gedaliah Schorr (1910-1979), *Rosh Yeshivah* of Yeshiva and Mesifta Torah Vodaath, pointed out that in a Torah scroll, if even one letter is missing the scroll is invalid. Every single letter is of paramount importance and, similarly, every member of *Klal Yisrael,* represented by a letter, is of paramount importance. Therefore, if even one Jew does not fulfill his potential as a loyal Torah Jew, it is a deficiency in *Klal Yisrael* as a whole. Every Jew, like every letter, has an essential role in the unit of *Klal Yisrael,* and we are all responsible for each other.

In discussing this role of communal responsibility, R' Yitzchok Dovid Grossman of Migdal HaEmek, Israel, retells one of the Dubno Maggid's classic parables.

A wealthy man had two sons living in a foreign country, the older one wealthy and the younger one poverty stricken. The man was about to marry off a daughter and, understandably, wanted his whole family to be together for the occasion. He sent his elder son a letter expressing his wish that both sons, along with their wives and children, should come from abroad to join in the family *simchah* (happy occasion). In the letter he wrote, "Enclosed are tickets for both your families. Any money that you expend in my honor will be reimbursed when you arrive."

Upon receiving the letter, the wealthy son took his wife and children to the most exclusive stores and fitted them out with magnificent clothing. "We are going to visit Grandfather," he said proudly. "We must look distinguished in his honor." No expense was withheld as hats, suits, dresses and shoes were all bought according to the latest fashion. The other brother, though, being poor, did not have either the time to spend shopping or the funds to lay out for new clothes. Although his family, too, looked forward to the upcoming trip, they understood that they would have to travel with their very modest wardrobes.

The day of the trip arrived and both brothers with their respective families boarded the plane. Hours later, when the plane finally arrived at its destination, their father was at the airport along with his new *mechutanim* (relatives through marriage), eagerly awaiting the arrival of his children and grandchildren.

The first to deplane was the wealthy brother and his family, all of whom were magnificently dressed. The beaming father was proud as he pointed to them and said for all to hear, "Here comes my eldest son with his wife and children. Are they not elegant?"

The new *mechutanim* nodded courteously.

Then the second brother approached. Despite his situation he had tried to look decent, but his poverty was obvious. His wife's outfit was out of style, and the clothes the children wore were obvious hand-me-downs, somewhat worn and ill fitting. The grandfather was humiliated by their appearance. "This is my second son and his family," he said quietly to the *mechutanim*. Once again they nodded. But the grandfather was enraged.

The wedding took place as planned, with the family enjoying their reunion. After the week of the *Sheva Berachos* (a reference to the seven blessings recited at each meal the bride and groom attend during the first week of marriage), the wealthy older brother came to his father and asked that he be reimbursed for all the expenses he had incurred.

"I don't owe you a thing!" the father exclaimed emphatically.

"But, Father," the son said in dismay, "you wrote that you would reimburse me for all the money that I spent."

"Let's look at the letter I wrote," said the father.

The son removed the letter from his pocket and gave it to his father. "Look here," the father said, "I wrote you, '. . . any monies that you expend in my honor will be reimbursed . . .' Now I ask you," said the father, "did you spend the money in my honor or in your own self-centered honor?"

"I did it for you," said the son, actually believing that he did.

"No you didn't," said the father. "If you were truly interested in my honor, you would have made sure that your brother did not look as shabby as he did. The way he and his family appeared at the airport was a disgrace and an embarrassment to me. Your having purchased all the fine clothes for yourself and your family was obviously for your benefit, not for mine!"

❦ ❦ ❦

The Dubno *Maggid* remarked, "Every day we say in our *Shacharis* (morning) prayers, '... בָּרוּךְ הוּא אֱלֹקֵינוּ שֶׁבְּרָאָנוּ לִכְבוֹדוֹ — Blessed is He our G-d, Who created us for His glory.' All of us were brought into this world to sanctify and glorify *Hashem.* This is done by learning *Hashem's* Torah and performing His *mitzvos.*

"However, if we are truly interested in לִכְבוֹדוֹ, seeing that *Hashem* is glorified, then we must be concerned that not only we, but all of *Hashem's* children act in consonance with the Torah's directives. It is the obligation of each Jew to feel a responsibility for another Jew's actions, and that is what *Chazal* (Talmudic Sages) meant by the teaching (*Shevuos* 39a) 'כָּל יִשְׂרָאֵל עֲרֵבִים זֶה לָזֶה — All (people) of Israel are liable for one another.' "

When R' Grossman tells this story, he adds, "We, as a nation, must view ourselves as a unit, not as a group of individuals."

◆§ Compared to Whom?

At a recent Torah Umesorah convention, R' Avrohom Yaakov HaKohen Pam, *Rosh Yeshivah* at Yeshivah Torah Vodaath, retold the following parable, which the Dubno *Maggid* (1740-1804) used to explain a verse. The verse in *Vayikra* (19:2) reads: "קְדֹשִׁים תִּהְיוּ כִּי קָדוֹשׁ אֲנִי ה' אֱלֹקֵיכֶם — You shall be holy, for I, *Hashem* your G-d, am Holy."

Many years ago a wealthy individual from a small town far away from any major metropolis made his way to the big city to visit with the *Rosh Yeshivah* of a prestigious yeshivah. "I am looking for a *chassan* (groom) for my daughter," the gentleman began. "She is my only daughter and I want only the best for her. You can be assured that the boy she will marry will be able to continue his Torah studies unimpeded. I will provide for both of them so that they will have no financial worries. Thus the young man will be able, in comfort, to attain the heights of Torah knowledge that he aspires to."

The *Rosh Yeshivah* saw that the man was very sincere, so he suggested a prominent *bachur* (yeshivah student) for his daughter. Indeed, the two eventually got married and went to live in the bride's small home town.

After the week of the *Sheva Berachos* (lit., Seven Blessings — recited at meals that the bride and groom attend during their first week of marriage), the young man sat down in the town's small *shul* to resume his Torah studies. His diligence and devotion were incredible. Hour after hour he would sit alone in the little *beis midrash* and learn without interruption. The months passed in this manner, and the father-in-law was extremely proud of his daughter's husband.

About a year after the wedding, the father-in-law noticed that the young man's diligence was beginning to slacken off. At first he would come to the *beis midrash* an hour later than usual, then he started to find excuses to leave earlier than in the past.

At first the father-in-law was hesitant to say anything, but when the young man began to skip a day or two of learning from time to time, he realized that he would have to intervene. He called the young man into his home. "My dear son," he began gently, "you know how proud I have always been of your learning and Torah accomplishments. The *Rosh Yeshivah* assured me a while ago that you would eventually be the greatest among your peers. But it grieves me to see what has become of your learning lately. I couldn't help but notice that there are days when you don't step into the *beis midrash* altogether. Is this how you will continue your progress?"

The young man looked at his father-in-law with surprise. "My dear father," he responded, "I have indeed achieved just what the *Rosh Yeshivah* said I would achieve. I am the greatest among my peers here in this town. Tell me honestly, is there anyone here who knows as much as I do? Is there anyone here who even spends half the time that I do in Torah study?"

The father-in-law looked at his son-in-law and said softly, "Think for a moment. To whom are you comparing yourself? To the simpletons of our town here? They know very little and they aspire to very little. You should be comparing yourself to the wonderful students you learned with back in your yeshivah days. They are the true barometer of your accomplishments."

R' Pam continued, "If a Jew looks around him he sees a world of immorality, deceit and fraud. He sees underhandedness and the insatiable pursuit of material goals. Thus he can easily rationalize to himself and say, 'By my performing even one *mitzvah* I have already achieved a much greater status than those members of the secular world.'

"A Jew might feel comfortable with the knowledge that even with the little that he does he has already achieved a degree of holiness far beyond those who do no *mitzvos* at all. Thus *Hashem* says, 'Don't compare your holiness to the holiness of others. Be holy for I am holy. Use Me, not the nations of the world, as a barometer and then you will know where you stand.' "

◆§ The Law and Beyond

R' Sholom Eisen, a *dayan* (Rabbinical judge) in Jerusalem for decades, spent a good deal of his day adjudicating cases in Rabbinical Court. However, that did not stop people from coming to his home incessantly to ask him their personal *she'eilos* (religious questions) as well.

Quite often, when these *she'eilos* were not of a private nature, R' Eisen's children stood by and listened so as to learn from their revered father's approach to *halachah.*

The following episode was retold by R' Eisen's son, R' Yaakov (of Montreal), who witnessed it many years ago.

It happened one afternoon that a very prominent *rebbetzin* (wife of a *rav*) came to R' Eisen with a *she'eilah.* This woman, known for her exceptional piety, lived alone, for her husband had passed away a number of years earlier. She was very poor and had very little to live on. That day she had gone to the local butcher and bought a chicken. When she cut it open, she noticed something in the chicken's entrails that might possibly render the chicken *treif* (non-kosher). As she was extremely scrupulous, she did not dare try to decide this religious question herself, but came to R' Eisen with the chicken in question to get his opinion.

The *Rav's* children had seen their father *paskin* (rule) on many similar situations, and thus they were quite surprised when they heard him say, "This is indeed a very difficult *she'eilah.* I am going to have to think about this. Please leave the chicken here and come back in an hour."

R' Eisen's children began to wonder. What could possibly have been so difficult for their father, who undoubtedly had seen hundreds of such cases before? The woman left, and once she was out of the house, the *Rav* called his wife into the room.

"The *rebbetzin* from Battai Natan (a housing complex) was just here with a chicken," R' Eisen began, "and there is no doubt in my mind that this chicken is *treif.* While I answer the other people who are waiting outside, please take this chicken to the butcher, get another one the exact same size as this one, and bring it back as soon as you can."

R' Eisen's wife immediately went to the local butcher, purchased a chicken similar in size to the one in question, and took it home. R' Eisen then cut the chicken in the exact same manner as the first one had been cut, and then waited for the *rebbetzin* of Battai Natan to return.

When she did come back R' Eisen greeted her and said, "Here is your chicken. You may go home and cook it." And then he added, "It is good that you didn't try to decide this question on your own." And then to be sure that she wouldn't use the present decision to decide a similar matter in the future, R' Eisen continued, "If a similar question arises on another occasion, be sure to bring it here for a decision."

Part E:

Pawns in the Hand of the King

☙ Rattled by an Ambush

One of the *talmidim* in Yeshivah Ohr Somayach in Jerusalem, who was originally from the Soviet Union, told a story — but not about himself. He had received a startling letter from a friend back home. He knew this friend, Ilya, to be an atheist. But his letter began, "Dear Boris, I know now that there is a G-d in this world." The letter then went on to detail this amazing story.

Ilya had been inducted into the Soviet Army. After a period of basic training he, along with hundreds of other soldiers, was sent to Afghanistan to wage war in the mountains against the soldiers of Kabul. Training for this kind of mountain warfare required specific preparations. Not only would the Soviet soldiers have to concern themselves with conventional military hardware, but here in the mountains, the elements, as well, would play a role. Extreme heat, rugged terrain and poisonous snakes all had to be taken into consideration.

As a youngster, Ilya had been a nature lover. Plants and animals were his hobby, and hiking was his pastime. For him, being quartered in this vast mountain region was part of the thrill of army life.

For days on end Ilya and his battalion were stationed in a strategic highroad area that overlooked miles and miles of flatlands. Every day Ilya would stroll off by himself, observing the plant and animal life that existed in the area. Of all that he saw, the snakes and scorpions fascinated him the most. Each morning he would take some food and feed the snakes that nested behind a quarry of rocks. It was almost as if he were their friend. The poisonous and dangerous snakes took whatever food Ilya offered, and retreated to their cove.

One day his battalion was informed by the commanding officer that they would be moving from this encampment. They would have to be ready to travel early the next day. The next morning, after packing, Ilya decided to 'say goodbye' to his friends the snakes by offering them food just one more time.

As Ilya came close to one large cobra, it suddenly uncoiled and stood erect, threateningly puffing out its hood, and positioned itself to spew its murderous venom. In training, the soldiers had been warned that when a cobra extends itself upright, one must stand immobile, for any movement could agitate the cobra which, in a flash, would lash out with its fangs, sink them into its victim's skin, and inject its deadly venom. Unless medical assistance were readily accessible, this would often mean death.

Ilya had no choice but to wait until the cobra recoiled. But it didn't. It remained upright, positioned as though it were ready to strike. Ilya was terrified. In a moment he could be killed. He could hear his battalion leaving the area. He wanted to yell for someone to wait for him, but he didn't dare.

For more than three hours the cobra seemed to stare right into Ilya's eyes, as Ilya cautiously glared back, trying not to make the last move of his life. Finally, after what seemed an eternity, the cobra recoiled and slid away. Ilya ran back to get his gear, then started running in the direction in which he thought the soldiers had gone.

For hours he searched for them. He made his way, tired and thirsty, towards a pass between two mountains. He was getting worried — and then he saw the first of them. The unmistakable Soviet soldier was sprawled on the mountain road, dead. Then he saw the rest of them — the soldiers he had been with were all lying dead on the ground! He ran towards them, his gun cocked as he whirled wildly, looking for the enemy in all directions. But all around him stillness prevailed. A silence of death. It was then he realized that his battalion had fallen victim to an Afghan ambush. Afghan soldiers had been lying in wait for this battalion to pass between the mountains, and then had killed all its members.

Ilya suddenly realized that he alone had been spared — by a cobra that he had fed every day. Ilya lifted his eyes towards the distant mountains and then to Heaven. A tear rolled down his face. He knew very well that only G-d's miracle had saved him.

He surveyed the vastness all around him and realized, for the first time in his life, that nothing was to be taken for granted. Everything in this world, even the seemingly self-motivated and self-contained laws of nature, was actually controlled by a higher force, that of *Hashem* in Heaven.

◆§ *Castaways*

The ways of *Hashem* are mysterious. David *HaMelech* wrote in *Tehillim* (92:7), "וּכְסִיל לֹא יָבִין אֶת זֹאת – simple people cannot understand this." Wise men, on the other hand, can only rest assured that there is a reason for every occurrence.

At times, what man considers to be a most wonderful happening turns out to be a disaster, and conversely, what one may perceive as an ill-fated occurrence turns out eventually to be a blessing in disguise. The way *Hashem* masks His intentions is known as *hester panim* (literally, hidden countenance). Rare are those who have the opportunity to see clearly through the veil that conceals G-d's intentions.

The following episode illustrates circumstances which, at the time of their occurrence, could easily have been perceived in one manner, but produced results which, later on, turned out to be incredibly different than at first thought.

Young Moshe Rabi was among the lucky ones. At least that's how it seemed at first. When the Nazi regime in Germany was beginning to rear its ugly head in 1939, a benefactor [R' Moshe Schneider] in England came forth to sponsor, as part of a children's transport, sixteen-year-old Moshe's trip from Frankfurt to London in the hope of sparing the youngsters the agony that was about to befall their fellow Jews at the hands of the Nazis.

However, shortly after arriving in England, Moshe was told that he would be taken to a refugee detention camp. It seemed that German spies had been infiltrating England in the guise of Jewish refugees, and Scotland Yard wasn't taking any chances. At first all enemy aliens were classified in one of three categories. Suspects having ties to the German armed forces, such as soldiers or sailors, were imprisoned; adult German aliens with other jobs had their travel restricted; and children were free to live with families that would house them. However, after Germany scored a great tactical victory in 1940 at Dunkirk, France, causing the retreat of hundreds of thousands of French and British soldiers, all German nationals — Jews and non-Jews alike — were herded together into camps set up first in London and then in Liverpool.

Conditions in the detention camps were horrible, as space was cramped and food was sparse. The internees complained bitterly, and soon British authorities offered anyone who desired it the opportunity to be deported to Canada. Many Jews, including Moshe, decided to leave the English camps, thinking that things could not possibly get worse. But they were wrong.

The German Jews were taken to an island where they boarded a boat called the *Dunera,* expecting to sail westward, towards Canada. Actually they had been misled. After numerous days at sea it became obvious to many on board that the *Dunera* was actually sailing south. After many inquiries the people on board were told the truth. They were on their way to Australia!

Throughout the trip the Jews were subjected to constant abuse and ridicule; they were harassed and hassled incessantly. None of them was allowed onto the top deck for a breath of fresh air; instead, they were fenced in behind barbed wire to make sure that they would remain on the lowest decks of the huge ship. Sailors, crewmen — and even the captain — would take the Jews' personal belongings away from them, claiming the items would be safer in the hands of the authorities. The British crewmen even issued receipts for the items they took, but the Jews soon realized that the receipts, like the crew's promises, were worthless.

The dejected travelers were lonely, frightened, and tense about the future. They had few, if any, possessions left. They had escaped from their homes, and were now being deported from their adopted homes. The passengers knew that the Pacific Ocean was teeming with German Navy ships laden with firepower. They felt helpless, not in control of their destiny.

English crew members had been following the news bulletins of the war over their radios. Things were not looking good for the British Army as Germany was scoring one tactical victory after another. Late one day the *Dunera* barely avoided a near catastrophe when a huge swell miraculously cast the ship out of the way of a fired torpedo. Although the ship was merely grazed by the missile, the English seamen were infuriated and humiliated by the thought that they had almost been blown out of the water. In a fit of rage they vented their wrath on the German nationals aboard.

With calculated cruelty, the British gathered the last possessions that the foreign passengers owned and cast them overboard into the raging waters of the Pacific. The final ties to their past lives — letters, small heirlooms and treasured books, the items that had made them feel human — were now gone forever. The dark of night mirrored their despair as Moshe and the others aboard cried out at this latest indignity. They no longer had anything tangible from the past — only memories. Numb and shattered, they watched their belongings bobbing and weaving in the sea, going under and rising again to the surface as they were tossed from wave to rising wave.

Eventually the *Dunera,* with its cargo of shattered souls, arrived in Sydney, Australia. All the passengers disembarked there. Soon after, the *Dunera* began its return voyage to England. A day or so after setting out, the *Dunera* with only its British crew members aboard was torpedoed by German submarines. It exploded, and all on board were killed.

A few years ago a film was released both in England and in Australia about the *Dunera*. The film was very uncomplimentary regarding the British crew members of the ship, as it criticized their callous and ruthless behavior towards the passengers on board. When the British Navy objected to the way its members were being depicted, the Parliament in London began an inquiry to ascertain whether, indeed, English shipmen decades ago had been cruel and inhumane.

As more facts about the incident came to the fore, the diary of the German commander who had torpedoed the *Dunera* was made public. In it were some incredible entries. It seems that the commander had actually tracked the *Dunera* on its way down to Australia. He had fired a torpedo at the huge ship and was surprised that it hadn't been a direct hit. Shortly afterwards he and his mates had been ready to torpedo the ship again and blow it up, but as they peered through their periscopes they noticed suitcases and other paraphernalia floating in the ocean not far from the *Dunera*. Thinking that the material afloat might be useful for intelligence gathering, they sent divers to retrieve the items.

When the items were brought aboard the German submarine they were examined carefully. The Germans saw that among the material gathered were personal letters written in fluent German, German books and mementos clearly from Germany. They then realized that there were German nationals on board the *Dunera*. Therefore, to spare the lives of their fellow countrymen who were obviously being taken from England to Australia, the German commander ordered his crew not to fire at the *Dunera*. He radioed all German boats in the area to avoid this ship, as his submarine alone would accompany the *Dunera* from a distance. And so it was, all the way to Sydney.

Once the boat had docked and the passengers disembarked, the commander felt assured that there were no more Germans on board. His conscience was now clear and, on the *Dunera's* return trip to England, the commander attacked and demolished the ship.

And so, what Moshe Rabi and his fellow Jews thought was the final indignity — the casting overboard of their remaining treasures — was actually an act of *hashgachah pratis* (Divine Providence) which saved them. What they perceived as the severance of their past was actually the bridge to their future.

Moshe Rabi, along with many of his family members, still live in Australia today where they are an integral part of the Melbourne Jewish community.

◆§ *Kaddish in the Capital*

When things go smoothly we usually take them for granted. It's when things occur which are out of the ordinary that we take notice and wonder. Then we first ask ourselves, "Why did *Hashem* make this happen?"

One couldn't blame R' Mordechai from Cleveland Heights

for wondering what he might have done to deserve his being so inconvenienced on his business trip, which was suddenly altered from its normal course. Now, though, looking back, he understands that the events of that autumn morning were nothing short of supernatural. He realizes today that he was but a pawn in the master plan of the King of the universe.

For years R' Mordechai has been careful to find a *minyan* in any city to which he travels on business. Soon after getting off a plane, while other passengers are still picking up their baggage, he is already searching through the local phone book for the name of the nearest *shul,* and calling for its *minyan* schedule. Perhaps, he figures, that is why he merited being part of this special story and its unusual *minyan*.

A group of four *frum* (religiously observant) businessmen from Cleveland had arranged to travel together by plane early one Sunday morning to a New York City trade show. It was *Rosh Chodesh* Elul and R' Mordechai, one of the businessmen, had assured the others that, provided their plane landed on time at LaGuardia Airport in New York City, they would be able to catch any of a number of *minyanim* for *Shacharis* in Manhattan and still be at the trade show when it opened at 9:00 A.M.

R' Mordechai was supposed to pick up the others at 5:00 A.M. to catch the flight an hour later. But he overslept, and at 5:30 his brother, a second member of the group, came frantically to his house to see what had happened. R' Mordechai awoke with a start and told his brother to get the others and go without him; he himself would have to make the next plane. The three others made their way to the airport as R' Mordechai frantically put his things together, dashing around to find his *tallis, tefillin,* attaché case, trade samples and car keys. Equipped with a cup of coffee and his radar detector, he drove with abandon and got to the plane just as the doors were about to be closed. The others were surprised that he had made it.

The plane took off from Cleveland's Hopkins Airport in perfect weather. But shortly after the flight was in progress the captain announced that he had just been informed that there was a thick blanket of clouds and fog enveloping the New York City area. He promised the passengers to keep them informed of any developments. The men began to get apprehensive, for they had not really left much time to get from the airport to a *minyan* and still be on time to the trade show.

The flight continued as passengers tried to figure out alternate ways of getting to their destinations if they couldn't land in New York. Soon the captain's voice came over the intercom again. The news was not good, he announced. The fog had traveled westward over the New Jersey border, and not only was it impossible to land in New York, it would be dangerous even to attempt a landing at Newark Airport. They would have to land further south — in Washington, D.C.

❦ ❦ ❦

On board with these businessmen was a small group of *chassidim*. They had come to spend *Shabbos* in Cleveland Heights with their *rebbe*, R' Mechele, and were returning to New York this morning as well. When the plane landed in Dulles Airport, in the nation's capital, the *chassidim* and the businessmen decided that perhaps they had better form a *minyan* right there, for by the time they could catch a connecting flight and land in New York, the time for reciting *Shema* would be long gone. They counted to see if they had ten. Indeed, the *chassidim* were six, and then they counted the businessmen: one, two, three — and R' Mordechai made four! They had their *minyan* — and only because R' Mordechai had caught the plane!

A member of the airline personnel designated a corner of the waiting room where they could say their morning prayers. The ten men congregated there, each in his *tallis* and *tefillin*. All this was in perfect view of any passersby who could watch the proceedings through the glass partition behind which the *mispalelim* stood.

As they were saying *Hallel*, a well-dressed man slowly and hesitantly walked into the area where they were *davening*. A few heads turned to see what he wanted. "Would you mind if I said *Kaddish?*" the man asked softly.

One of the businessmen, R' Yankel, was taken aback. The man

hardly looked Jewish. How did he even know about *Kaddish,* and what did he want with it? It was then that R' Yankel noticed that the man was wearing a black ribbon on his lapel. (Numerous Reform Jews who do not observe the ritual of rending a garment as a sign of mourning wear a black ribbon instead.)

R' Yankel motioned to the man to wait for a few moments and he did so. At the appropriate time R' Yankel went over to the man, gave him a *siddur* and a *yarmulke,* helped him don a pair of *tefillin* and said, "You may begin the *Kaddish.*" The man looked around uneasily, then began. "*Yisgadal veyiskadash* ..." he whispered, and burst into tears. He regained his composure and continued, "... *shemei rabbah* ..." The men answered *Amen* with reverence. The gentleman struggled through the remainder of the words, as the men of the *minyan* helped him get through the entire *Kaddish.*

When he finished, he nodded his head in thanks and asked, "Is there another one to recite later?" They told him that there was. He waited patiently and then after the *davening* they motioned to him once again to begin. And once again as he said the *Kaddish* he burst into tears. All in the *minyan* could not help but be touched by the sensitivity and sadness of the man.

When *Shacharis* ended, one of the *chassidim* went over to the gentleman and introduced himself. After a few moments of conversation the *chassid* said, "I couldn't help but notice that you were so emotionally torn as you prayed. Is everything all right with you?"

It was then that the gentleman told this incredible story.

"You see," he began, "my father died just a few days ago, and last night he came to me in a dream and said to me, 'Robert, how come you're not saying *Kaddish* for me?'

"In my dream I replied, 'Dad, I hardly know how to say *Kaddish*, and besides, there are no synagogues where I live and I am always traveling.'

" 'I need you to say *Kaddish,*' my father insisted to me. I kept repeating that I just could not get to a place where I could say *Kaddish* for him. It was then that he asked me, 'But what if I send you a *minyan?* Would you then say *Kaddish?*'

" 'Of course I would,' I replied, and that's when I woke up. I couldn't believe that dream. I was trembling as I awakened. As I was getting dressed I managed to convince myself that there was really nothing to that dream. But then I came to the airport to catch a flight, and there, to my unbelieving eyes, were all of you praying in a *minyan* — in the *minyan* that was obviously meant for me!"

◆§ *A Tehillim — Israeli Bound*

The words of *Tehillim* (*Psalms*), written primarily by David *HaMelech,* speak for us and speak to us. On one hand, they portray the trials and triumphs of King David's life, yet simultaneously they manage, through the eloquence of expressed emotion, to reflect the joys and sorrows of all men — past, present, and future. And because *Tehillim* reflects the entire gamut of human emotions, it is understandable that it is the one book with which almost any Jew can identify. From the simplest Jew, sitting alone in a corner of the synagogue, to the great Torah sage leading his followers in prayer — men and women throughout the centuries have found solace and comfort in the tear-drenched pages of their *Tehillim*.

The following remarkable story about a man and his *Tehillim* bears witness to this special affinity.

In the American yeshivos that Moshe had attended as a youngster, he didn't seem any different from the dozens of other boys who had been his classmates. His parents, Holocaust survivors, were thrilled to be alive in America, and were gratified to have a child who could attend a religious school in New York, unhindered.

However, Moshe had a sharp and probing mind. From the stories that occasionally filtered down through his parents, he learned that his European ancestors, traced back scores of years, were of chassidic origin. The family's allegiance had been with the *Rebbe* of Belz.

Throughout his youth Moshe had attended Belzer functions, and had even been present when the Belzer *Rebbe* came to New

York. Nevertheless, *chassidus* was a fascination in his mind, not in his heart. At every event that he attended, he felt he was on the periphery, an outsider looking in. And then . . . he went to Belgium.

The Belzer *Rebbe* had come to Antwerp from Israel to dedicate a new building that had just been completed. Hundreds of Belzer *chassidim* from all over the world had gathered that *Shabbos* to be with the *Rebbe*.

Friday night, as the *Rebbe* began to chant *Lechu Neranenah* (the opening prayer of the Friday-evening service), the multitude of *chassidim* joined in. Their voices rose and reached a deafening crescendo as they swayed in waves to the *Rebbe's* piercing prayers. The storming tide of overwhelming voices swept away any lingering doubts that Moshe may have had in his heart. Alone in a corner he burst into tears as he was engulfed by deep emotion. Suddenly he felt connected to *chassidus* and to the *chassidim* around him. His heart had been touched to the core.

Within a year, his *Shabbos* mode of dress was transformed from American elegance to chassidic royalty. He now wore a *bekesha* (long black satin jacket), and one Friday evening, right before *Kabbalas Shabbos*, Moshe was adorned — by the Belzer *Rebbe* — with his first *shtreimel*.

As he and his wife became more involved with Belzer institutions, both in the United States and in Israel, Moshe began to assume an active role in the financial stability of Yeshivas Belz. Soon he became the chairman of the annual fund-raising *Melaveh Malkah*, which brought him into close association with the *Rebbe* as he made many trips to visit him in Israel.

On one of these trips, the *Rebbe* called him into his private study to thank him for the devoted work he was doing for Belz. The *Rebbe* presented him with a *Sefer Tehillim* (Book of *Psalms*) and instructed Moshe to recite *Tehillim* daily after *Shacharis* (morning prayers). The *Tehillim* became one of Moshe's most treasured possessions. Every morning without fail, Moshe recited the chapters appropriate for that particular day, thereby completing all of *Tehillim* every month. Wherever he went, he made sure to take with him his precious leather-bound *Tehillim* that the *Rebbe* had inscribed. In times of crisis and in times of joy, the words of King David brought him solace; the gift from the *Rebbe* gave him comfort.

❦ ❦ ❦

When the time came for the *Rebbe's* son to celebrate his *Bar Mitzvah,* Moshe and his family joined thousands of Belzer *chassidim* from throughout the Jewish world, and journeyed to Israel to join in the festivities.

On Friday morning Moshe and his family went to the *Kosel* to daven *Shacharis.* Afterwards Moshe ran some errands before returning to the hotel and beginning to prepare for the busy *Shabbos* that was ahead. It wasn't until later in the afternoon that Moshe reached into his *tallis* bag to get a *siddur,* and felt that something was missing! He searched furiously through the bag. His *tallis* was there, his *tefillin* were there, but the *Tehillim* — it was gone! It was only an hour and a half before *Shabbos!* Where in the world was he going to find his *Tehillim?*

He began a frantic search around the room; it wasn't there. He ran down to the hotel dining room where they had eaten breakfast. It wasn't there. He ran to the hotel lobby. It was not there, either. His heart fell. How could he possibly retrace his steps of the whole day? There was not enough time left before *Shabbos*!

He began to think fast. Where did he have it last? Where had he seen it for sure? Of course. It was at the *Kosel*, after *Shacharis*. He had said *Tehillim* that morning just as he did every day, and he definitely had his *Tehillim* then. But how could he get to the *Kosel* and back before *Shabbos*? His wife tried to talk him out of going back there, but he wouldn't hear of it. He was going back. Maybe he had placed the *sefer* on one of the tables. There wouldn't be many people there now; it would be easy to find. Or so he hoped.

Taking along one of his sons, Moshe caught a cab and headed for the *Kosel*. Once there, they frantically searched the tables with their neatly stacked piles of *siddurim* and *Chumashim,* ready for the *Shabbos* crowd. No luck. They went to the guards in the booth before the entrance to the *Kosel,* and asked if anyone had turned anything in. Yes — a camera and some film — but no *Tehillim.*

They asked the policeman standing guard near the wash basins, but no one had given him anything, either.

Moshe was now beside himself with frustration and disappointment. He tried to mentally retrace his route that day. Where had he gone after leaving the *Kosel?* He had been to numerous stores, to the *mikveh,* to Har HaMenuchos (a cemetery where many *tzaddikim* are buried) and *Kever Rachel.* There was no way he could get to all those places before *Shabbos!* He had gone home that morning by bus, and in his mind he could picture the bus driver. Maybe someone had turned something in to him. In New York, the policy of the drivers was to search the bus after the last stop; maybe they did that in Israel, too. Maybe he would be lucky and get the same driver on the final route of the day . . .

Moshe and his son climbed the hill leading away from the plaza of the *Kosel*, and went to the semicircular bus stop so familiar to thousands of tourists and Israelis who take countless buses which begin their routes there throughout the day and night. The bus came up the hill, swung around to where a crowd of people was waiting, and everyone began to get on. It was the last bus before *Shabbos* that would head towards the *Tachanah Merkazit* (Central Bus Station).

As he and his son boarded the bus, Moshe realized that he did not recognize the driver. As he was getting his *cartisia* (bus ticket) punched, he desperately, almost pleadingly, asked the driver, "Did anyone return a book to you? I lost my precious *Tehillim* this morning."

The driver said that no one had returned anything to him, nor had he found anything during his routine searches of the bus after completing each route that day. Moshe and his son sat down near the back of the bus, on the right side, their eyes searching the floor, the overhead racks — but knowing in their hearts that it was hopeless. This was the wrong bus, and time was running out. They would make it back to the hotel just minutes before *Shabbos*, and there was no time to check the other places he had visited earlier. He was shattered.

Still, Moshe could not rest. Instinctively his eyes darted back and forth, examining the crevices of the bus, studying the passengers.

On one side of him sat a young man with his wife and two children. They, too, had boarded the bus at the *Kosel*. They were a religious couple and were involved in an animated conversation with their children. The young man seemed to be explaining the sights and sounds of Jerusalem to his family. Moshe watched and listened to the young man for a few moments.

Then he saw it. It was on the young man's lap, upside down. Moshe couldn't be sure, but it was a leather-bound book, the same color — and seemingly the same thickness — as his *Tehillim*. Moshe's heart was pounding as he delicately interrupted the man's conversation and said in Hebrew, "*Slichah* (excuse me), but is that your book?"

"Actually not," replied the man in surprise. "I found it."

"You what?" Moshe almost shouted. Other passengers on the crowded bus turned around in unison. Moshe reached across and picked up the book. It felt familiar. He turned it over. He opened it to the *Rebbe's* inscription, but couldn't read it because his eyes were awash with tears. He did not realize it, but he was creating a spectacle on the bus, crying uncontrollably as he held the precious *Tehillim* in both his hands.

"This is my treasured *Tehillim*. I can't believe it. How and where did you find it? Was it on this bus?" The questions were tumbling over each other.

By now many others on the bus had turned around to see what the commotion was about. "No," the young man said, amazed at finding himself involved in such an unusual set of circumstances. "I actually found it on another bus on the way to the *Kosel*."

"You mean you didn't find it right now?" Moshe asked incredulously.

"No," the gentleman laughed, not believing what was happening. "It was on the bus on the way here, stuck between two seats. I saw that it was a *Tehillim* and I just didn't know what to do with it. So I decided I would take it with me to the *Kosel*, and then take it to the Lost and Found Office at the *Tachanah Merkazit* upon our return to the city. As a matter of fact," continued the young man, "that's where we were going right now."

Moshe couldn't thank the gentleman enough for his sincerity and integrity. Neither of them could get over the *hashgachah pratis* (Divine Providence) they had experienced: how *Hashem* had orchestrated that the item found on one bus would be returned to its rightful owner on another bus.

As Moshe walked back to the hotel he lifted his eyes to gaze at the magnificent sun dipping beyond the hills of Jerusalem. He remembered the words that he had often said (*Tehillim* 121:1,2), "I raise my eyes towards the mountains, from where will my help come? My help is from *Hashem,* Creator of heaven and earth."

Clutching the *Tehillim* firmly in his hand, his mood — like the sun in the distance — was a glowing gold.

◆§ *A Matter of Time*

Most people feel they are invulnerable. They believe that nothing will ever occur to disturb or disrupt their regular routine of life. Even David *HaMelech* wrote (*Tehillim* 30:7) "וַאֲנִי אָמַרְתִּי בְשַׁלְוִי בַּל אֶמּוֹט לְעוֹלָם — I had said in my tranquility, 'I will never falter.' " In reality, though, almost anything (good or otherwise) can happen to almost anyone. It is foolish to think that 'things' happen only to others, for to the 'other fellow,' you are the 'other fellow.'

R' Chezkel* (1901-1964) of Jerusalem perhaps understood this lesson as well as anyone. On a spiritual level, R' Chezkel was a much-heralded *tzaddik* and *talmid chacham* known throughout Israel. He was a *talmid* of the Stutchiner *Rav,* R' Leib Chasman (who later became the *Mashgiach* of Chevron Yeshivah); he was a *melamed* for more than twenty years in the Chayei Olam yeshivah in the Old City of Jerusalem, and was the founder of the first yeshivah in Haifa. Physically, he was a man of extraordinary

---

* The name has been fictionalized at the family's request. Stories about R' Chezkel include "Dead or Alive," p. 237; and two stories in *The Maggid Speaks,* "Seventeen Soldiers . . . Lives on the Line," p. 42, and "Yitzchak the Shikker," p. 128.

strength and stamina. It is said that in his youth he once single-handedly held a door closed as twenty Arabs on the other side of the door tried to ram it in, intent on attacking the Jews in the building.

Yet at age forty-eight R' Chezkel was stricken with a terrible illness which caused him to lose one of his legs. For the next fifteen years of his life he suffered great pain and was confined to a wheelchair. Before he passed away on the 25th day of Shevat (the day of R' Yisroel Salanter's *yahrzeit*, it was noted), he wrote in his will that his tombstone should simply state: "Here lies a man who suffered greatly, a man who did not attain everything he could have."

In further humility, he also insisted that he not be buried in the *chelkas harabbanim* (the section reserved for rabbis) in the cemetery on Har HaMenuchos, but rather that he be buried with the simple people, those who were Sabbath observers and put on *tefillin* every day.

R' Chezkel hated any form of *machlokes* (argument or fight). In his will he advised his children, "If you are praying in *shul* and you hear two people arguing, then even if you are in the middle of the recitation of *Shema*, walk away, so that you are not near people who are in dispute and discord."

R' Chezkel was as humble as he was great, and although his life was peppered with fascinating vignettes and episodes, he rarely ever spoke about these incidents. The only exception he made was at certain family *simchos* where he would recount, in fascinating poetry, some of the colorful incidents he had experienced.

At a *Sheva Berachos* for his youngest son, R' Chezkel detailed in poetry the following incredible story.

❦ ❦ ❦

R' Chezkel lived in an apartment complex called Brodie's Houses. One afternoon, wishing to get some fresh air, he wheeled himself out into the courtyard where he sat reading from a *sefer*. Suddenly he heard an argument erupt between a young woman and an old man.

Despising arguments, he turned to wheel himself back into his home. However, he could not help but overhear the bitter words exchanged by the two people. The woman was shouting, "That apartment should belong to me! I have a growing family! I have a whole life to live! My children and I are the ones who deserve the new available apartment."

The older gentleman retorted, "I have been on the waiting list for years! I have priority! The apartment should really be mine!"

It seems that spacious apartments were at a premium in Brodie's Houses, and now that one was finally available these two people were arguing as to whom the landlord should grant it to. Things got heated very quickly, and as R' Chezkel was closing the door of his home behind him, he could hear the woman snapping disdainfully at the old man, "Your life is almost over! I have so many years ahead of me — it is I who deserve the apartment!"

The old man retorted, "Only G-d knows how many years anyone has left."

With that R' Chezkel closed the door behind him, stung by the bitterness and rancor of the dispute he had just overheard.

During certain periods of unrest, Arabs were constantly tossing grenades and bombs at random into the courtyards and market places of Jerusalem, killing and maiming innocent people. Two days after he had overheard the argument between the young woman and the old man, R' Chezkel was sitting in his living room, when he heard the frightening sound of a bomb whizzing over his building and landing in the courtyard of Brodie's Houses. There were screams of pain, and in a moment pandemonium broke loose as people ran to get away from the area.

R' Chezkel, though, was sure that he had heard his own son scream out, and so as quickly as he could he wheeled himself out into the open courtyard. There, to his utter dismay, was his son lying on the ground, wounded by the shrapnel from a grenade that had been tossed by an Arab. The boy was bleeding profusely and R' Chezkel tried to get out of his wheelchair to lift his son.

As he bent over his injured son, an ambulance happened to be speeding by. Concerned people, who had run over to help, quickly flagged it down. The wounded child was carried into the ambulance and rushed to the hospital where his life was saved.

Since there was already another patient in the ambulance, R' Chezkel could not accompany his son. When he looked around after his son had been taken away in the ambulance, he noticed that two others in the courtyard had also been hit during the terrorist attack: the old man and the young woman whose argument he had overheard only two days earlier. The young woman, tragically, had been killed, whereas the old man, although wounded, survived.

Now years later, as he told this story at his son's *Sheva Berachos,* R' Chezkel was publicly thanking *Hashem* — as he had done privately a thousand times before — for sending the ambulance to him just when his son so desperately needed it, and for saving his son's life. But even on this special night of joy, R' Chezkel could not refrain from expressing his sadness regarding the false sense of security that the unfortunate woman had seemed to have. In magnificent prose, which he sang (in Yiddish) to the well-known *grammen* (poetry) tune in Jerusalem, R' Chezkel described the incident of the two people arguing and the subsequent bombing.

He sang two lines — which showed both foresight and insight — in a slow, deeply emotional voice, as though quoting the old man as he answered the woman carrying the child when they first argued. The lines contained a sobering thought for the haughty and the careless:

> *Zai nisht azoi hais, zai a bissele kelter,*
> *Vile a mensch vaist nisht ver is yinger tzu elter.*
> (Don't be so hot, let your temper turn cold,
> For a man doesn't know, who's young and who's old!)

⦁§ *Flight Made in Heaven*

There is a well-known expression (based on *Iyov* 22:28): "צַדִּיק גּוֹזֵר וְהַקָּדוֹשׁ בָּרוּךְ הוּא מְקַיֵּם — That which a *tzaddik* decrees, *Hashem* fulfills." This happens not only when a *tzaddik* says something forcefully, but often, even a remark made in passing is later borne out as fact. The following incredible incident was first related to me by R' Yitzchok Dershowitz of Lakewood, New Jersey, who is a repository of stories about his late *rebbe* R' Aharon Kotler (1891-1962). R' Menachem Fink, the son of the central figure in this episode, supplemented the various details.

R' Yaakov Fink (1902-1984), a noted *talmid chacham* and author, was the *Rav HaRoshi* (Chief Rabbi) of the Jewish community in Argentina. He had served the community there for over a decade after having served as *Rav* in Rio de Janeiro, Brazil, for seven years. Now on a trip to *Eretz Yisrael*, he had been offered an attractive rabbinic position in a small Israeli town and he was tempted to accept it, for he felt that he had already had enough of life in the Diaspora. Besides, he had family in Israel, and that made the offer even more inviting. He decided to seek counsel from a Torah sage.

After much discussion he still had not made up his mind and so, when he was in America on his way home from Israel, he stopped in Lakewood, New Jersey, to spend a *Shabbos* with an old acquaintance, the *Rosh Yeshivah* and *gadol hador* (great Torah sage), R' Aharon Kotler.

R' Aharon had his finger on the pulse of every Jewish community in the world, and he inquired about the doings of *Yiddishkeit* in Argentina. R' Fink told him that he was considering leaving. "How can you think like that?" asked R' Aharon incredulously. "There is still so much to do there! And besides, if you leave, who would go there to take your place?"

The two men discussed R' Yaakov's responsibilities to his community, and finally R' Aharon said, "Don't worry — some day we shall go to *Eretz Yisrael* together." R' Aharon explained that he himself had a role to play in America — as did R' Fink in Argentina — and thus they should both remain where they were.

R' Fink was very moved by his words. When he returned to Argentina he gave much thought to R' Aharon's exhortations and decided to stay on a while longer. He remained for a few more years, but when he was offered the position of *Av Beis Din* (head of the Rabbinical Court) in Haifa, he decided once and for all to leave

Argentina and accept the position in Israel. He bade his friends goodbye, settled all his matters in Argentina, and packed his belongings for the move to Israel.

R' Fink and his wife decided that on their way to *Eretz Yisrael* they would make a stop in Montreux, Switzerland, to spend a *Shabbos* with R' Yaakov Yechiel Weinberg, the world-renowned *talmid chacham* and author of the famous responsa, *Sridei Aish.* From Switzerland they would travel to Paris, where they would board their connecting flight to *Eretz Yisrael.*

On the morning of the final leg of their journey, they went to Orly Airport in France with great anticipation. Finally they were 'going home.' But at the airport they noticed an unusual sight. Tens of American *yeshivah bachurim* were rushing about, obviously attending to some important matter. R' Fink did not understand what was happening. He went over to one of the *bachurim* and said, "Excuse me, but what are all of you doing here in France and where are you headed?"

"We're accompanying the *Rosh Yeshivah* to *Eretz Yisrael,"* one of them answered, looking forlorn.

"What are you talking about?" R' Fink asked.

"Don't you know?" they asked. "R' Aharon Kotler was *niftar* (passed away) and we are taking him to his final resting place in *Eretz Yisrael.* We just came from America."

R' Fink was astounded that he would have the *zechus* (merit) to accompany the great R' Aharon on his final trip.

During the flight, as R' Fink reflected on all his personal connections with R' Aharon, it suddenly dawned on him, to his great astonishment, that indeed he was going to *Eretz Yisrael* together with R' Aharon, just as the *Rosh Yeshivah* had said they would, many years before!

Free Loan

The Ponevezher *Rav,* R' Yosef Kahaneman (1886-1969), was noted for his tireless efforts in raising funds for the yeshivos he founded. Whether it was for his yeshivah in the city of Ponevezh (Lithuania) itself, or for the Yeshivas Ponevezh he established many years later in Bnei Brak, the strength and stamina he expended on their behalf were far beyond what was expected of a man his age.

R' Berel Wein of Monsey tells how once, in Miami, he met the Ponevezher *Rav*, who was there to solicit contributions for his world-famous yeshivah. The *Rav* and R' Wein met early in the morning, and together they went to see people throughout the day. By late afternoon R' Wein, more than forty years younger than the elderly *Rav*, said to R' Kahaneman, "Let's go home for a while and rest. We have the whole evening's work ahead of us."

The *Rav* looked at his younger counterpart and, with a weary smile, said, "Now is not the time to rest. There will be plenty of time to rest — in the World to Come."

The following story was related by R' David Cohen of Brooklyn, who heard it personally from the Ponevezher *Rav*.

One afternoon, while R' Kahaneman was still in Lithuania, he was returning by train from a trip he had made to numerous towns for the benefit of his yeshivah. The people he had spoken with had not been too helpful, and the amount of money he had raised fell far short of the amount needed. He had hoped to raise one thousand rubles, but had managed to collect only three hundred.

On the same train, R' Chaim Ozer Grodzinsky (1863-1939), *Rav* of Vilna and one of the *gedolei hador* (outstanding Torah scholars) of his time, was returning home from Russia. R' Chaim Ozer, along with the Rogatchover *Gaon*, R' Yosef Rosen (1858-1936), and the Brisker *Rav*, R' Chaim Soloveitchik (1853-1918), had been called together to comprise a *beis din* to settle an inheritance dispute involving the fabulous wealth of a certain Jewish tea magnate. The family squabbles and fights were such that the greatest Jewish authorities were asked to adjudicate the matter. Now that the case had been settled, R' Chaim Ozer was returning home.

When the Ponevezher *Rav* and R' Chaim Ozer met on the train, they greeted each other warmly. During their conversation the Ponevezher *Rav* told R' Chaim Ozer that his fund-raising trip had not been successful. He had hoped to raise enough money to cover the deficit of the yeshivah, which had been met with short-term loans, but he had fallen far short of his intended goal.

"What amount are you short?" asked R' Chaim Ozer.

"Seven hundred rubles," said the Ponevezher *Rav* dejectedly.

R' Chaim Ozer reached into his pocket, took out an envelope and said, "Here it is — the exact amount you need — seven hundred rubles."

The Ponevezher *Rav* was stunned. How did R' Chaim Ozer happen to have just that particular amount, and why would he give it to him right then and there? R' Chaim Ozer smiled and said, "You know that I just came back from a *din Torah* regarding a tea magnate's estate in Russia. In reality we did not come to a final conclusion of the case. Nevertheless, the parties involved insisted that we take *psak gelt* (money for the time spent in evaluating and judging the case). I felt very uncomfortable taking the money, for in actuality we did not reach a conclusive *psak*. Thus I vowed that I would give all the money I received to charity. The amount they gave me was seven hundred rubles, exactly the amount that you need. It was *hashgachah pratis* (Divine Providence) that caused us to meet. The money is yours."

Whenever the Ponevezher *Rav* repeated this story he would say, "The Talmud (*Beitzah* 15b) tells us: *Hashem* says, 'לְווּ עָלַי ... וַאֲנִי פּוֹרֵעַ — Borrow money on My behalf [i.e., for your *Shabbos* expenses] . . . and I will pay you back.' I borrowed money [for the yeshivah] for the sake of *Hashem's* Torah, and He reimbursed me — to the penny."

◆§ *A Light for Hope*

The year 1929 is remembered well as the year of the stock-market crash and the start of the Great Depression.

However, that very same year, in another part of the world, a different type of cataclysmic event occurred. On a Friday afternoon in Chevron, one of the holiest cities in *Eretz Yisrael*, a horrifying massacre of Jews was carried out by bloodthirsty Arabs. Arab murderers ran through the Slobodka Yeshivah, Knesses Yisroel, where they slaughtered yeshivah *bachurim* and, in a wild maniacal rage, stormed houses, killing and butchering Jews in one of the cruelest and most sadistic episodes in modern times. In total, more than one hundred Jews were killed.

Very few Jews who were seen by Arabs on that tragic day in Chevron survived the rampage of terror. Two yeshivah students were trapped in one of the homes which the Arabs had forcibly entered. As the Arabs ran from room to room, beating and attacking Jews, these two were also pounced on and thrown down. They remained immobile, lying on the floor among others who had, unfortunately, been killed. The Arabs thought that they had murdered everyone in the room. They returned several times to look over the bodies, until they were convinced that indeed everyone there was dead. The two *talmidim* lay there, frozen in terror, for what seemed like hours, until they felt it was safe to move around, get out of that death-filled room and escape from the house.

One of those survivors was the noted R' Meir Chodosh (1898-1989), who eventually became the *Mashgiach* of the Knesses Yisroel yeshivah after it moved to the Achvah section of Jerusalem, where it was renamed Yeshivas Chevron. He served in the capacity of *Mashgiach* for more than fifty years, teaching literally thousands of *bachurim* who came to learn in this famous yeshivah.

Over the years, in his many lectures to the *bachurim,* R' Meir Chodosh often discussed the concept of never abandoning hope. He would cite the famous talmudic teaching "אֲפִילוּ חֶרֶב חַדָּה מוּנַּחַת עַל צַוָּארוֹ שֶׁל אָדָם אַל יִמְנַע עַצְמוֹ מִן הָרַחֲמִים — Though a sharp sword may rest on a man's neck, he should nevertheless not desist from prayer (nor abandon hope for survival)" (*Berachos* 10a).

For years people thought that he expounded this thought because he had survived against all odds that Friday in Chevron. However, one day as he was discussing the topic of never losing faith in *Hashem,* he told the following amazing story. When he finished telling the story he revealed that it was this episode, more than anything else in his life, that had given him the courage and fortitude not to abandon hope on that nightmarish afternoon in Chevron.

The story was first told to me by R' Sholom Schwadron and then again by R' Meir's son, R' Moshe Chodosh, *Rosh Yeshivah* of Yeshivah Ohr Elchonon in Jerusalem, who filled in many details.

In the early 1900's, R' Binyamin Chodosh (R' Meir's father) came to America to raise funds for his poverty-stricken family back home in Lithuania, and to investigate whether life in America would be suitable for him and his family. After a short stay he determined that indeed they would all be better off in America, and so he wrote to his family members, instructing them to procure passports for their move to the United States.

R' Meir at the time was in his early teens, and well aware of the strict Lithuanian law which stated that no one could be issued a passport from any municipality unless he first produced an official birth certificate from the town where he had been born. Young Meir would have to travel from Panitz, where his family lived, to Miadel, the city of his birth. Due to infrequent train service and poor connections, the trip would take a number of days.

The young boy Meir had no choice but to make the trip back to Miadel, even though the journey would most likely be dangerous. The unrest in that part of the world, which was to be the harbinger of World War I, had already begun, resulting in a tremendous upheaval of authority and government. As the power of the central government weakened and disintegrated, political bands began to seize municipalities and claim territorial control.*

In many towns chaos reigned, as the residents never knew which

* See "An Ember Ablaze," earlier in this volume.

political faction was in charge. No one knew from which quarter threats and demands would next be issued.

As R' Meir got off the train in a small village deep in Lithuania, he was approached by a police officer. "What are you doing in this town?" the officer asked, brandishing his club.

R' Meir was taken aback by the officer's gruffness. "I am traveling back to Miadel so that I can get a passport," came the reply.

"That's a lie!" the officer retorted. "No parent would allow a child your age to travel alone these days!"

Meir became frightened and flustered, and as the officer peppered him with questions, the soft-spoken boy answered "No" to questions he should have answered "Yes," and "Yes" to questions he should have answered "No." Soon, in his nervousness, he became trapped by his own words as he contradicted himself hopelessly, until the officer finally grabbed him by the shirt, lifted him a foot off the ground and yelled, "You are a traitor! A spy! Come with me!"

The young boy was terrified because he knew that he was at the officer's mercy. The officer could do whatever he pleased, and no one would dare stop him. Meir was taken to police headquarters where he was questioned mercilessly.

By midday the heat was unbearable. When the interrogating officers left the room to go for lunch, Meir remained alone with the officer who had brought him in. Still enraged that he had not been able to get the 'truth' from the boy, the officer announced that he would take him to the courtyard outside and get rid of him once and for all.

Holding his rifle against the frightened boy's back, the officer pushed him out into the blazing sun. Meir was so scared that he could hardly walk. "Stand against the wall!" the officer yelled.

Meir walked towards the wall, saying those chapters of *Tehillim* (*Psalms*) which he knew by heart. "Turn around, you traitor!" came the order.

Meir turned around slowly as the officer began to shout and to curse the young boy's heritage. The facts that Meir was a Jew, was from a distant city, and did not know anyone in that town — all counted against him.

"Pick up your head!" the officer ordered.

But Meir couldn't budge. He wanted to, but he simply couldn't. He was frozen in fear. The more the officer yelled, the more Meir wished he could obey — but he was paralyzed by terror. Finally, as the officer reached the peak of his maniacal rage, a superior officer appeared in a window that overlooked the courtyard.

"What's all the yelling about?" he shouted down towards the officer. "Have you gone mad?"

The officer retorted that he had captured a traitor — a spy — and he was about to kill him. From the second-story window, the short frail lad looked even skinnier and shorter than he actually was. "Leave him alone!" the commanding officer ordered. "Go find someone your own size to pick on, and stop yelling so I can get some sleep on this hot afternoon!"

And with that Meir was miraculously set free.

When Meir left police headquarters he ran as fast as he could towards what he now viewed as a new lease on life. He made many vows along the way regarding his future Torah study and *avodas* (service to) *Hashem.* Years later he admitted that, due to his human frailties, his commitment to those vows slackened off somewhat as the story of his unexpected survival began to recede into the depths of his memory. But one thing always stayed with him, and that was the strong belief that *Hashem's* help can come even at the very last moment in the face of seemingly imminent danger.

It was this lesson that he had learned years earlier which pulled him through the horror of Chevron.

In telling over this story, R' Meir said that he was never really sure why *Hashem* had seen fit to spare his life twice.

Perhaps it was so that he could become what his name portended – Meir – a light and inspiration for thousands of *talmidim.*

◆§ *Air Male*

David *HaMelech,* whose adversaries caused him endless suffering, wrote words of encouragement to others who might be downcast because of their seemingly insurmountable problems. He advised, "הַשְׁלֵךְ עַל ה׳ יְהָבְךָ, וְהוּא יְכַלְכְּלֶךָ — Cast your burden upon Hashem, and He will sustain you" (*Tehillim* 55:23).

We ourselves echo these encouraging words every *Shabbos* morning when we recite the moving prayer of *Nishmas*, "פּוֹדֶה וּמַצִּיל וּמְפַרְנֵס וְעוֹנֶה וּמְרַחֵם בְּכָל עֵת צָרָה וְצוּקָה — [*Hashem*] liberates, rescues, sustains, answers and is merciful in every time of distress and anguish."

The following story, told by R' Yaakov Kaminetzky (1892-1986) to R' Dovid Trenk of Adelphia, New Jersey, depicts, almost literally, a desperate woman's total dependence on *Hashem*, just as David *HaMelech* had encouraged.

Chiyena Miriam Feder, whose father had died when she was a little girl, lived in the town of Mir, near the Polish-Lithuanian border. As she came of age, she and her poverty-stricken mother realized that although all her friends were getting married, she was having a very difficult time finding a *shidduch* (suitable marriage partner). Chiyena Miriam, who was exceedingly short, had very definite ideas about the type of young man she wished to marry — and that was not helping matters, either.

She was not interested in marrying a working man who would undoubtedly provide her with financial security. She wanted her life's companion to be one whose life was dedicated to Torah, one who after marriage would remain as a student in the great yeshivah of Mir and become a *talmid chacham* (Torah scholar). To marry someone like that would require financial support from her side of the family. But without a father, there was no one she could count on.

She worked as a librarian and tried to put together what money she could. Months of waiting turned to years. Chiyena Miriam became more and more depressed as she saw the friends with whom she had grown up becoming busier and busier with their growing families while she struggled on, seemingly doomed to a life of loneliness.

One day, as she sat in the library mulling over her situation, she decided to write a letter to the only one who could help her — her

Father in Heaven, the Father of all mankind — *Hashem.*

Through the ink of her pen flowed the sadness of her heart as she transcribed the verbal prayers of the past few years onto the sheet of paper that now bore the burden of her pain. Once again she outlined the type of young man she so desperately sought: One involved with Torah, possessing exceptional *midos* (character traits), who would not consider her abject poverty a burden. She ended the letter with, "You, *Hashem,* Who supports the poor and uplifts the downtrodden, can surely answer my prayers. I look to You every day. Your devoted daughter, Chiyena Miriam."

She sealed the letter, put it into an envelope and on the outside wrote simply in Hebrew "לְאָבִי שֶׁבַּשָּׁמַיִם (To my Father in Heaven)."

She walked to a park outside the town of Mir, and held the letter loosely up in the air, pointing skyward. As soon as she felt a gust of wind she opened her hand and watched as the letter was carried off by the breeze. Then she walked directly home.

❦ ❦ ❦

Twenty-one years earlier, R' Yitzchok Yechiel Davidowitz, *Rav* in the town of Karelitz [whose daughter Faya Gittel was to be the mother of R' Moshe Feinstein (1895-1986)], had passed away. A few nights after his passing, a young, expectant woman in Karelitz, a Mrs. Sonenzon, dreamed that she would have a boy who would become a great *tzaddik,* and that she should name him after the *Rav* who had recently passed away. And soon her son Yitzchok Yechiel Sonenzon was born. As had been foretold in the dream, young Yitzchok Yechiel blossomed rapidly. At age twenty-one he was already known as an exceptional *talmid chacham.*

One day, as Yitzchok Yechiel was strolling through the park to refresh his spirits, he noticed a sealed envelope on the ground and bent to pick it up. Hoping to be able to return the letter to its owner, he checked the address on it and was surprised when he saw to Whom the letter was addressed.

Unable to contain his curiosity as to its contents, Yitzchok Yechiel opened the letter and read it. He was awed! He read it a second, and then a third time. He was moved by the pain and the sincerity of the writer, whoever she was.

He returned to the *beis midrash* (study hall), but couldn't keep his mind on learning. He went to discuss the matter with R' Elya Boruch Kamai (1840-1917), the *Rav* of the city (and first *Rosh Yeshivah* of the Mirrer Yeshivah). After a short discussion he told R' Elya Boruch that he would consider marrying this girl.

Inquiries were made, and eventually Yitzchok Yechiel married Chiyena Miriam, who was six years older than him. She had taken the words, "Cast your burden upon *Hashem*," literally. "And He sustained her."

And just as his wife desired, R' Yitzchock Yechiel went on to achieve great heights in the Torah world. He became the *Mashgiach* in a yeshivah in Minsk where such notables as R' Yaakov Kaminetzky, R' Yaakov Ruderman (1900-1987) and R' Avrohom Kalmanowitz (1891-1965) studied as youngsters. He also authored *sefarim:* one on *Mishnayos* and a second, *Derech Adam,* on *tefillah.* [One of their grandchildren, R' Yisroel Sonenzon, now lives in Lakewood, New Jersey, with his family.]

◈ *In the Nick of Time*

Often timing is everything. Most of us would like to have things happen when we think 'the right time has come.' But as King Solomon wrote in *Mishlei* (19:21), "רַבּוֹת מַחֲשָׁבוֹת בְּלֶב אִישׁ וַעֲצַת ה׳ הִיא תָקוּם — There are many thoughts in the mind of man, but it is G-d's master plan that shall prevail."

At times it seems that our well-intentioned plans are being unnecessarily delayed, and this increases our frustration. If we are fortunate, though, we are blessed by eventually being allowed to understand what G-d's master plan actually is. The following story contains a unique ending to a seemingly troublesome sequence of events.

Mr. Alex Steinberg (1910-1977) of Kew Gardens Hills, New York — a gentleman of the old school — was a well-known and beloved philanthropist who was involved in many Torah causes throughout his four decades of devotion to public life. Though his ready smile and open hand were extended to everyone, one of his pet projects was the welfare of Yeshivah and Mesifta Torah Vodaath in Brooklyn, where he served as a member of the Board of Directors. Every Sunday morning, without fail, he would travel to the yeshivah to discuss the financial health of the institution.

One afternoon a man approached Mr. Steinberg and presented him with two *chalafim* (knives used in *shechitah*). He explained that he was not a religious man and had been left these *chalafim* by his late father, who had been a *shochet* a number of years ago. "I am sure you will know what to do with these," the man said confidently. "Whatever you decide is okay with me."

Mr. Steinberg knew that Torah Vodaath gave a *semichah* class and that part of the curriculum involved studying the laws of *kashrus,* starting with the laws of *shechitah.* He decided to bring the *chalafim* to the yeshivah office so that they could be given to the *semichah* class.

Mr. Steinberg kept the knives in the back seat of his car all week long to be sure that he would not forget to bring them to the yeshivah on Sunday. However, on Thursday afternoon he parked his car in Manhattan, and when he returned to it he realized that the *chalafim* were gone.

Mr. Steinberg was disturbed that someone had stolen the knives and was apprehensive that they would probably use them for some purpose less than "kosher." He was also disappointed that he would not be able to present them to the young men of the *semichah* class. After a few days, though, he forgot about the incident.

Mr. Steinberg, a traveling salesman, was accustomed to buying a new car every two years, and he usually gave the used car to his son, R' Peretz. This car was no different, and after he was given the car by his father, R' Peretz kept it for close to a year and then sold it to a used-car dealer. A day after the sale, the dealer called R' Peretz and said that he had found something in the car which, perhaps, he would want to come and pick up.

R' Peretz who thought that he had thoroughly cleaned and emptied the car before selling it, was surprised that something of value — something that would merit the dealer's calling him — could still be in the car. "What did you find?" he asked.

"Two long knives in a case," the dealer replied, sounding surprised that a rabbi would carry such dangerous items around with him.

When R' Peretz went back to the dealer to claim the knives, he realized at once that they were the *chalafim* his father had thought were stolen more than two years earlier. It soon became obvious that the thin case containing the *chalafim* had slipped through the crevice behind the back seat and landed in a space between the trunk and the padding of the rear seat, where no one had ever thought to look for them. R' Peretz thanked the dealer and took the two *chalafim* home with him.

The very next morning an elderly man came to *daven* in the Young Israel of Queens Valley, where R' Peretz is the *Rav*. After *Shacharis* the man approached R' Peretz and showed him a letter that he had just received from his brother, a *shochet* in Kiev, Russia.

His brother wrote that he desperately needed money to buy *chalafim* so that he could continue *shechting* for the people in his community.

"Can he use *chalafim* instead of money?" R' Peretz asked the gentleman.

"Of course," exclaimed the visitor. "That's exactly what he needs!"

"Then maybe I can help you," said R' Peretz, incredulous at the timing of the return of the *chalafim*. Later that day R' Peretz spoke with his father. They had the *chalafim* checked to be sure that there were no nicks or scratches along their blades, and within days arrangements were made for the *chalafim*, which had hidden themselves for more than two years, to be sent to Kiev.

> There is a Talmudic dictum (*Shabbos* 32a) "מְגַלְגְּלִין זְכוּת עַל יְדֵי זַכַּאי — [*Hashem* sees to it that] things of merit come about by those who are meritorious themselves." This story speaks for itself.

◆§ A Megillah with Mazal

The following incredible story, told by Mr. Heshy Millet of Brooklyn, would be practically unbelievable except that Mr. Millet himself was centrally involved in the incident.

It has been noted that the Hebrew word מַזָּל – *mazal* (lit., good fortune) may be seen as an acronym for three words: מָקוֹם (place), זְמַן (time), and לָשׁוֹן (language), indicating that if one is fortunate enough to be at the right place at the right time and to say the right things – that's *mazal*. The *hashgachah pratis* that caused a remarkable juxtaposition of events portrays an unusual aspect of *mazal*.

In the *shul* where Mr. Millet *davens* regularly there is an older gentleman who comes to *daven* as well, but only for six months of the year. The other six months he spends in the warmer climate of Florida. The people in *shul* have come to expect the gentleman to leave New York shortly after *Sukkos* and to return from Florida shortly before *Pesach*.

One year, though, the gentleman appeared in *shul* just a day or two after *Purim*, a number of weeks before his usual date of return. When Mr. Millet saw the old man he said, "I see you've returned earlier this year. Is everything okay?"

"Not really," said the old man. "I received a call from a family member here in Brooklyn telling me that my house had been broken into, and so I had to come back to file insurance claims and see exactly what was and what was not taken."

Mr. Millet expressed his regrets about the incident and related that there had been a rash of robberies recently in the neighborhood. "Was anything of value taken from your home?" asked Mr. Millet, duly concerned.

"Yes," said the old man sadly. "I don't care about all the other items they took, but they took a small handwritten *Megillah* (Scroll of *Esther*) that I got from my grandfather. It has been in our family, handed down from generation to generation, for close to three hundred years!"

"You're kidding!" exclaimed Mr. Millet.

"No," replied the gentleman sadly. "That *Megillah* has been a precious heirloom in our family."

But the gentleman had not understood why Mr. Millet was so taken aback. Mr. Millet tried to control himself as he asked the next question, because he was aware that the gentleman had already had two heart attacks and he certainly didn't wish to give him a third. "What if I told you," Mr. Millet began, slowly and softly, "that I could get back your *Megillah* for you in half an hour?"

The gentleman tried to force a smile. "Please, Heshy," he said. "Don't be foolish. The robbery happened a week ago. I am afraid it is long gone."

Mr. Millet told the man to wait at home by the phone while he ran back to his own home to make a call himself. He dialed the number of his nephew, Mr. Yaakov Wolf, who owns an appliance repair shop in Boro Park.

Aside from his repair shop in Boro Park, Yaakov Wolf had been renting a separate room in an apartment building, where he kept his tools and other paraphernalia. Numerous times robbers had broken into that basement room and taken old appliances and tools which they probably resold. Just two days earlier Yaakov had reported to his uncle, who owned the building, that the room had been burglarized once again, this time on a Friday night. "Not only did they steal some tools," Yaakov complained, "but they had a beer party down there as well. Bottles and cans were left all over the place. What a mess!"

The next day Yaakov called his uncle again. This time he told him what he found when he began to clean up and take inventory of what still remained. He noticed that the robbers had left other things there aside from their beer bottles. He bent to pick up what he thought was a roll of cardboard — but when he had it in his hand he gasped. It was a small *Megillah* written on parchment!

How could that *Megillah* have gotten there? He had never owned one like it and no one he knew had ever brought one like that to him. He was puzzled. But as he continued cleaning up, it suddenly dawned on him. Maybe the robbers had stolen the *Megillah* along with other things from someone's home, and, not knowing what it was, just decided to toss it away somewhere.

As Mr. Millet dialed quickly, he hoped that Yaakov hadn't yet sold or given away that *Megillah*. "Yaakov," he yelled into the telephone as soon as he recognized his nephew's voice, "do you still have that *Megillah* you found?"

"Yes, I do," Yaakov replied. "But why do you ask?"

"I think I know to whom it belongs," exclaimed Mr. Millet excitedly. And he went on to tell him about the robbery at the home of the older gentleman who lived in Flatbush. "I can't believe that this is a mere coincidence," Mr. Millet explained. "It seems that amazing *hashgachah pratis* is at work here."

Within half an hour Mr. Millet went to Boro Park, got the *Megillah* from his nephew, and came back to the home of the elderly gentleman waiting by the phone. He rang the bell of the old man's home, and was welcomed in.

"Is this your *Megillah?*" Mr. Millet asked, sensing that it was.

The gentleman took the ancient scroll in his hands, looked at it carefully, then caressed it gently. He closed his eyes and smiled softly, not believing what he was holding. It was as though a heavy burden had been lifted from his worried, broken heart.

Mr. Millet didn't even wait for the reply to his question. Instead, he went to the phone to call his nephew and tell him that the two of them had been fortunate, for together they had fulfilled the *mitzvah* of *hashavas aveidah* (returning a lost item) in an incredible way.

Of Twigs and a Deathbed

In the Boro Park section of Brooklyn there stands a yeshivah called Emek Halachah. Its *Rosh Yeshivah,* R' Tuvya Goldstein, a world-renowned *posek* (halachic decisor), is known for the intimacy he shared with the *gedolim* of the pre-war generation.

He studied for years under R' Elchonon Wasserman in Baranovich, and later was a student of R' Boruch Ber Lebowitz in Kaminetz. He was often in the presence of R' Chaim Ozer Grodzinsky in Vilna, and more recently shared a special friendship with R' Moshe Feinstein in New York.

Yet this venerable Torah scholar did not always have the good fortune of being surrounded by the walls of the *beis midrash* (study hall). For a number of years he, along with eleven other young men from Kaminetz, were imprisoned and confined to a Siberian labor camp. I was fortunate to be present when R' Tuvya recounted a phenomenal story of intimidation, terror and deliverance in which he was involved. Although this episode occurred more than four decades ago, as R' Tuvya retold it, he relived the incident as though it had happened yesterday.

The year was 1943, and the Germans had effected their invasion into Stalingrad, Russia. The war for the Russians was at its peak, and everyone in the country was expected to do his share for the welfare of the Motherland. In labor camps the work intensified. In the one where R' Tuvya and the other yeshivah *bachurim* were confined, they were told that they would be gathering materials necessary to build planes for the Soviet army.

Until the Germans invaded Russia, R' Tuvya and the other *bachurim* were able to avoid working on *Shabbos*. After the invasion, however, the intensity of the war increased and they were forced to work seven days every week.

They were told by their *nashelnyk* (field director) that their division would have to clear the timber, which consisted of chopped tree trunks, twigs and branches, from an area measuring about two square miles. All lumber, large and small, was to be carried to a nearby river and sent downstream, where other workers would be waiting to take the wood to the industrial plants that manufactured airplanes.

The *nashelnyk* told the prisoners that he would return in three hours to check their progress. Mistakenly, R' Tuvya and the others thought they would be left unobserved. They didn't realize that the *nashelnyk* actually climbed to the top of a deserted hill and watched to see how they were working. What the *nashelnyk* saw, first puzzled, then confused, and finally infuriated him.

As the *nashelnyk* left them, R' Tuvya and his yeshivah friends huddled together. They decided that if they already had to work on *Shabbos*, they would try to minimize *chilul Shabbos* (desecration of the Sabbath) in any way they could. They decided they would implement two halachic concepts.

The first is known as שְׁנַיִם שֶׁעֲשׂוּהוּ (Two who perform it). One of the thirty-nine *Avos Melachah* (primary violations of the Sabbath) is carrying. The Talmud (*Shabbos* 92b) explains that the Torah law prohibiting this refers to cases in which one person alone carries something in a public domain. However, if two together carry something that can normally be carried by one person, it is not a Torah violation but rather a Rabbinic (and thus a lesser) violation. Thus, all afternoon R' Tuvya and the eleven others carried branches and even small pieces of lumber in groups of two or three.

As the *nashelnyk* observed them from afar, he was confused. It was understandable that two or three people were needed to carry a huge piece of wood; however, there were literally hundreds of little twigs, each maybe four or five inches long, and soon the *nashelnyk* realized that even these tiny twigs were being carried by at least two *bachurim* at a time. He could not believe his eyes. Why did it take two healthy young men to carry one twig? But that was not the worst of it.

The yeshivah *bachurim* had remembered another *halachah:* פָּחוֹת פָּחוֹת מִד' אַמּוֹת (Carrying less than four cubits at a time). The violation of carrying, prescribed by the Torah, referred to cases in which one carried something for the distance of four cubits (between six and eight feet) (*Shabbos* 153b). However, if one carried something for a distance of less than four cubits, rested, and then continued on his way — again carrying for less than four cubits — that was not a Torah violation, but merely a Rabbinic violation. And so, two or three boys would pick up a piece of wood and start walking. They would pace off three cubits, rest a moment and then resume walking, again measuring as they walked three cubits, at which point they would stop for a moment, and then continue on.

That looked fine to the *nashelnyk* when they were carrying huge logs, but these fellows were following the same routine even when they were carrying a twig! Two boys would pick up a three-inch twig, walk three or four steps towards the river, stop and rest a moment and then walk again a few steps, and stop and rest again. The *nashelnyk* thought he would explode.

This went on for close to three hours, and all the while R' Tuvya and his friends, disregarding the fact that the work was extremely tedious and difficult, were content in having minimized their *chilul Shabbos* by way of implementing some of the Rabbinic rulings they had learned in the yeshivah.

After three hours the *nashelnyk* made his way to the yeshivah *bachurim*. "You fellows were not working well today," he scowled at them.

"We worked very diligently," they retorted. "We cleared almost the entire area."

"You fellows were playing games. I was watching the whole time," the *nashelnyk* replied.

Nothing more was said, and by six o'clock everyone was back in the barracks, having been given their minimal amount of hard bread and water. Usually everyone was asleep by six o'clock because they had to get up early the next morning to head out to the labor fields. However, that night at seven o'clock, when all should already have been asleep, the wake-up bell clanged with sudden ferocity. The men in the barracks jumped from their beds with a start. There must be an emergency, they reasoned, because that bell meant that everyone had to gather at once in the central auditorium.

Everyone dressed in a hurry and proceeded to the central hall, where they were instructed to take seats. The twelve *bachurim* entered the hall with everyone else, but at once they were told to separate themselves from the crowd. Twelve chairs had been set aside for them, apart from everyone else, and there they were instructed to seat themselves. R' Tuvya and his friends suddenly realized that they were in trouble. It dawned on them that maybe the *nashelnyk* had reported them to higher officials! In a few moments their worst fears were confirmed. Five stocky frowning officers took their seats at a table facing the assembled inmates, and called the meeting to order. Standing off to a side with a sneering expression of vengeance was the *nashelnyk* himself.

"Your Honor," he began, as he faced one of the 'judges,' "I bring before you a group of people who are sabotaging our efforts against the enemy. Germany has attacked the Motherland and we here at this labor camp were given the honor to prepare materials for planes to crush the enemy. Instead of working tirelessly for our victory, these twelve healthy young men staged a comic theatrical play out in the fields. Everything they did, they did in pairs. Even the smallest twig required two of them to carry it. Then, as if that twig were too heavy for both of them, they would rest every few meters as though they were exhausted from their difficult work."

The close to three hundred other laborers that comprised the audience sneered with derision at these traitors. And then, to dramatize the foolishness of it all, the *nashelnyk* called one of the people from the audience to act out this scenario with him. The *nashelnyk* and another laborer carried a twig across the front hall together, walked a few feet, stopped, and then walked again. The audience roared with laughter. To the twelve *bachurim*, however, this was no joking matter.

The presiding judge looked sternly at them and asked for an explanation. None of the young men spoke fluent Russian, but one of the *bachurim* thought he could make himself understood reasonably well. He stood up nervously as all eyes turned to him, and he said, "We have all worked hard for the sake of the Motherland, but being that today was our Sabbath, we tried to do things in a manner that would not desecrate our Holy Day." He then tried to explain as best he could to people without any Talmudic background the laws of שְׁנַיִם שֶׁעֲשׂוּהוּ and פָּחוּת פָּחוּת מִד׳ אַמּוֹת.

The judges listened carefully, and then one of them said, "You can't tell me that this is part of your religion. I read about Moses; he was a very smart man and there is no way that he would instruct two people to carry one twig! That's not intelligent, and Moses was very intelligent!"

Try as they did, the *bachurim* could not make the *nashelnyk* or the judges understand why they had acted the way they did. The judge went into a long dissertation about traitors and counter-revolutionaries. He peered down at the Jewish boys and said, "At this very moment our enemies, the Germans, are killing your parents, your brothers and sisters. The United States, France, England and the Soviet Union have all banded together to get rid of the enemy. We are unified. Where is your loyalty?" he roared. He accused the twelve *bachurim* of being spies, and ordered two soldiers with bayonets to stand on either side of the chairs where the *bachurim* were seated. They were to be taken to jail where they would await further sentencing.

R' Tuvya and the boys huddled together. They decided to say *Viduy* (confession), which a Jewish person says when he is about to die. They knew the *Viduy* of R' Nissim Gaon, which is a shorter version than the regular *Viduy*, and quietly they began saying the words they knew to themselves. Not one of them thought they would live until the next morning.

The 'case' continued for hours as the judges and the *nashelnyk* took turns lecturing to everyone about the great war efforts of the Soviet Union. It was already after ten o'clock when suddenly the judges stood up as they noticed a group of people entering through the door at the opposite end of the room. Everyone turned to see what had caught the judges' eyes.

Into the room walked six Russian men dressed in the full uniform of the Moscow Interior Central Committee. The judges immediately recognized them as those who came once a year to check on the conditions of the laborers. They never came at night, because no one worked at night. Why were they here now?

The presiding judge invited the six men to come up front as officers scampered like frightened cats to get the deepest cushioned chairs for these officials. Once they were seated, the presiding judge, seeking to make a favorable impression on his superiors, had the *nashelnyk* begin his theatrics again.

Two laborers were called from the audience to show how the yeshivah *bachurim* had carried out their orders of the day. Once again the audience laughed in derision. Even the stern-faced officers from Moscow couldn't hold back their weak smiles. The more the *nashelnyk* called these boys traitors and saboteurs, the more the

Moscow officials seemed to be pleased. That is, all of them except one. He stared ahead, stony faced. Every once in a while he would glance from the yeshivah *bachurim* to the *nashelnyk*. As the harangue continued about unity, the Motherland and the enemy, this expressionless official bent towards the chairman of the group and muttered a few words. He was requesting permission to take the twelve young men into a different room to talk with them privately. He was granted permission. He approached the presiding judge, spoke to him quietly for a moment, and the twelve were ordered to follow him outside.

The Soviet officer motioned to the young men to enter a side room, and he followed behind them. He closed the door and looked over the terrified young *bachurim*. They were standing stiffly at attention, not knowing what to expect next.

"*Zets zach* (sit down)," he said to them in Yiddish. They froze with terror. Was this a ploy? How did this officer know Yiddish? The officer then smiled warmly and said, "*Ah guta vuch!* (A good week to you!)" This was the traditional greeting used by Jews the world over after *Shabbos*. For the first time in hours they relaxed. The officer continued reassuringly, "*Ich bin a Yid* (I am a Jew)."

They sat down as he asked them, "What is going on here?" in a voice indicating that he was on their side.

They explained to him in Yiddish, as best they could, the concepts they had tried to put into practice that afternoon to avoid desecrating the *Shabbos*. And then the officer told them his story.

"Let me tell you about myself," he said. "I am a Jew but I am also a Communist. A few years ago my mother died, but as she lay on her deathbed she called me to her bedside and said, 'I want to be able to die in peace. I know you are a Communist but I want you to promise me that someday you will do something to help a religious Jew.' It was her last and only request of me, and I promised her that someday I would fulfill her plea. I believe in my heart that now is the time, because I see that a power beyond my control brought me here to you. We never come to these camps after dark. But tonight, as we were driving, our car broke down. We had no idea where we could stay overnight until we saw the lights of this auditorium. We walked over here, right into the middle of your 'trial.' "

He asked the boys who their *rebbe* was and they told him that it was R' Boruch Ber Lebowitz who came from Slutzk. The officer was interested. He had an uncle who came from Slutzk. They talked for a few more minutes and then the officer said, "Let me speak for you when we return to them. I will take care of you."

R' Tuvya and the other *bachurim* were speechless. If ever *Hashem* had sent a messenger, here he was! Their hearts pounded in frenzied anticipation. A hundred thoughts crisscrossed their minds. Would this fellow *Yid* be able to overturn this kangaroo court? . . . Could he sway the opinions of the majority? . . . May *Hashem* bless the memory of that mother of his! "יַעַנְךָ ה׳ בְּיוֹם צָרָה — *Hashem* answer us on this day of suffering," they prayed. "Help us get out of this alive . . ."

The young men followed the officer into the auditorium. They took their seats and the officer immediately addressed both the *nashelnyk* and the judge. "You insist that these people are counter-revolutionary," he said. "But how have they been working until now? Have they not been loyal to the Motherland?"

"Yes, yes," stammered the *nashelnyk*. "I don't know what happened to them today, but yes, they were always loyal. As a matter of fact, just this past Thursday night we had a late-night delivery of heavy chains, and when I asked for volunteers to unload the boat, no one would come out of bed to help me except these twelve fellows."

"That's exactly what I mean to point out," cried the officer. "They are extremely loyal in our fight against the enemy. It's obvious that just today they changed their work habits because of this religion of theirs."

The yeshivah *bachurim* had told this officer that they were being given less food than many of the other workers in the camp. And so, while he had the judges listening intently to him, he continued to speak on their behalf. "It is my impression," he said, "that these workers are among the most loyal in the division, but how can they produce when they are given merely half the amount of bread that others are given? Others get 800 grams of bread a day, and they have to exist on merely 400! They have to be fed more and then they will be able to work even better!"

The other five officers agreed with the reasoning of their comrade from the Interior Ministry. The judges, sensing that the men from Moscow were leaning favorably towards the yeshivah *bachurim,* softened their attitudes towards them as well. The case was soon closed, and everyone was sent back to their rooms. No punishments were meted out to anyone.

R' Tuvya says that from the next day on, the *nashelnyk* completely changed his demeanor towards the *bachurim.* He became their good friend, often sharing with them news from the war front, information which he did not share with others. They were never again challenged by the *nashelnyk,* and life for them — while never pleasant — was, from that moment on, tolerable.

> When R' Tuvya finished this story he smiled and said with pleasure, "Most Jews have the opportunity to *lain* (read) *Megillas Esther,* with its varied cast of characters and its complex plot — which ends with deliverance from death at the hands of the enemy. I lived through a *megillah* in which we were saved from imminent danger and saw the hidden hand of *Hashem* revealed. We witnessed the numerous things that all came together — a Jewish mother's final wish, a car breaking down just outside our quarters, Moscow ministers traveling at night, the minister having an uncle in Slutzk — all so that our lives should be saved. And not only that," he continued, "but who would believe that because of that incident we began to receive double the amount of bread we had been given until then? It was an outright miracle — nothing short of that — an outright miracle."

The Seed Grew in Berlin

David *HaMelech* exclaimed (*Tehillim* 104:24): "מָה רַבּוּ מַעֲשֶׂיךָ ה׳, כֻּלָּם בְּחָכְמָה עָשִׂיתָ — How great are Your works, *Hashem,* with wisdom You made them all." The word רַבּוּ (lit., great) can also mean 'abundant' (see *Radak* ibid.). Thus David *HaMelech's* words imply that at times *Hashem* orchestrates many different and seemingly unrelated events. It is when the disparate occurrences suddenly begin to interact that one realizes *Hashem's* wisdom in attaining a desired result.

The following intricate story involving plots and subplots is a case in point. It was told by R' Zelig Prag, a *mechanech* (Torah educator) in Brooklyn.

A few weeks before the *Pesach* holiday during World War I, the Jewish chaplain of the German Armed Forces, Rabbi Dr. Naftoli Carlebach, received a letter from a Jewish soldier fighting on the front.

The soldier wrote that he came from a small town where he was the one who always baked *matzos* for all the townsfolk. "*Pesach* is approaching," the young man wrote, "and if I don't return home before *Yom Tov* there will be no one there who can bake the *matzos*. Is there any way that you can intercede on my behalf with the Minister of the Armed Forces so that I may be allowed to return home just for this period?"

R' Carlebach read and reread the letter, touched by the sincerity and sensitivity of the young soldier. But what in reality could a chaplain do? The world was aflame in war and the German army was an integral spark in the conflagration. R' Carlebach was sure that the Minister of War wouldn't give him the time of day.

But as he thought about the situation, he said to himself, "A Jew is pleading, and if that's the case then I must share his burden and do whatever I can." Thus R' Carlebach traveled to Berlin to make an appointment with the Minister of War.

He sat patiently in the waiting room together with captains, lieutenants and generals. But merely five minutes after he had presented his credentials to the Minister's secretary, she called his name and said to him, "The Minister will see you now."

R' Carlebach was surprised to be ushered in so quickly. He had taken along with him a *Mishnayos* to study during what he thought would surely be an hour or more of waiting. When he came into the room, the Minister of War was standing behind his desk. As R' Carlebach nodded his head and extended his hand in greeting, the Minister said, "You look exactly like your father."

R' Carlebach was shocked! It was true that everyone told him he looked like his late father, but how did the Minister of War know that? "You knew my father?" R' Carlebach asked incredulously.

"Yes, I did," the Minister answered. "Sit down," he continued. "It's a long story that you are probably not aware of."

And this is the story that the Minister, in middle of a raging war, with countless people waiting outside his office to talk to him, told the *Rav*.

❦ ❦ ❦

"When your father was a young man, he wanted to build a nursing home for elderly Orthodox Jews in Berlin. He tried to raise money for the project but, for the most part, was unsuccessful. Seeing that he wasn't getting close to his goal, he decided to approach the Minister of Finance of the German Empire, who himself was a Jew.

"Many people discouraged your father, telling him that it was a waste of time to see the Minister because he was a Reform Jew and therefore would not allocate any funds at all for your father's project, which was for Orthodox Jews. Your father felt, though, that having exhausted all other channels, he might as well try this last one.

"He came to the office of the Finance Minister in Berlin and asked that he be given an appointment. He was told by the secretary to wait, and she went in to clear his request with the Minister. In a few moments she came out of his chambers, walked directly over to your father and said, 'The Minister will see you at once!'

"Your father was startled. He had not imagined that he would be seen so quickly. As he walked into the office of the Minister, the Minister said to him, 'I was expecting you.'

" 'You were?' your father asked, not believing what he had heard.

" 'Yes,' said the Minister. 'Let me tell you why.'

"And then the Minister told him the following:

> Last night I had a very confusing and disturbing dream. I dreamt that there was a group of rabbis sitting around a

table, and on the table was a large, dried-out seed. Each of the rabbis peered at the seed and said that it could never be revived. It was already too dried out and there was no hope for it in the future. One rabbi, though, looked at the seed and said, "No, it's not too late. If the seed is nurtured properly there is still a chance that it may grow." And then I woke up.

Thinking about the dream, I decided that the seed represented myself. And I made up my mind that if a rabbi, any rabbi, would come to my office today, I would consider it a sign that my interpretation of the dream was correct. And now you have come to me, so tell me what I can do for you.

"Your father," the Minister of War continued, "told the Minister of Finance of his desire to build an old-age home for Orthodox Jews. After listening to his idea, the Minister of Finance said that he would help him as much as was feasible. Indeed, a magnificent home was built for those elderly people. Furthermore, because of his association with your father, the Minister began returning to his religion, and by the time he died he was a religious man. Before he passed on, he specified in his will that no one was to eulogize him except your father. And that's exactly how it was. At the funeral no one spoke except your father.

"At that time," said the Minister of War, interrupting himself, "I was then a young officer working at military headquarters, and as a government official, I attended that funeral.

"I want you to know that I have been trained as a soldier to kill and to torture," the Minister continued. "There is very little that fazes me. I had never cried as an adult. But when your father spoke, his words were so eloquent and so moving that I cried like a child."

He paused for a moment as he recalled the poignant moments of that day long ago. "I have never forgotten the words or the face of your father. Thus, when I heard the name Carlebach I had to see if you were a relative. It is obvious to me that you are his son. Tell me then, how can I help you?"

R' Carlebach, who was by then trembling, explained the situation about the soldier who requested a leave of absence to be able to bake *matzos* for the people of his home town. Permission was granted. R' Carlebach thanked the Minister for his graciousness and the Minister, in turn, thanked the *Rav* for having come to meet him.

◆§ *Dead or Alive*

The following story was told to R' Sholom Schwadron, the *Maggid* of Jerusalem, by his *mechutan* (relation by marriage) R' Shimon Lazer Meletzky. The story concerns R' Chezkel whom we have met earlier in "A Matter of Time" (page 206).

Besides being fascinating, this episode has an inherent lesson. The good deeds that a man does do not go for naught. *Hashem* remembers.

When he was drafted into the Russian Army in the early 1900's, Chezkel was but a youngster of nineteen. After a short stint of basic training during World War I, he was sent to a battlefield located outside of Stutchin, his home town in Russia. For hours on end, the fighting and shooting between Russian and Polish soldiers would go on, and then there would be an interlude during which the soldiers would retreat to their foxholes for rest and cover.

It happened that during a raging battle, Chezkel was positioned next to another Jewish soldier, Mendel (not his real name). A shot rang out. Chezkel turned and saw that Mendel had been seriously wounded. Almost at once medics came to Mendel's assistance, but they realized immediately that he was losing his life. As the furious battle raged on, Chezkel came over to see if he could be of help. He could see that Mendel was trying to talk to him. The poor young soldier was gasping for breath. "Chezkel," he managed to mutter, "see to it that I get taken to *kever Yisrael* (a Jewish cemetery)." And with those words he expired.

Choked with tears, Chezkel covered Mendel gently and went back into the thick of the battle. Pretty soon there was a lull in the fighting, and Chezkel ran back to the body of the slain soldier, determined to fulfill his last wish. He picked up Mendel, slung him over his shoulder and began the trek from the battlefield into the town of Stutchin, which was more than two miles away.

Chezkel knew that if he were caught leaving his battalion he could be tried and sent to prison or, even worse, sentenced to death on grounds of desertion. But he knew the paramount importance of the words of the Talmud (*Taanis* 21a), "מִצְוָה לְקַיֵּם דִּבְרֵי הַמֵּת — It is obligatory to carry out the final wishes of a man about to die," and so he risked his life to do what had to be done.

[When R' Chezkel would retell this story years later he would describe how, on his way to Stutchin, he passed numerous captains, colonels and lieutenants of the Russian Army, yet miraculously not one said a word to him. It was as though he and the dead soldier were invisible!]

He walked as fast as his feet could carry him, trying to balance Mendel on his shoulders. Finally he reached Stutchin. Being a native of the city, he knew where to contact the *chevra kaddisha* (burial society). Assured that they would give the slain soldier proper ritualistic burial, he quickly gave them the body, and that evening he returned to the battlefront.

Within a few months Germany became victorious over Russia and thousands of Russian soldiers were captured, Chezkel among them. He was told that he would be serving in the army, but not as a soldier in battle. The Germans feared that Chezkel, as well as other members of the Russian army, would turn against the victors. Thus he was given a menial job — to watch the sheep in the meadow and report anything suspicious that he might observe.

Chezkel was warned numerous times that should he show even the slightest degree of disloyalty to the German army he would be subject to the death penalty.

For weeks he grazed the sheep and watched for movement in the distant hills, without incident. Then one afternoon he heard a shot ring out in the distance. He ran to where the noise came from and saw a German soldier lying on the ground, bleeding profusely from a gunshot wound. Try as he could to help the fallen soldier, the wound was too serious and Chezkel could not do enough to save him. Within minutes the soldier was dead.

As Chezkel was bending over the fallen soldier, some German officers came to see what had occurred. Their first reaction was to believe that the Russian shepherd had killed their fellow officer. Protest as he did that he was merely trying to give medical assistance, the officers grabbed Chezkel, handcuffed him and dragged him to the authorities, who immediately threw him into prison.

Throughout intense questioning and threats by the authorities all afternoon, Chezkel maintained his innocence, but the authorities would not believe him. At night they transferred Chezkel into a solitary confinement cell which was so narrow that he was able neither to lie down nor to sit up. It was a tall thin cell, barely large enough for a human being to stand upright in.

In sheer terror, Chezkel *davened Maariv* (evening prayers) in the dark confines of his cell. He had been given no opportunity to contact any of his relatives, and for all he knew he could be put to death without his family even being notified.

Chezkel had been told that he would be tried early in the morning. He was frightened and exhausted but could not get to sleep, for there was no position that he could find for himself which would be comfortable.

He tried to doze off even as he was standing. Time passed slowly until suddenly, in the cell where there was no room for anyone else, he saw before him the young Jewish soldier whom he had brought to *kever Yisrael* just a few months earlier. Chezkel was startled. Was this a dream? Was this really happening? Chezkel tried to move and respond to the presence that was before him, but he couldn't.

Suddenly the soldier was speaking to him. "Chezkel, I've come to tell you that you have nothing to worry about. You will be saved. They will threaten you and even take you to be killed, but don't worry — even if it seems impossible, you will be spared. You brought me to *kever Yisrael* at the risk of your own life. That *zechus* (merit) will stand by you." And with that he disappeared.

Chezkel opened his eyes but could see nothing in the darkness of his cell. He tried to get his bearings. Had he slept? Was it morning? Chezkel couldn't be sure whether what he thought happened had actually happened. It surely was a dream, but was it a real message or was his subconscious mind playing tricks on him? In a confused state, his mind swayed from elation as he felt reassured to despair as he feared that it was merely a hallucination.

After what seemed like hours, he was taken from the cell and brought to a makeshift courtroom. The prosecutor made his case, 'proving' beyond a shadow of a doubt that Chezkel 'the traitor' had killed the soldier in an act of treason. Using crooked logic, the prosecutor convinced the court that Chezkel, who was legally allowed to carry ammunition, had killed the soldier when he thought no one was looking. Chezkel had no one to speak on his behalf. Although he denied all accusations, his protests were to no avail.

He was found guilty and taken out to be shot by a firing squad. Five soldiers, cocked rifles on their shoulders, waited to receive their orders to fire. The commander in charge barked "One!," yelling it with gusto for all to hear. The gathered crowd of army personnel became hushed into stony silence. "Two!" the commander yelled. Chezkel, who was blindfolded, saw his parents, his home and family pass before his tightly shut eyes. He tried to say *Shema Yisrael*, but was too terrified to move his lips. He was going to the *Olam HaEmes* (the Eternal World of Truth) — at least that!

But suddenly there was a commotion as people began to yell. Chezkel became even more frightened and confused. As his eyes were covered, he had no idea what was going on. He did not see that a horseman was frantically charging towards the assembled crowd, waving a paper and screaming as he approached. "Hold the fire! Hold the fire!"

The soldiers of the firing squad lowered their rifles as they looked towards their commander for direction. The rider jumped off his horse, walked briskly up to the commander and announced, "They just found this note in the fallen soldier's pocket. In it he wrote that, in a state of depression, he was taking his own life." Then, pointing to Chezkel, the messenger said, "The man you have blindfolded there is innocent!"

And with that Chezkel was saved.

The way he had treated the dead kept him alive.

Part F:

Views and Perspectives

◆ A Prisoner's Decree

The Skulener *Rebbe,* R' Eliezer Zisya Portugal (1896-1982), was known throughout the world for his boundless *ahavas Yisrael* (love of a fellow Jew). He and his wife personally adopted close to 400 children after World War II and took care of their needs, both physical and spiritual. His Chessed L'Avraham organization, for the benefit of thousands who needed help at the time (and which, under the leadership and guidance of his son and successor, R' Yisroel Avraham Portugal, gives succor to emigrants from behind the Iron Curtain and from Iran), is a role model for other organizations involved in the same type of work.

The following story was heard from the *Rebbe* by R' Kalman Drebin of Brooklyn:

As a young man in Rumania, the *Rebbe* encouraged both young and old alike to come closer to belief in *Hashem.* He encouraged young men not to enter the Rumanian armed forces, for to do so would irrevocably tear them away from the paths of *Yiddishkeit.* Instead, he exhorted them to attend a yeshivah where they would be involved with Torah studies, a move which would assure them of remaining true to the traditions and heritage of their forefathers.

One day someone reported to the Rumanian authorities that a certain R' Portugal was instructing youths on how to avoid being drafted by the army. When the authorities checked into the matter, they found that the allegations were indeed true. In a fury, they arrested the *Rebbe* and had him imprisoned. The police put him into solitary confinement, took away his *yarmulke* and glasses and left him alone in a dark, dirty cell. The *Rebbe* was a frail, sickly man, and now in the cold and damp dungeon — where the only place he could sit or rest was on the chilly, moist earth — he thought that his end was near.

From the cell he had very little contact with the outside world, nor had he any idea how long he would be there. The authorities had threatened that they would leave him there forever. He wanted to *daven,* but he had no head covering, so he took the jacket that he was wearing, pulled it up over his head and began to sing aloud the prayers that he knew by heart.

It is known that the *Rebbe's Shacharis* could at times take up to four hours, and his recitation of *Shema* during a weekday *Maariv* could take up to twenty-five minutes; thus, on a regular basis he was always meticulous with every word of the prayers, and in this extraordinary situation he was even more so.

There in prison, with no other matters to claim his time or attention, he would recite the *Shacharis* service. Every word was uttered with heartfelt emotion, every phrase pronounced with piercing passion. The *Rebbe* came to the prayer of *Baruch She'amar*. This particular prayer begins with a series of phrases in which we bless various aspects of *Hashem*.

The *Rebbe* concentrated on each phrase as he never had before: "בָּרוּךְ שֶׁאָמַר וְהָיָה הָעוֹלָם — Blessed is He Who spoke, and the world came into being; בָּרוּךְ אוֹמֵר וְעֹשֶׂה — Blessed is He Who speaks and does; בָּרוּךְ גּוֹזֵר וּמְקַיֵּם — Blessed is He Who decrees and fulfills." As the *Rebbe* uttered this last phrase, a question occurred to him. Why was this particular phrase mentioned here? It seemed out of context with this whole prayer. For the term גּוֹזֵר, decrees, usually signifies an edict of a harsh nature, and not desirable to man. Moreover, we say that He not only makes decrees, but He even fulfills them! The *Rebbe* was puzzled, because all the other phrases in this prayer seem to describe positive aspects that man would rejoice over. For example, "בָּרוּךְ מְרַחֵם עַל הָאָרֶץ — Blessed is He Who has mercy on the earth; בָּרוּךְ מְשַׁלֵּם שָׂכָר טוֹב לִירֵאָיו — Blessed is He Who gives good reward to those who fear Him; בָּרוּךְ חַי לָעַד וְקַיָּם לָנֶצַח — Blessed is He Who lives forever," and so on. How does "גּוֹזֵר וּמְקַיֵּם — decrees and fulfills" — fit in here?

Suddenly the *Rebbe* became annoyed with himself. The question about the phrase belonging in this text was so obvious, why hadn't he thought about it before? For years and years he had been praying this prayer daily, and not once did the thought occur to him that גּוֹזֵר וּמְקַיֵּם seemed out of place. Why hadn't he thought about it before?

He became despondent, for he felt that perhaps until now he had not been praying with the proper focus on the words of the prayers he was saying every day. He said to himself, "I am not moving from this place until I figure out why that phrase is there."

He kept repeating the phrase, trying to force an answer into his head. And then, after a very long while, it came to him! He became ecstatic! He was simply overjoyed, because now he felt that he understood why גּוֹזֵר וּמְקַיֵּם actually did belong in this prayer.

The word קַיֵּם, aside from meaning fulfill, also means to exist and endure, prevail and persevere. And that is what is meant here, thought the *Rebbe*. Sometimes *Hashem* must decree something against man. He must make him suffer, for whatever reason *Hashem* deems it necessary. But at the same time, *Hashem* gives man the power and strength to endure and prevail, to enable him to come through this decree and withstand it. And that is what is meant in the expression גּוֹזֵר וּמְקַיֵּם.

The *Rebbe* realized that he himself, at that moment, was the victim of a decree. But he was positive from that moment on that he would also be a מְקַיֵּם, one who has endured the decree. He no longer was depressed. He was positive that it was only a matter of time until he would be saved, and indeed, within a few short days, at the intervention of people on the outside, the *Rebbe* was released by the Rumanian authorities.

The *Rebbe* was so touched by this episode that every year on the *yahrzeit* of his release from that prison he would recount this incident and explain to all his listeners the new and encouraging meaning he found in the words גּוֹזֵר וּמְקַיֵּם. He would thus impart to all who listened never to be broken by events, for *Hashem*, even in His decrees, gives strength to His people.

⊰§ *A Kernel of Truth*

R' Shmuel Salant (1838-1909), the *Rav* of Jerusalem for more than thirty years (from 1878 to 1909), was known not only for his brilliance in Torah scholarship, but for the very novel approach he had in solving difficult problems. The following episode is a case in point.

In Jerusalem, a young man was married just a few days before the *Pesach* holiday, and, following the custom of many families, he and his new wife went to spend *Yom Tov* in the home of her parents. In Israel, Jews celebrate only one *Pesach Seder* (unlike in the Diaspora, where they celebrate two), and so the level of anticipation before the first night of *Yom Tov* was especially high.

The tables in the home of his in-laws were beautifully set, and all were dressed in their *Yom Tov* best, including the *chassan* who wore his new *shtreimel* (rounded beaver hat, worn by many Chassidic and Yerushalmi Jews on *Shabbos* and holidays). The *Seder* began and everything progressed smoothly. The children recited the *Mah Nishtanah*, the *Haggadah* was read, and the *matzah* and *maror* (bitter herbs) were eaten. Finally the meal was served. However, as the new *chassan* was eating his soup, he suddenly noticed a wheat kernel floating in his plate.

He was shocked! A wheat kernel in hot soup — surely that was *chametz*, a most flagrant violation of the holiday! How could *chametz* be served in his mother-in-law's house? He had been under the impression that the family he was marrying into was strictly observant, and now it seemed they were lax.

He could not hide his displeasure, and soon others around him began wondering out loud how the wheat kernel had gotten into the soup. The mother-in-law herself was humiliated, for indeed she was extremely meticulous in her Passover preparations. How could *chametz* have gotten into the food she had prepared so carefully? Did that not make the rest of the food suspect?

The mood of the evening was shattered as everyone — especially the *chassan* — became disenchanted. The *Seder* continued and finally ended, and everyone left the table silent and subdued.

The next morning in *shul*, after the *davening* had been completed, R' Shmuel Salant innocently approached the father-in-law and asked cheerfully, "And so, how is the young couple?" The father-in-law could not mask his sullen face. His eyes told the *Rav* that something was amiss.

R' Shmuel approached the *chassan*. "How is the *Yom Tov* going for you?" he asked, waiting for some hint of reaction from the young man. The *chassan* looked down dejectedly and his feelings of disappointment were quite obvious. "Fine, fine," he answered unconvincingly.

"What's wrong?" asked R' Shmuel, addressing both the *chassan* and his father-in-law.

Within a few moments he heard the story of how, to the embarrassment of all, a wheat kernel — *chametz* — had been found in the *chassan's* soup. The *Rav* listened intently and then suddenly said, "Quickly, both of you, come out of the *shul* at once."

Together the *Rav* and the two men went outside. R' Shmuel asked that someone bring him a rag. The older man and his son-in-law looked at each other with surprise, as a rag was brought to the *Rav*. "Now give me your *shtreimel*," the *Rav* said to the young man.

R' Shmuel Salant then took the *shtreimel* and began rubbing the top of it vehemently with the rag. To the shock of those who had gathered around, two wheat kernels fell out of the top lining of the *shtreimel!*

As the kernels fell to the ground, R' Shmuel exclaimed, "It's exactly as I suspected. Last *Shabbos* at the *Aufruf* (when the *chassan* is called to the Torah reading before he gets married), the children all threw wheat kernels at you after you had your *aliyah*, and some of the kernels got stuck in your *shtreimel!*" (It was the custom in Jerusalem at the time to throw either wheat or barley kernels at the *chassan* during his *Aufruf* to symbolize the blessing of growth and prosperity. Today many throw sweet candies instead.)

R' Shmuel smiled and added, "And that is why your soup and no one else's had a wheat kernel. It fell from your *shtreimel!*"

When R' Sholom retells this incident, he smiles and says, "This teaches us, of course, that before you accuse anyone of having committed a wrong, you had better check your own *shtreimel* first! For the very transgression you are so sure another person caused may actually have been of your own doing."

◆§ *Signs of Distinction*

Who are we to judge others? What do we know of the experiences that others have lived through and not talked about? Can we say with certainty who is a *tzaddik* and who is not? Do we have the infinite wisdom it takes to see a man in his totality? In this powerful episode we get an insight of how great people view seemingly simple people. This incident was retold by R' Isaac Handler of Brooklyn.

The Satmar *Rebbe,* R' Yoel Teitelbaum (1887-1979), visited *Eretz Yisrael* in the late 1940's. He was followed wherever he went by his loyal *chassidim,* who cleaved to every word he uttered and scrutinized every move he made. Many in Israel sought his blessing and came to visit him every day.

R' Asher Zelig Margolis, a well-known *talmid chacham* and author of chassidic and kabbalistic *sefarim,* was one of those who followed the *Rebbe* throughout his sojourn in Israel. R' Margolis revered the *Rebbe* and was despondent when he realized that the *Rebbe* would soon be leaving the Holy Land for America.

"*Rebbe,*" R' Asher Zelig said to the Satmar *Rebbe,* "now that you will be leaving, to whom will we be able to give a *kvittel* (a note, given to a *rebbe,* which contains a personal request for a blessing)?"

The Satmar *Rebbe* looked at R' Asher Zelig and replied, "Go into any of the Jerusalem *shtieblach* (small synagogues) in the morning. If you see a man — bearded or not — and he is putting on *tefillin,* and under the *tefillin* on his arm you see numbers [that the Nazis tattooed onto the arms of those in the concentration camps] — such a man is worthy for you to give a *kvittel* to!"

◆§ *Of Tea and Tehillim*

Sometimes a short pithy comment is so classic as to have a meaning almost as broad as life itself. In this homey little incident, the beauty and warmth of a few simple words stand out remarkably.

On a recent Friday night in Jerusalem, R' Michoel Levy, a school principal from Brooklyn, went to visit R' Yisroel Grossman, the renowned *dayan*, at his home in the old Battei Varshaw section of Jerusalem. It was already quite late when R' Levy made his way up the rickety stairs to R' Yisroel's home, and R' Levy wondered if he might not be disturbing someone at this late hour.

However, as he entered the door he was enthusiastically greeted by both R' Yisroel and his wife, the *rebbetzin*. The men sat down at the table and the *rebbetzin* offered R' Levy a cup of tea. " Please don't bother. I just finished eating," he protested, but the *rebbetzin* insisted it would be no trouble.

Once again, R' Levy tried to dissuade her from preparing anything. The *rebbetzin* looked at her visitor and said in a motherly manner, in Yiddish, "There are two things that can never hurt a *Yid*. *Ah glezeleh tay* (a glass of tea) *und a kapital Tehillim* (and the recitation of a chapter of *Psalms*)." She paused for a moment and then added, softly and with emphasis, *"Uber baida darfen zain varehm!* (But both have to be warm!)"

Warmth and enthusiasm enhance everything we do. The lesson of the hot tea and the passionate *Tehillim* is that to be effective, one must be vibrant. The lukewarm and the lifeless usually are left standing by the wayside.

◆§ *The Potential of the Poor*

R' Yitzchok Hutner (1904-1980), the *Rosh Yeshivah* of Yeshivas Chaim Berlin, once told the following story to R' Aharon Kotler (1891-1962). R' Aharon, who was the recognized *gadol* of his era and founder of the Beth Medrash Govoha in Lakewood, New Jersey, found the story so moving that it literally brought him to tears.

R' Hutner relished repeating this inspirational incident, for it was characteristic of the insight and perception of another *gadol* of a previous era, the Brisker *Rav*, R' Yehoshua Leib Diskin (1817-1898).

In Europe, many years ago, a man was looking for a *shidduch* (partner in marriage) for his daughter. A certain *bachur* was suggested as a suitable match, but after making some inquiries the prospective father-in-law was having serious doubts about him. The young man in question indeed had a reputation as being very pious and sincere, and was known for his exceptional *hasmadah* (diligence in Torah study). However, it was also known that he didn't possess a very sharp mind and that his comprehension of Torah matters was certainly not outstanding.

The father of the girl was in a quandary, for he wanted only the very best *bachur* for his daughter and this fellow seemed to be lacking in superior abilities. He decided to seek the counsel of the Brisker *Rav*, R' Yehoshua Leib, and thus he traveled to meet him.

He explained the situation to the *Rav* who listened patiently to the troubled man. When he had finished, the *Rav* said thoughtfully, "Let me tell you a teaching of *Chazal*. It is mentioned in *Avos* 4:11: 'כָּל הַמְקַיֵּם אֶת הַתּוֹרָה מֵעֹנִי סוֹפוֹ לְקַיְּמָהּ מֵעֹשֶׁר — Whoever fulfills the Torah despite poverty, will ultimately fulfill it (Torah) in wealth.' It is my understanding," said the *Rav*, "that this Talmudic teaching refers not only to money but to talent and ability as well. Let me explain."

The Brisker *Rav* went on. "The assurance of our *Chazal* that lies in this teaching must be interpreted broadly. Just as we are guaranteed that those who uphold Torah and *mitzvos*, even though they are poor and lack financial means, will eventually attain affluence so that they will then be able to uphold the Torah from a position of wealth, in the very same way those who are diligent in their studies and keep at them even though they lack great depth of understanding — and thus could be considered poor in this respect — are also assured of 'wealth,' they will attain great heights in Torah. Thus, if the young man in question is indeed diligent in his learning and sincere in his performance of *mitzvos*, even though he may be 'poor' due to his lack of exceptional comprehension at this moment, in time he will surely attain 'wealth' — in this case, superior comprehension — and achieve prominence in Torah. I therefore suggest," concluded the *Rav,* "that you agree to the *shidduch* because this young man will someday achieve the eminence in Torah that you are looking for."

Listening to the *Rav* expound on the *mishnah* and its new application, the gentleman now saw matters from a different perspective. He agreed to the marriage of the young man to his daughter. The *chassan* eventually became the world-renowned Aishishoker *Rav,* R' Yosef Zundel, a scholar who authored many *sefarim* on *Shulchan Aruch,* including the noted *Chedrei Deah.*

The lesson of this incident seems beautifully obvious. It's not always those who possess natural talents who reach the pinnacle of achievement, but rather those who are diligent. For as the diligent pursue their goals, they acquire along the way the necessary faculties to attain their sought-after success.

"But the question is," asked R' Hutner, "what was it that made R' Aharon cry when he heard this story? I believe," he answered, "there is an element of *siyata d'shmaya* (Divine assistance) bestowed on someone who is intensely involved in the battle to overcome his 'poverty' in Torah so as to achieve 'wealth' in Torah. R' Aharon was born with the G-d-given gift of genius and brilliance and thus never had this struggle, so he was never the beneficiary of this aspect of *siyata d'shmaya*. For R' Aharon not to be the recipient of any aspect of *siyata d'shmaya* in Torah, regardless of the reason, was in his mind indeed something to cry about."

◆§ An Act of Shame

In the winter of 1939, the economic situation of Yeshivah Rabbeinu Yisroel Meyer HaKohen (Chofetz Chaim) in Brooklyn was critical. America was still trying to come out of the Depression, and with the financial flourish that would accompany World War II still two years away, Yeshivah Chofetz Chaim, like other yeshivos in America, found itself struggling for survival.

The yeshivah couldn't pay its coal bill, and the *bachurim* (young boys) learning in the yeshivah's building on South 9th Street in the Williamsburg section of Brooklyn were so cold that they sat in the *beis midrash* with their coats on. To keep warm, a few boys at a time would go downstairs to learn in the dining area adjacent to the kitchen, taking turns, so that they could absorb some of the steam emanating from the large pot of soup being cooked for lunch.

To try and alleviate some of the yeshivah's financial problems, R' Dovid Leibowitz (1890-1941), its *Rosh Yeshivah* and founder, undertook to make a trip to Miami where he made appointments to meet with some wealthy people whom, he thought, would be able to help the yeshivah in its plight. Accompanying him was one of his beloved *talmidim*, R' Abba Zalka Gewirtz.

The long train ride, which was to take from Wednesday night until Friday morning, was not all that comfortable for they could not even afford accommodations in a Pullman car which provided sleeping berths. Thus, throughout the trip, they had to get whatever rest they could while sitting erect.

Finally they arrived in Miami. They came to town with great anticipation, hoping to be able to get the yeshivah on a solid financial footing. They made their way to the home of a prominent person in the community, on whom they thought they could rely for assistance. They arrived just at the appointed time, knocked on the door, and were greeted by their host with something less than enthusiasm. R' Dovid tried to explain that they had just come from New York on an important mission to save their yeshivah from going under. But the man had very little time or patience for them. He told them to leave at once as he had no desire to hear their story.

R' Dovid, in his ever-gracious manner, thanked the man for his time, but the young *talmid* Abba Zalka was incensed.

As they made their way out onto the sunny, tree-lined street, Abba Zalka said to his *rebbe,* "That was a terrible way to treat you. Where is *kavod haTorah?*"

R' Dovid sighed and smiled. "You are mistaken," he said lovingly to his *talmid.* "The man gave us a great honor."

"Honor?" the surprised *talmid* asked. "He hardly gave us the time of day, and he certainly didn't act with respect."

"Let me explain," said R' Dovid. "The prophet Yechezkel (Ezekiel) was known as יְחֶזְקֵאל בֶּן בּוּזִי — Yechezkel ben (son of) Buzi (*Yechezkel* 1:3). *Chazal* say (see *Vayikra Rabbah* 2:8) that *Buzi* was actually a title for the family of Yechezkel. בּוּזִי, coming from the word בוז — meaning 'shame' — signified that this family was willing to suffer shame and embarrassment as long as they were doing anything that would honor or glorify *Hashem* and his Torah. But why would the verse ascribe to a noble family a title which connotes forever disgrace and contempt?

"The answer is," continued R' Dovid, "that *Chazal* are telling us that it is an honor to be abused or mistreated for the sake of Torah. It is indeed proper and fitting for people to be remembered that way, for it depicts the exalted life they lived.

"Thus this man's action now makes us part of an exclusive group to which we should be proud to belong. We are from Yechezkel ben Buzi's people! And all because we came here for *kavod Shamayim* (honor of *Hashem* in Heaven)."

Perhaps those who have had the opportunity to raise funds, even for a most charitable cause, will find solace in this story. Scorn and abuse are often, unfortunately, part of the burden one must bear in the field of fundraising. R' Dovid Leibowitz taught that when involved with a noteworthy Torah cause, one should not swallow humiliation and disappointment while in the service of *Hashem* as if they are bitter pills. Rather one should wear them as badges of honor, similar to the way the Buzi family was commemorated forever.

⁂ Truth on the Line

The *Sefer Daniel* states, "יָהֵב חָכְמְתָא לְחַכִּימִין — [*Hashem*] gives wisdom to the wise" (*Daniel* 2:21). The obvious question is: Why give wisdom to the wise? It would seem that it is the foolish who really need it. The answer is: Only the wise know how to utilize their wisdom properly (see *Midrash Rabbah* 1:7:5). The following story, which reminds one of Shlomo *HaMelech's* wisdom, is a case in point.

R' Eliyahu Chaim Meisel, the Lodzer *Rav* (d. 1912), was once confronted by two hysterical women who came to his home to seek a settlement of their argument.

The two women shared the same clothesline on which they hung their laundry out to dry. The line was stretched across a courtyard, from a hook outside one woman's window to a second hook outside the other woman's window. The two would normally take turns using the line, but this time there seemed to have been some confusion, and both women were claiming ownership of the laundry which had been hung out to dry.

Unable to resolve their argument, they decided to bring the whole load of laundry to the home of the *rav*, and let him determine its ownership.

R' Eliyahu Chaim listened to the arguments of both women, as each claimed with certainty that she was right. After listening carefully, he instructed the women to leave the laundry on his table in a huge pile and go out of the room. He then called in his own wife, the *rebbetzin*.

"Do me a favor," he requested her, "and please bring in a large batch of our laundry. First mark each item in a secret way so that the mark is not easily discernible, and then mix all of it together with the laundry that is on the table."

The *rebbetzin* did as her husband requested, and brought in a recently dried load of laundry, which she marked carefully. She showed the *rav* exactly where every item was marked and then she mixed her laundry together with the pile of laundry that already was on the *rav's* table. The *rebbetzin* left the room through one door and the *rav* called in one of the two women who had been waiting outside a second door.

"Please select from this pile the laundry that is yours," the *rav* said. Carefully and diligently the woman picked out a shirt from this side, a sock from the second side, making sure to choose only those items she was positive were hers. She continued to select a good deal of what was on the table, but not one item that belonged to the *rebbetzin.* The *rav* told her to put everything back into the pile and mix it all up again. Then he called in the second woman.

The *rav* told her, as well, to choose the laundry that was hers. As she picked up each item she announced in a defiant tone that it was unquestionably hers. She went through the entire bundle of laundry, exclaiming that each article — even those put in by the *rebbetzin* — was hers. The *rav* realized that this was the woman who had been lying, for she was taking items that were definitely not hers.

He then called back the first woman and told her to select once again what was hers. The *rebbetzin* then came in and took the marked laundry that was her own. And the lying woman was finally left with what was really hers — a very small amount of the laundry.

◆§ *A Poor Man's Bell*

At a *bar mitzvah* celebration, R' Moshe Chodosh, the *Rosh Yeshivah* of Yeshivas Ohr Elchonon in Jerusalem, retold the following parable from the Dubno *Maggid,* R' Yaakov Krantz (1740-1804).

The parable illustrates beautifully how one cannot simply view things superficially. There is usually more than what meets the eye, and it is the intelligent person who seeks to understand all aspects of life in more depth.

A certain poor fellow, R' Yonah, was invited to a meal at a wealthy man's house. When he entered the mansion, R' Yonah was overwhelmed by the opulence he beheld — such magnificent wall hangings, such gorgeous furniture, such bright chandeliers. Soon he was ushered into a large splendid dining room. First, everyone munched on various delicacies already on the table, and then the first course was served.

When all the diners were finished with their portions the rich man, who was seated at the head of the table, tinkled a bell that stood to the right of his place setting. Almost at once waiters came in to remove the dishes and bring in the next course. R' Yonah was amazed. He had never seen a bell like that before.

After the second course was completed, the host again tinkled the bell, and again the waiters came in swiftly to remove the dishes and bring in yet more food. R' Yonah was immensely impressed. He decided he would have to get one of those bells for his home as well.

When the meal was finally over and everyone had left the dining room, R' Yonah quickly walked to the head of the table to take a close-up look at what the bell was made of. It was a simple metal bell with a wooden handle. R' Yonah decided he would buy an even fancier bell for himself. He would get one of silver plate.

The next day he purchased a silver-plated bell and ran home excitedly to his wife and children. "Our days of hunger are over!" he exclaimed happily. "Wait until you see what I brought home! We won't be starving any longer."

He immediately placed the bell on the table and told his family to take their regular seats. He then tinkled the bell with conviction. He waited for the waiter to walk in — but nothing happened! He shook it again, and still no one responded. "I can't understand it!" he muttered angrily. "When the rich man tinkled his bell, all that food was served — and here nothing is happening!"

The distraught man returned the bell to the store where he had purchased it. "This bell you sold me is useless. I got no response when I rang it."

❦ ❦ ❦

"The obvious reason nothing happened," said the Dubno *Maggid*, "is because there is neither a waiter nor food in the poor man's house. The bell works to summon someone or something that is there to be summoned. Much preparation is necessary before the bell can accomplish anything."

"In some ways many of us are like this poor man," continued the Dubno *Maggid*. "For example, the Torah (*Bamidbar* 15:39) tells us — and we recite it in the *Shema* every day — that we should look at our *tzitzis* so that we will be reminded of our obligations to perform all of *Hashem's mitzvos*.

"There are many people, though, who can look at a pair of *tzitzis* and not be reminded of anything. On the surface all they see are strands of wool hanging from a four-cornered cloth. It is only if one is learned and understands how the *tzitzis* represent the 613 *mitzvos*, and one has studied what the 613 *mitzvos* are, that he can appreciate what his viewing of *tzitzis* should accomplish. Merely to look at them without any preparation — with no studying ahead of time — is like pressing the bell without having arranged for anyone to respond."

R' Chodosh added, "This same idea of preparation is true regarding every Jewish boy who becomes thirteen years old. Simply reaching the age of *bar mitzvah* does not give a boy an understanding as to what his Torah obligations are. Only if parents and teachers prepare a child in depth, properly, before he is recognized by *halachah* as an adult, will his life have any true religious significance afterwards.

"Otherwise," said R' Chodosh, "the boy's new birthday is merely a noisy bell heralding just another day of his life."

◆§ *View from the Top*

When the first *Rebbe* of Ger, the *Chidushei HaRim*, R' Yitzchak Mayer Alter (1789-1866), was very ill and realized that he was nearing the end of his life, he summoned his young grandson,*

* The *Chidushei HaRim's* son R' Avraham Mordechai would have become *Rebbe* at his father's passing. However, he passed away at a young age during his father's lifetime. His son Aryeh Leib was just twelve years old at the time. From then on, the *Chidushei HaRim* raised his grandson.

R' Yehudah Aryeh Leib Alter (1847-1903), later to be known as the *Sfas Emes*, to his private room. The elderly *Rebbe* informed the young man that he was to become the next *Rebbe* of Ger.

R' Yehudah Aryeh Leib, who was barely nineteen at the time, became very frightened. "How can I ever replace you?" he said to his ailing grandfather. "You are a *talmid chacham* of world repute. All the *chassidim* love you, admire you, and have followed you. How can I even consider myself as your replacement? How can I ever reach your spiritual heights?"

The *Chidushei HaRim* peered at his grandson with fatherly concern and understanding. "Let me tell you a story," he said. "There was once a man who wished to climb a very high and steep mountain. For weeks and weeks he struggled to get to the top, and finally, after making a great effort and enduring tremendous hardship and pain, he reached the summit. He was exhilarated. He had accomplished what he had set out to do, and he felt quite positive that very few people, if any, would have been willing to go through what he had gone through to get to the top.

"As he was walking around on the mountain's peak, he was astonished to hear voices nearby. He ran to see where the voices were coming from, and soon he saw a group of people. 'How did you people get up here?' he asked in amazement.

" 'You are not the only one who worked so hard to get up here,' they told him. 'Others before you have also done the same. Indeed, there are but a few of us, but we did survive the struggle. If you wish, you can join us here.'

"The surprised climber looked at the group before him, and when his eyes fell upon a young boy he was astounded. He turned to the child and said in amazement, 'How did you get up here? Did you climb all the way up as well?'

" 'No,' said the boy softly, 'I didn't. I was born up here.' "

A child on the mountain begins life with a higher perspective than even a giant in the valley. Thus, by virtue of the fact that R' Yehudah Aryeh Leib was born and reared in the homes of his illustrious father and grandfather, he acquired traits of prominence and distinction and he became fit, in the eyes of his grandfather, to be the next *Rebbe.*

In our lives as well, if one is blessed with the good fortune to live in a neighborhood where observance of *Yiddishkeit* is no problem and where getting kosher food is no hassle, he has the obligation to live his life by maintaining the loftiest Torah standards. For if one, by the grace of *Hashem,* received the privilege of being born 'on top of the mountain,' he also has the responsibility to achieve goals that tower over those of people with lesser opportunities.

Count Down

It is said that when the *Sfas Emes,* R' Yehudah Aryeh Leib Alter (1847-1903), passed away, and his children were returning from the cemetery, the oldest son, R' Avrohom Mordechai (1866-1948; who succeeded his father as the next Gerrer *Rebbe*), turned to his younger brother and said, "*Baruch Hashem* (thank G-d), our father merited to have אֲרִיכַת יָמִים, *arichas yamim* (longevity)."

A younger brother, surprised by this remark, replied, "Actually, our father didn't live to an old age at all! He was merely fifty-six years old and one can hardly consider that longevity."

R' Avrohom Mordechai cast his eyes heavenward and replied, "It's true that he didn't have אֲרִיכַת שָׁנִים (lit., long years) but he definitely had אֲרִיכַת יָמִים (lit., long days)."

No one can be guaranteed אֲרִיכַת שָׁנִים, long (and numerous) years, but everyone, by using their time wisely — by being involved primarily with important rather than insignificant matters — can assure themselves אֲרִיכַת יָמִים (long and productive days).

As R' Berel Wein, *Rosh Yeshivah* of Yeshivah Shaarei Torah of Rockland County, once remarked in reference to *Sefiras Haomer,* during which we fulfill the Biblical commandment to count the days from *Pesach* to *Shavuos,* "A Jew must not merely count (his) days, but rather make his days count."

What Noise?

The Netziv, R' Naftali Tzvi Yehudah Berlin (1817-1893), the *Rosh Yeshivah* of the Volozhiner yeshivah, loved each of his *talmidim* as a father loves a child. Every student's personal concerns were his concerns. He worried and fretted about their health and eating habits as much as he cared about their accomplishments in learning.

During one particular *zman* (semester) there was a terrible fire in the yeshivah and a good part of the *beis midrash* was rendered unusable. Many of the *talmidim* needed a place to study, and so the Netziv himself offered that the top floor of his home be converted into a temporary *beis midrash.*

The din caused by the studying of the *talmidim* was constant. Many of the yeshivah's *masmidim* (diligent students) would study late into the night, while others would get up very early to begin their studies even before *Shacharis.*

One evening a man from a nearby town came to visit the Netziv. As he entered the *rav's* home, he was struck by the constant noise coming from the floor above him. The blend of booming voices coming from *talmidim* intensely debating with each other or singing aloud as they studied seemed to him almost deafening.

"*Rebbe,*" he said, "how can you sleep at night with all that noise going on?" The Netziv smiled at the man as he replied, "There was once a man who owned a wheat-grinding mill. He lived next door to his plant, and day and night he could hear the constant banging and clattering of the machinery in his place of business. As long as he could hear that noise in the background he was able to go on with his regular activities. If ever the noise stopped he would become frantic, because that meant the process of his business had shut down.

"My role in life," continued the Netziv, "is to see to it that these boys have a place to learn and that their Torah studies continue constantly. It is only when I hear their learning that I can rest peacefully. To me that is not noise — it is music to my ears!"

The Netziv, then, was like a father who, without paying specific attention, hears his child playing and chattering in the background. Only when it becomes suddenly quiet does the concerned father begin to worry.

◈§ *Struggles*

When one of Iyov's friends, Eliphaz HaTeimani, tried to console Iyov about the difficult situation of poverty and suffering that had befallen him, Eliphaz said, "כִּי אָדָם לְעָמָל יוּלָּד – Man, though, is born to toil" (*Iyov* 5:7). The Talmud (*Sanhedrin* 99b) on this verse notes that although it is inevitable that man must labor in this world, fortunate is the one who can [fulfill his obligation of] labor by his diligent study of Torah.

In this touching incident involving two Torah luminaries, R' Shimon Shkop (1860-1939) and the Netziv, R' Naftali Tzvi Yehudah Berlin (1817-1893), we get a rare glimpse of the intense emotional involvement they had with their Torah studies. Their עֲמֵלוּת בַּתּוֹרָה (toil in Torah) becomes obvious.

This incident, retold by R' Avrohom Shkop of Brooklyn, grandson of R' Shimon, happened when R' Shimon was but a young *bachur* studying in the yeshivah in Volozhin. (R' Shimon was later to become the noted *Rosh Yeshivah* of the yeshivah in Grodno, Poland, and author of the well-known work, *She'or Yoshov.*)

The Volozhiner yeshivah, under the direction of its *Rosh Yeshivah*, the Netziv, had instituted a rotation system so that there would be some students learning in the *beis midrash* at all hours of the day and night. Thus, one could walk into the main study hall at even two or three o'clock in the morning and find a group of boys learning there, and this group would be relieved by yet another group a few hours later.

The Netziv, who considered the voices of boys learning Torah to be music to his ears, took particular pleasure in walking into the *beis midrash* well past midnight and observing his *talmidim* studying diligently.

On one such late night he was walking in the *beis midrash* when he noticed the young boy Shimon crying to himself. Knowing that this child came from an extremely poor family, he approached the boy and said softly, "Are you missing anything, my child?"

"No," replied the boy, looking up with tear-filled eyes. "I have what I need."

"Then why are you crying so?" asked the Netziv with concern.

The boy looked down at his *Gemara* and said, with obvious shame and disappointment, "I have been trying to figure out this *Rashbam* for a few hours already, and I just can't seem to understand it."

The Netziv looked down at the *Gemara* and said to the boy, "Let me see which *Rashbam* you are referring to." (According to R' Zelig Epstein, *Rosh Yeshivah* of Yeshivah Shaar HaTorah, it was the *Rashbam* in *Bava Basra* 29b, ד"ה אנא בשכוני.)

The saintly *Rosh Yeshivah* lifted his eyes from the *Gemara* and turned to the boy. He smiled at him, placed his hands on the young student's forehead and kissed him. "My child," he began, "may *Hashem* bless you. I myself had such trouble with this very *Rashbam* that I went to the *kever* (gravesite) of R' Chaim Volozhiner numerous times and prayed to G-d that He grant me wisdom in understanding this troublesome *Rashbam!*"

"This one little story," said R' Avrohom Shkop, "illuminates simultaneously so much about my grandfather R' Shimon, about the Netziv and about the level of Torah study in Volozhin."

◈ *Public Eye or Private I?*

R' Avrohom Kabalkin, a noted Torah scholar and author in Jerusalem, told the following story during a lecture on the conflict regarding the responsibility one has to himself versus the responsibility he has to others.

A group of people once came to the Chofetz Chaim's yeshivah in Radin to select, from among the students, a *Rosh Yeshivah* for a yeshivah in their own home town. They had done their research before their trip and so, once they reached the Chofetz Chaim's *beis midrash,* they went directly to the candidate they deemed most qualified, an established *talmid chacham* with an impeccable reputation.

However, when they offered the man the position of *Rosh Yeshivah,* he respectfully declined it. He explained that he still wanted to grow in learning and thus could not leave the confines of the *beis midrash.*

Naturally the people were disappointed, and so they made their way to the Chofetz Chaim himself to tell him what had transpired. After listening to what they had to say, the Chofetz Chaim asked that someone get a message to the young man saying that he wished to see him.

When they were alone, the Chofetz Chaim told the young man the following parable.

> There once was a shoemaker who was an exceptional craftsman. Every pair of shoes he made was exquisite in detail. It took him weeks to complete just one pair, and the price he charged for a pair was one hundred rubles. Understandably, because making these shoes was so time consuming, he could only produce a limited number of pairs a year, and these were the only type he made.
>
> One day a representative of a large shoe company approached him with an offer. He said that the company wanted to hire the shoemaker to make shoes for them, and if he accepted he would be able to produce hundreds of pairs of shoes a year. The shoemaker was surprised by the promise that his output would increase so dramatically, but he had a question. "How much would each pair sell for?" he asked.
>
> "Ten rubles," came the reply.
>
> "I can't do that," the shoemaker said. "The shoes I make sell for one hundred rubles. Look at the difference!"

"But sir," the representative retorted, "you make just a few pairs of shoes a year, which sell for a sum total of maybe one thousand rubles. If, however, you make the shoes we suggest, you might be getting only ten rubles a pair — but in the end you will have made five thousand rubles!"

"So it is with you," said the Chofetz Chaim. "It's true that your own learning will be enhanced if you continue here in the *beis midrash*. However, if you accept the position of *Rosh Yeshivah* you will enhance the learning of countless *talmidim*. Although it may be on a lower level than that which you are capable of, in the long run the sum total of all that the *talmidim* may accomplish because of you will be much more profitable . . . even for you."

☙ *Rebuke and Remorse*

A man's personality is a blend of his temperament and disposition. Most people have within themselves the positive capacities to be cheerful, respectful or charitable, as well as the ability to show concern, compassion or humility when these characteristics are called for. How rare, though, is the individual with the inner strength and courage to readily admit guilt when he realizes he had been wrong! How unusual is the person with the stamina to remain silent when he is criticized unduly! The Talmud (*Yoma* 23a) has only the highest praises for those of such noble character. In this touching story, retold by R' Sholom Schwadron of Jerusalem, we see these remarkable elements of character in all parties involved.

The Kalisher *Rav*, R' Meir Auerbach (1815-1878), the author of *Imrei Binah*, lived in the Old City of Jerusalem. Above his home was the *shul* of which he was the *Rav*. One afternoon R' Auerbach heard very loud rumbling noises coming from upstairs. He surmised that children were probably running around in the *beis midrash*, and this disturbed him.

He thought that they might settle down after a while, but the noise only got worse. Soon he heard a tremendous clatter as a heavy wooden table overturned and crashed to the floor. This frightened the *Rav,* and he ran upstairs to see what had happened. The children heard him climbing up the creaky stairs and ran to hide from his rebuke and wrath.

One young boy named Chaim (the son of R' Zalman, see "A Little Boy's Esrog"), who had nothing to do with the others, had been sitting and learning by himself. He was so absorbed in his studies that he didn't realize that the troublemakers had scampered out. When the Kalisher *Rav* finally made it into the *beis midrash,* the only child he saw was Chaim, looking perfectly innocent.

"You can't fool me by sitting there and appearing so blameless!" the *Rav* stormed. "What do you and your friends think this is? A playground? You have no *derech eretz* (respect) for a holy place!" On and on the *Rav* continued, warning Chaim that he wouldn't allow either him or the others to come back if they ever again behaved in this manner.

Chaim sat silently, listening respectfully and not answering a word. The other children, meanwhile, who were hiding nearby, heard everything that was going on. When the *Rav* went back downstairs into his house, the other children came out of hiding and went down to the Kalisher *Rav.*

They knocked on his door and asked if they could talk to him for a moment. Surprised by their sudden appearance, he let them in. "We have a confession to make," one of them said. "It was we who knocked over the table upstairs. By mistake you scolded the wrong boy. We all went to hide when we heard you coming, but that boy Chaim was sitting and learning the whole time that we were running around up there. It was our fault, not his."

[At this point R' Sholom sighs and says, "Look at the children of years ago!"]

The *Rav* was amazed at their integrity and he immediately went upstairs, hoping the child was still there. When he saw that Chaim was indeed still sitting by the *Gemara* he bent over the young boy, kissed him on the forehead and said softly, "Please forgive me. The children just told me that you had nothing to do with them. I am sorry that I scolded you. I apologize." The *Rav* paused for a moment and then said, "But I must ask you, why didn't you say anything to me when you realized that I was criticizing you for no reason?"

Chaim looked up at the *Rav* and said respectfully, "It says in *Tehillim* (69:13), 'יָשִׂיחוּ בִי יֹשְׁבֵי שָׁעַר' — They gossip about me, those [drunkards] who sit by the gate.' David *HaMelech* was upset," the boy explained, "because unscrupulous people were criticizing him for no reason. But if the revered Kalisher *Rav* criticized me, then even if I didn't deserve his rebuke for this reason then I surely must have deserved it for something else."

"May *Hashem* bless you," said the Kalisher *Rav*, as he kissed the child once again.

The *Rav* never forgot the boy, and for years he always inquired as to his whereabouts and doings. Years later when Chaim married, the Kalisher *Rav*, who was a man of considerable wealth, came to his home and gave him a bag containing a small fortune. "I have been waiting for years to give you this gift," the *Rav* said. "I want you to be able to continue your Torah studies without any hindrances. May G-d bless you with all that is good."

Truly Extraordinary

The following story was told by R' Avrohom Respler, principal of Yeshivah Toras Emes, Brooklyn, N.Y., at a *Melaveh Malkah* honoring members of Hatzoloh, the dedicated group of men who provide emergency medical services in many communities.

The Ostrovtzer *Rebbe*, R' Meir Yechiel Halevi (1852-1928), was known for his brilliance in Torah knowledge and, specifically, for the phenomenal mathematical computations he came up with that gave insight into segments of the *Chumash* and *Talmud*. (Many of them are recorded in his *sefer*, *Meir Einei Chachamim*.)

One day R' Chaim Ozer Grodzinsky (1863-1939), the *Rav* of Vilna and *gadol hador*, met R' Meir Yechiel. "Tell me *a gut vort* (lit., a good word — Torah insight)," R' Chaim Ozer asked of the *Rebbe*.

R' Meir Yechiel, who was very humble, declined, saying that he didn't feel he had anything worthwhile to repeat. R' Chaim Ozer, who was aware of R' Meir Yechiel's sparkling knowledge, insisted that the *Rebbe* tell him something — anything — and so the *Rebbe*, in deference to R' Chaim Ozer, repeated a Torah thought which he had originated.

R' Chaim Ozer was astounded at what he heard and proclaimed, "You are truly a *gavra rabbah* (an extraordinary individual)."

"Oh no," insisted the *Rebbe*. "I am certainly not one who can be called a *gavra rabbah*."

"If not you," retorted R' Chaim Ozer, "then who does deserve that title?"

"Those who relieve the burdens of fellow Jews," answered the *Rebbe*. "And let me show proof," he added.

"You see, the Talmud (*Makkos* 22b) states, 'There are certain people who are so silly. They stand up to honor a *Sefer Torah* when it passes by, but they don't stand up for a *gavra rabbah* that passes by.' " The *Rebbe* then asked, "But just who is a *gavra rabbah?* The Talmud itself answers the question," he continued.

"A *gavra rabbah* [is one like] the *Chazal* who had the authority to proclaim that when the Torah stated (*Devarim* 25:3) that a man should get forty lashes for violating a Biblical prohibition, what was actually meant was that he should get thirty-nine (see *Gur Aryeh*, ibid.). Now," continued the *Rebbe*, "if the Talmud meant that a *gavra rabbah* was merely one who could change what it seemingly says in the Torah (modifying forty lashes to thirty-nine), then the Talmud could have used proof from a different source. Regarding *Sefiras HaOmer*, the Torah states (*Vayikra* 23:16) that fifty days should be counted. Yet *Chazal* went ahead and said that one counts only forty-nine. But the Talmud did not deem that a proof as to who is to be called a *gavra rabbah*. Why not?"

The *Rebbe* smiled and answered the question himself. "You see, one who changes a count of fifty days to a count of forty-nine days is merely making a fine Talmudic deduction, a nice *pshat* (learned thought). But one who minimizes the pain and suffering of a fellow

Jew by modifying forty lashes to thirty-nine, so that he doesn't get smitten that one extra blow, that indeed is a *gavra rabbah*.

"Thus," said the Ostrovtzer *Rebbe* to R' Chaim Ozer, "you, and not I, are the one who is truly a *gavra rabbah*, for by virtue of the fact that you collect such phenomenal amounts of money and dispense it to orphans and widows, you relieve their burdens and pain, thus meriting that exalted title of *gavra rabbah*."

"This," said R' Respler aptly, "applies as well to the dedicated people of Hatzoloh and any others who minimize the suffering of Jews. They are truly in the category of *gavra rabbah*."

◆§ *Waters of Purity*

The last *mishnah* in *Yoma* (8:9) is well known. In it, R' Akiva explains how fortunate the Jewish people are, for it is *Hashem* alone, our Father in Heaven, who purifies them although they have sinned.

The *mishnah* cites two verses supporting this premise. The first, taken from *Yechezkel* (36:25), states, "וְזָרַקְתִּי עֲלֵיכֶם מַיִם טְהוֹרִים וּטְהַרְתֶּם — And I [*Hashem*] will sprinkle pure water on you, that you may be cleansed." The *mishnah* then cites another verse, this one from *Yirmiyahu* (17:13), "מִקְוֵה יִשְׂרָאֵל ה׳ — The *Mikveh* of Israel is *Hashem*." R' Akiva explains, "Just as a *mikveh* purifies those who have become defiled, so too will *Hashem* purify the Jewish nation."

R' Yaakov Galinsky once posed the following question: "The second verse, with its reference to *Hashem* as though He Himself were the *mikveh* purifying Israel, seems so encompassing and brings across the point so well, why was it necessary for R' Akiva to quote the other verse with regard to *Hashem's* sprinkling pure water?"

R' Galinsky answered his own question with a thoughtful

parable. "It is similar," he said, "to two patients who share a room in a hospital. Both are suffering from the same severe illness: both are bedridden and must take medication to survive. The future looks bleak for each of them. However, there is one major difference between the two. The first patient can at least reach out for his pills lying on the tray in front of him, and extend his hand for the cup of water which will help him swallow the pills. The second patient, though, is so weak that he has no strength to even get his own medication. He is totally dependent on others to administer his medicine. And if indeed no one arrives to assist him, his end will surely come.

"And that is what R' Akiva is teaching," said R' Galinsky. "There are two types of repentant Jews. The first kind — those who repent on their own volition — come, so to speak, to the *mikveh* to be purified. Regarding them, the *mishnah* cites the verse, "The *Mikveh* of Israel is *Hashem*. However, there are certain Jews who have, unfortunately, strayed so far from the true paths of *Yiddishkeit* that it seems almost futile to hope that they will return. In those instances, though, *Hashem* does not wait for a man to come to the *mikveh* to be purified, but rather *Hashem* 'goes out' to the individual and 'sprinkles pure water' on the defiled Jew, so that he may be purified and return to the fold.

"How lucky indeed are the Jewish people," R' Galinsky continued, "that *Hashem* does not forsake them. Even when some of them are rebelling against Him and not looking to be purified, *Hashem*, in His mercy, sprinkles water on them [with an unexpected incident or a sudden occurrence that awakens them from their spiritual slumber] so that they may return to Him."

Thus the occurrence of an extraordinary event in which one becomes aware of *Hashem's* greatness is merely a "sprinkling of water" to make sure one's *emunah* (faith) blossoms and grows.

The Whole Picture

Many people habitually jump to conclusions. They are under the erroneous impression that within a very short period of time they can grasp and evaluate a situation entirely. The Chofetz Chaim (R' Yisroel Meir HaKohen, 1838-1933) used a whimsical little parable to illustrate this flawed way of thinking.

A traveling businessman once stayed for a *Shabbos* in a small village far away from his home town. Curious as to who was who in the town, he made some inquiries and was informed as to who was the *Rav*, who were the prominent and respected members of the community and who were the ordinary folk in the neighborhood.

Shabbos morning, during the Torah reading he was surprised by what he observed. Instead of giving the *Rav* an *aliyah*, the *gabbai* gave one to a simple member of the community. And then to compound this grievous action, instead of calling prominent members to recite the blessings for the next few *aliyos*, the *gabbai* called a few simple workers of the town to recite them. Finally one important gentleman was called to the Torah. But then, to top off everything, the local shoemaker was given *Maftir* (the final and prestigious *aliyah*).

The visitor rushed up to the *gabbai* afterwards and said, "You've done everything all wrong. First of all, you didn't give the *Rav* an *aliyah*. Secondly, you bypassed prominent members of the community, and I know who they are, because I checked them all out yesterday. Then you gave very ordinary men the other *aliyos* — and *Maftir* you gave to the shoemaker! I really don't think you know what you are doing."

The *gabbai* smiled at the man and said, "My dear friend, you are here just a short time and already you are drawing conclusions. If you would have done a bit more research you would have found out that the *Rav* was given the prominent *aliyah* last week. Other important members of our *shul* received *aliyos* just a few weeks ago. The shoemaker who was called up today has *yahrzeit* this week, and another of those called to the Torah had a child just two days ago — therefore they both were given *aliyos*. It would have been better if you would have tried to get the total picture before you drew your quick conclusions."

"The same," said the Chofetz Chaim, "is with our evaluations of how *Hashem* conducts this world. Often we see how certain good people suffer and bad people are blessed with success. It almost doesn't seem fair, but the truth is," continued the Chofetz Chaim, "that each of us is here in this world a relatively short time. What is seventy or eighty years out of a span of thousands? In our finite capacity we cannot see the total picture of *Hashem's* plan. Each one of us must have complete faith that what *Hashem* causes to happen is all logical and reasonable. If it does not appear so to us, it is because we cannot understand the entire scope of what must transpire in this world, as we are only visitors here for a short time."

◆§ *Eternal Wellspring*

The Talmud (*Bava Kamma* 17a) notes that water is an apt metaphor for Torah, for the Torah is a wellspring of knowledge and fountain of advice for every Jew. Additionally, the Talmud (*Taanis* 7a) states that just as water on the elevated portions of a mountain trickles downward to the lower points, so, too, Torah does not remain with those who are haughty but rather with those who are humble. R' Chaim Tihrer of Chernovitz in *Be'er Mayim Chaim* (*Bechukosai*) depicts a scenario that carries this metaphor one step further.

There was once a man who owned a magnificent piece of property on which there was a wellspring. The spring water always tasted delicious, was always perfectly pure, and could be counted on to be refreshing.

After living in the community for a while the man wished to acknowledge his neighbors' kindness. He called them together and offered them the opportunity to share his water. "I cannot have you come here," he told them, "but you may each draw from the water by building pipelines from your yard to mine. The water will funnel through these pipes into basins or pools in your own yards, from which you will then be able to drink and enjoy these pure waters."

The people were thrilled to have that opportunity, but in order for them to enjoy this pure water at its best, each of them had to make sure of two things. First he had to see to the condition of the pipes. These had to be made of material that would not rust, for rust would tarnish the water. And, of course, the pipes would have to be kept perfectly clean, free from any soil, debris or mud.

Secondly, each person had to be sure that the basin in which the water would be stored would be kept clean at all times, so that when the people finally drank from the water, it would indeed be clear, refreshing and unpolluted.

The *Be'er Mayim Chaim* explains, for us to enjoy and be enriched by Torah in its purest sense, we must be sure that those whom we choose to transmit it to us (see *Avos* 1:6), our *rebbeim* and teachers, are pure in their *hashkafos* (outlooks and perspectives), so that there is no dilution of *halachah*. Even more importantly, we who are the receptacles of Torah must rid ourselves of impurities, of bad *middos* (characteristics) and behavior. Only then can we be assured that the Torah within us will enrich our lives the way it was originally meant to do.

◆§ *An Enemy's Praise*

The Chasam Sofer, R' Moshe Sofer (1762-1839), once learned of a malicious incident which had almost occurred in the city of Pressburg, where he was *Rav*. As he contemplated what might have happened, he suddenly arrived at a new understanding of verses in *Tehillim* which had puzzled *Chazal*.

The Talmud (*Pesachim* 118b) points out two seemingly contradictory verses written by David *HaMelech* in the 117th Psalm. "Praise *Hashem*, all you peoples; laud Him, all you nations. For His kindness to us (the Jewish nation) was overwhelming . . ." Why, asked Chazal, would nations praise

Hashem because good things happened to the Jews? It's more likely that such events would cause them grief, not happiness. If anything, the nations of the world would heap praises upon G-d only if wonderful things happened to them or if, Heaven forbid, terrible things happened to the Jewish people!

A new explanation came to the Chasam Sofer when he became aware of the following story:

There was a very wealthy man living in Pressburg who, even though he was blind, lived alone and managed somehow to take care of himself.

One day a group of young hoodlums, jealous of the blind man's money, conceived an amateurish plan to enter his home and rob him of his belongings. They knew that each morning the man would go out for a little stroll. Every day his routine was the same. He would leave his home at a certain time and take a walk through the park, following the same path he had taken the day before — and the day before that. He became a familiar figure to other daily strollers there.

The hoodlums decided they would come very early one morning and dig a deep hole in the path where the man normally walked. They figured that he would surely trip and fall into the hole. They then would rush from their hiding places nearby, pretend to be good Samaritans and offer to carry him home. Once they were in his house, they would take whatever expensive items they wanted.

The morning came and they dug the hole, then camouflaged it with leaves so that no one else would notice it and steer the blind man away from it. Then the hooligans waited behind some trees as the blind man began his daily stroll in the park. They watched anxiously as he came within ten feet of where the trap was. Suddenly the blind man turned around and started back home! They couldn't believe their eyes! He had never done that before! It seems that just that particular morning he was a bit tired and therefore decided to cut short his walk. Their evil scheme was foiled!

When the Chasam Sofer heard about this, he remarked: "Now I

understand the *pshat* (meaning) in (the aforementioned verses of) *Tehillim.* Could this blind man possibly be thankful that he was not robbed? Of course not! He wasn't even aware of the fact that others were plotting against him. *Hashem* had protected him and he hadn't even realized it. Only the hoodlums themselves — and nobody else — could 'appreciate' the hand of G-d causing this man to suddenly become tired. And that is what David *HaMelech* meant. So many times the nations of the world have plotted and schemed against the Jews, and their plans have been foiled by the hand of G-d. However, only the nations themselves knew how their evil plots were foiled by *Hashem*. The Jews themselves didn't realize it. Thus the meaning of David *HaMelech's* words is as follows: Because *Hashem* showed kindness to the Jews (by thwarting the evil plans against them), the nations of the world should praise *Hashem,* because they, more than anyone, could recognize the Hand of *Hashem*.

R' Yaakov Galinsky, the noted lecturer on *mussar* from Bnei Brak, points out that it is very much the same in our daily lives as well. We must constantly be grateful to *Hashem* — not only for the good that He has caused to happen to us, but also for the evil that He turned away from us — that we are not even aware of! The accident that didn't happen, the illness that didn't occur, the loss that did not transpire — our gratitude should know no bounds!

◆§ *People of Valor*

When R' Elya Lopian (1872-1970) was the *Mashgiach* in the *yeshivah ketanah* (elementary school) in Kelm, he traveled to numerous cities to raise funds on behalf of the yeshivah. On one occasion when he was in Radin, he was invited to spend a *Shabbos* with the Chofetz Chaim. It became an especially memorable *Shabbos* for R' Elya, and often he would repeat both what he had heard and what he had seen in the home of the Chofetz Chaim.

Among the things that R' Elya described was how the Chofetz Chaim recited *Aishes Chayil* (taken from *Mishlei* 31:10-31). Every word that the Chofetz Chaim uttered was recited slowly and carefully. However, when he came to the verse (31:23) "נוֹדָע בַּשְּׁעָרִים בַּעְלָהּ, בְּשִׁבְתּוֹ עִם זִקְנֵי אָרֶץ — Her husband is known at the Gates, when he sits with the Elders of the land," the Chofetz Chaim began translating and speaking in Yiddish.

"*Aishes Chayil* is a parable for the Torah," began the Chofetz Chaim. "But if the Torah is referred to as 'אֵשֶׁת חַיִל — the wife of valor,' then who is 'בַּעְלָהּ — her husband'?"

The Chofetz Chaim answered his own question. "The one who studies Torah, he is considered 'בַּעְלָהּ — her husband.'

"But how is one to know if this 'husband' has been loyal and faithful to his 'wife' (the Torah)?" continued the Chofetz Chaim.

The Chofetz Chaim explained that, in this context, 'being faithful' means having a proficient knowledge of Torah. If someone is very knowledgeable in all aspects of Torah, he is considered to be a 'loyal husband.' However, it is not up to us to judge who is really knowledgeable and who is not. For if a man cites a passage in Torah or a citation from the *Gemara* or even a *halachah* from the *Shulchan Aruch,* it may simply mean that he learned or heard it recently. Conversely, there are those who purposely conceal the scope of their Torah knowledge, and thus the wide breadth of their Torah learning remains a secret.

The Chofetz Chaim proclaimed, "The only way to know if someone is truly proficient and accomplished in Torah is if he is tested. And everyone will indeed be tested! And that is what this phrase in *Aishes Chayil* teaches us. This ultimate test will take place when one is about to enter the Gates of Heaven [in the World to Come]. There each person will be tested by the Elders of his own generation, for only they, who lived through the same times, could possibly know what the trials and tribulations of the people of that particular generation really were, what the lures were, what the opportunities were. They will be able to judge accurately how much a person knows and how much he should have known."

The Chofetz Chaim continued. "That is the meaning of this verse. 'נוֹדָע בַּשְּׁעָרִים בַּעְלָהּ' — Her husband's Torah knowledge will be known, 'בְּשִׁבְתּוֹ עִם זִקְנֵי אָרֶץ' — when he has the opportunity to sit [for that final test] with the Elders of the land in the World to Come."

❦ ❦ ❦

The Chofetz Chaim then turned to R' Elya Lopian, who was at that time involved in teaching young boys, and said, "[If this is the case] how can boys even think of leaving a yeshivah before they are proficient in two of the six *sedarim* (sections) of Talmud?"

A Financial Lesson

R' Yosef Leib Bloch (1860-1930), the Telsher *Rav*, once went to the home of a philanthropist to collect funds for a worthy cause. The philanthropist understood at once the purpose of the *Rav's* visit and thus, once the *Rav* was seated and they had exchanged the usual pleasantries, the philanthropist said, "*Rebbe*, I know that you are here to raise money, and I intend to give you money for whichever cause you came. However, while you are here, please tell me a *gut vort* (a stimulating Torah thought)."

The *Rav* smiled and obliged readily by giving the gentleman a new perspective on man and his finances.

"The Talmud (*Bechoros* 58b) teaches us," R' Bloch began, "that when an individual had to give his yearly tithe (one tenth) of his animals to the *Kohen* (priest) as part of the *mitzvah* of giving *maaser*, he had to follow a painstaking procedure.

"He had to assemble all the animals that had been born during the past year and place them in a corral. One by one they would pass through a narrow gateway where he, the owner, would stand and count them as they walked by. He would count aloud — one, two, three, four ... — and then, as every tenth animal came through, he would mark the back of that particular animal with a red stripe. Thus the tenth animal, the twentieth, the thirtieth, and so on, would be easily recognized by their red stripes, and when he was finished counting and marking, the owner would know which ones to give to the *Kohen*.

"But did you ever wonder," asked R' Bloch, "why the owner had to go to so much trouble? He could easily have tallied the number of new animals he had, divided that amount by ten and still given the proper portion to the *Kohen*. Why the procedure with the counting and marking? Seemingly, it just made things more difficult."

R' Yosef Leib answered his own question. "There is much to learn from this procedure. A man looking over his stock of animals might think to himself, 'How can I give away a tenth of all these animals? It's too large an amount; I can't afford to give so much away.' Thus *Hashem* tells him, 'Here, count your animals. This one is for you, this one is for you, this one is for you . . . the tenth one is for Me. Now again, this one is for you, this one is for you, this one is for you . . . and the twentieth one is for Me.' In this manner, a person comes to realize and appreciate the abundance of the worldly possessions that *Hashem* has granted him. What he gives in return (to the *Kohen*, and thus to *Hashem*) is actually minuscule in comparison."

When R' Sholom Schwadron tells this story he adds, "If I were that philanthropist, I would have doubled my intended donation just for that *vort!*"

◆§ *Words of Healing*

Shlomo *HaMelech* wrote: "וּלְשׁוֹן חֲכָמִים מַרְפֵּא — And the language of wise men heals" (*Mishlei* 12:18). He was referring to the kind words of inspiration and encouragement usually spoken by [Torah] scholars (see *Metzudos David,* ibid.). However, in this story told by R' Chaim Kreiswirth, the Chief Rabbi of Belgium, one sees how King Solomon's words are true in their literal meaning as well.

A number of years ago, a very prominent *rav* in Europe became gravely ill. He was taken to a hospital where he underwent serious surgery. The family waited anxiously for the doctor's diagnosis, and when it came they were devastated.